Preface

ABERDARE. GOODWICK. CARDIFF, Carmarthen and Brittany. These are places that I love. I have visited some European countries but, by modern standards, I am not well-travelled. However, my mind and emotions have taken me to extreme places – places so dark that they were beyond description, to hospitals where I was treated for psychiatric and neurological conditions with some methods that have fallen out of favour. These include continual narcosis, abreaction, ether abreaction as well as so many sessions of ECT (electro-convulsive therapy) that I cannot recall how many I underwent. I envied my friends who had leucotomies and insulin coma therapy.

I have also been privileged to be taken on journeys of light. I had great fun with my grandparents (born towards the end of the nineteenth century); I have known joy with the family that I never expected to have; there have been occasions when, through meditation or prayer, I have been lifted out of my body to experience something approaching ecstasy.

Fit for a Purpose is an autobiography – the journey of my life as it has been so far. When I refer to my parents in the book, I often call them Lew and Nancy. They were *good* people (my mother was generous and entertaining, my father was thoughtful, hard-working and loyal) but, when I suffered a phase of disturbed behaviour at the age of eleven, our relationship was strained as they didn't know how to deal with my symptoms. (Few people would have done in 1955 – any deviations from 'normal' behaviour were hidden away and kept secret. In 1955, the new anti-psychotics and antidepressants were not yet available and, if the 'problem' was not kept secret within the home, the sufferer was likely

5

to be put in a long-term institution with limited chance of returning to a normal life or employment.) So when another major episode surfaced in 1962, I felt unable to tell my parents about it. The illness was very prolonged and it took years of hospital stays before a double diagnosis was agreed upon and successfully treated. As a child I had called my parents Mummy and Daddy, but the difficulties during and after my illnesses made this impossible for me. They became 'my mother' and 'my father'. This didn't provide me with a way of addressing them personally and, when things were easier in my mid-twenties, we were all happier when I found a solution – unusual for the time. I called them by their Christian names – Lew and Nancy.

This is the story of what I have seen, observed, struggled with and loved. I can write about it because I have been made to 'face my shadow'. I try to be fair and, whenever there were differences of opinion, I have searched deep within myself to see all sides of an argument because this is a more honest way of being at peace with the past. It leads to forgiveness and healing. And it clears a space for the present.

If I had not encountered all the problems along the road, my life would have followed very different pathways. I don't regret anything. I am 'fit for the purpose' for which I have been created.

Diana Gruffydd Williams
May 2018

FIT FOR A PURPOSE

DIANA GRUFFYDD WILLIAMS

First impression: 2018

© Copyright Diana Gruffydd Williams and Y Lolfa Cyf., 2018

Cover photograph: Cati Davies
Cover design: Y Lolfa

ISBN: 978 1 78461 524 6

Published and printed in Wales
on paper from well-maintained forests by
Y Lolfa Cyf., Talybont, Ceredigion SY24 5HE
website www.ylolfa.com
e-mail ylolfa@ylolfa.com
tel 01970 832 304
fax 832 782

Contents

1

War Wounds

OCTOBER 1944. LEWIS Williams was serving abroad in the Royal Engineers. It had been a long war. Back home in Aberdare, south Wales, his wife, Nancy, went into labour. The wards of the local hospital were filled with wounded soldiers, so I was born in my grandfather's house.

Compared with many others, we were fortunate. Inevitably in the war years there was the ongoing fear of a loved one being killed in action – or returning with a broken spirit. But whenever Nancy had letters from Lew, he sounded cheerful enough and hopeful. They had married in 1942 and longed for the short idylls when Lew was on leave. They were a passionate couple.

Nancy's father, Henry Griffiths, had a large house in Abernant – a pleasant area of Aberdare. Nancy had never left. Even when she was training to be a teacher at Swansea she came home for the weekends. Before and during her pregnancy she made the train journey daily to and from Pontlottyn where she taught. Nancy was close to her daddy – the man I would call Data.

Lew's parents lived down in the Valleys town of Aberdare, about a mile away. Their house was a little miner's terrace without a bathroom. But it was always a place of welcome, acceptance and love. Nancy, whose own mother had died when she was just four, called her mother-in-law Mother – something that gave her great comfort. Her father-in-law amused her with his humour and easy nature. I called these grandparents Nana and Daddy Bom (his name was Tom).

So there were the three of us living in Aberdare – and a father I had never met. Obviously, I didn't understand the war, the rations and the restrictions. Like any other baby I had basic needs which were ably met. But before long, the routine was broken suddenly and disturbingly.

My mother, Nancy, developed 'milk fever'; a problem that would be treated quickly and effectively now, but it was often fatal then. Nancy was very ill. I was immediately weaned off her breast. Tins of national dried milk were bought for a bottle. Nancy remained in bed, weak and scared. Her best friend from college came to visit her, fearing that it might be the last. She offered to adopt me if Nancy didn't pull through. Nancy recovered, though she remained nervous. She had had spinal problems as a child and these returned. The illness had traumatised her and she missed Lew.

After this setback the routine of my life resumed. Nancy did what she could, when she could, and we continued living in Data's home. Most days Data took me down to see Nana and Daddy Bom. I stayed there with my three grandparents who all loved me to distraction.

I only have one memory of those early days. Data had wrapped me up in a shawl. (It was a traditional Welsh way of carrying a baby, with the shawl wrapped around the adult and baby, twisted round firmly so that the adult had free hands and the infant had the security of being warm and intimately close to the adult.) We were leaving Nana and Daddy Bom's house when Data showed me the moon before he swaddled me up. Maybe I fell asleep or maybe I just enjoyed the cosiness as the next thing I remembered was Data loosening the shawl outside 1 College Street, Abernant, to show me the moon again before taking me inside.

I was nearly two when I saw my father for the first time. I am told that I kicked this stranger who had stepped into our lives. Lew had hoped for a hero's welcome – and he *had* one. He came to live with Data, Nancy and me. There was plenty of room for us all.

In the next six months or so there were tensions amongst the adults which I would have picked up at a fundamental level. As an adult, I've analysed what was going on between them, so that I can understand the complex dynamics.

My father, Lew, had lost nearly a decade of his youth in military service and the war. He never spoke about what happened but the experiences would have been enough to radically alter his way of thinking and feeling. He was deeply in love with Nancy but they had never had the chance to spend more than a few days together as husband and wife at that time. His own childhood had been hard. As a young lad it was clear that Lew was very gifted academically, so Nana stopped speaking Welsh (his examinations would have to be taken in English) and watched over him as he did his homework. Lew passed all his tests and examinations. In fact, he did so well that he won a scholarship to the University of Southampton to read mathematics. Nothing like that had ever happened in the family, and he was looking forward to the challenge. But, within weeks of arriving in Southampton, he was called home. His father, my Daddy Bom, was seriously ill. There was no income back home to keep his parents or to maintain him on his university course. He qualified later as a teacher in Bangor, north Wales, but he had lost the opportunity to graduate. So, by the time he married, his life was already littered with many disappointments.

Nana was a wonderful lady. Practical, determined, hard working, uncompromising, she was a woman whom other people sought out in time of need – to deliver their babies, give advice, lay out the dead. She did it all cheerfully and ably. She had been the driving force behind Lew's early success and, although she was delighted and relieved when Lew returned safely from the war, she didn't want him or his family to be restricted in any way.

Daddy Bom had worked in the coal mines as a boy. There hadn't been an alternative. A funny, affectionate and gentle man, by the time I was born he was already suffering from the early stages of pneumoconiosis. His ability to work physically was limited. In a less emphatic way than Nana, he also wanted the best for us.

Nancy's life had been more privileged in many ways, but early traumas had left permanent scars. When she was four, her mother Jane died very suddenly of influenza and pneumonia. One of her few memories of her mother was that of being lifted up to kiss her in her coffin. A few years later, she had a new stepmother. Nancy was an emotionally needy girl but her stepmother, though very gifted artistically and musically, was a bit aloof from the children. Nancy respected her though, and, during one of her college holidays, they were both in the same room at home when her stepmother fell and died immediately. Soon after she qualified Nancy met Lew, and yearned for the comfort of his love. War prevented that, so she grew even closer to Data.

Data was one of those people who was loved by everyone. He was gregarious, affable – and he had a permanent twinkle in his eye. Data had worked as a collier but he saved enough money to rent a china and hardware shop in Abercynon (a few miles from Aberdare). He later bought the property and the family lived above the shop. One of Harry and Jane's five children died in infancy but they had four others – Peggy, Nancy, Owen and Nesta. Nesta was only a baby when her mother died. Data looked after Peggy, Nancy and Owen but felt that Nesta needed the sort of care that he could not provide. Nesta was fostered by trusted family friends. Data remarried – then his second wife died. By the time I was born, his children had all left home – except Nancy. His home was comfortable enough to accommodate us all.

After the relief of getting back safely from the war, it was understandable that Lew found it hard to see how much I doted on Data – and he on me. Nancy was permanently living for the first time with Lew. She had been no further than Pembrokeshire in her life but Lew had travelled widely during the war.

One place where he had been stationed was Essex. He was told that there would be good prospects for him there when peace

12

came. Aberdare had been a thriving town with the coming of the Industrial Revolution, but in the 1940s it had become depressed: the hills were bleak and black from the coal mines. Lew made enquiries about a teaching post in Essex. He got the job, planned the move – but had not anticipated the negative reactions.

Data was unaware of the plans but the time came when he had to be told. He was cuddling me in a reclining chair when Nancy entered the room. She tried to tell him gently but he broke down.

'Do anything you like to me,' he wept. 'But don't take this child away from me.'

2

Exile

IT'S DIFFICULT TO know when and where personal memories begin, where they merge with given information and where hearing about past events becomes an envisaged memory. Conscious of this, this is how our exile seemed to be. And an exile it *was*.

The train journey to Essex was long and necessitated several changes of trains. I cannot recall it but, somehow, I absorbed the sadness. Maybe it was Data's grief that affected me. Maybe it was saying goodbye to Nana and Daddy Bom as well. I was just aware of a darkness that changed my young life. It literally changed the way I was. I probably picked up Nancy's fear. And I probably sensed Lew's determination to make the move successful and his frustration that we were not all overjoyed. I was born in 1 College Street, Abernant, Aberdare, and I had felt secure and happy there.

When we moved to Essex I no longer had Data's blanket to hide in. Nancy bought a pram. It was very hard to find accommodation in post-war Britain but we had been promised rooms in the school house which was the home of Miss Bates, the headmistress of the local infants' school in the village of Ingatestone. I remember Miss Bates. She was a spinster, wore thick glasses, and although she smiled sometimes she was strict. When we moved into her home, life was not easy. Noise in the evenings was frowned upon. Miss Bates had early nights. Lew paid for the rooms but we had a landlady who lived-in.

Lew had to work long hours. There was the journey to and from Brentwood every day to the secondary modern school where he was teaching. He carried his treasured briefcase with the lessons he had prepared, exam papers that he was marking, homework, and so on. On top of that, he took on evening classes to bring home some extra money. The evening work earned him an extra ten shillings a week. Necessary as all this was, it made the days long and lonely for Nancy.

Nancy was desperately unhappy. Today, she would probably have been diagnosed as clinically depressed. But then, she just had to tolerate the black moods. Essex is one of the flattest counties in England. Nancy couldn't get used to it. At every turn she expected to see a mountain. But there wasn't even a hill in Ingatestone. The flatness of the Essex accent seemed to convey no emotion. She longed for the Welsh lilts. She took me down in my pram past the 'rec' (recreational ground), and over towards the railway station. She must have been sorely tempted to get on one of the trains and make her way back 'home'.

It was a bleak time for the three of us. I didn't really understand what was happening. When my parents were offered a prefab, they accepted straightaway. We were going to be independent at last! Our prefab was typical of those post-war buildings. Lacking character, it was essentially something that would today be called a 'flat-pack' home. It was solid enough and we had a dining room cum kitchen, a sitting room, two bedrooms and a bathroom. It stood in a little plot of land slightly bigger than itself, so we had a small garden. There was a cupboard in the kitchen. Because of rationing it was never full. There was Camp Coffee, tea and a few jars of 'supplements' that were bought to help me thrive. I had become a *very* quiet little girl with a poor appetite. Scott's Emulsion, dark brown glass jars of horrible-tasting malt, cod liver oil – it must have cost my parents a fortune.

Then, one day, something happened that changed the balance in the lives of the three of us – and it was never healed. I was three years old. Lew was working long hours. Nancy was still unhappy. She took me by bus into the nearest town,

Chelmsford. We must have gone in to get some shopping and we were waiting at the bus stop to go back to Ingatestone. Nancy held my hand. Then, in a moment that is the nightmare of every parent, she unwittingly let go of it. I wandered onto the edge of the road. Before Nancy was aware of anything being amiss, a passing lorry had dragged me along by its wheels. I have no conscious memory of this and don't even know if I was taken to hospital. Whether I did or not, I returned to our prefab – paralysed.

I remained like that for five months and Nancy had to nurse me. I was unable to do anything for myself. Nancy, a hard-working woman who was scrupulous about my care, became even more depressed. Such mistakes do happen but it was understandable that Lew was furious about the accident. He must have been desperate. Nothing was working out to plan and, as I lay in bed unable to move, there was no guarantee that I would recover.

Nancy was never able to recall this episode in our life without bursting into tears. Her response to the mere mention of it meant that it was impossible for me to get an objective idea of exactly what happened. I don't think the guilt ever left her. When, as an adult, I asked Lew about it, he said that it was in the past. The tension in the prefab must have been unbearable at times and I sometimes wonder if I felt safe enough to recover. With modern technology and the advances in neurology, it might have been possible to make an accurate diagnosis. But nothing like that was available then. Nana eventually wrote to say that, for my sake and the sake of their marriage, there had to be forgiveness. They had to move on. Nancy was always grateful for her intervention.

I recovered. Once again, I was a little girl who could do all the things that she had done before. Then, straightaway, I became ill again. There were no vaccinations available for whooping cough in the 1940s. I developed the disease and was told that I nearly died of it. Nancy nursed me while Lew continued working his long hours. When I still had whooping cough I contracted gastroenteritis. No one knew much about dehydration. Again, I hovered on the edge of death. I recovered.

Nancy was deeply unhappy, and at the end of her tether. Like a horse that has constantly been pulling against restraints that were impossible for her to bear, she was ready to break loose and go mad. Lew was probably at the end of his tether too. But he couldn't show it. His only aim had been to build a brighter future for us. On three occasions, his only daughter had fought for her life. Nancy had told him that she couldn't go through with another pregnancy. I was their only hope, their pride and joy. I *had* to live. Things *had* to change for the better.

In the end, Nancy went to see the doctor. Perceiving her depression, he said that she had to do one of two things. She had to take a job – or return to Wales. I'm sure that she would have preferred it if we'd packed our bags and returned home, but Lew had set his heart upon this better future. There were terrible rows at home. My parents were both strong-minded and volatile. For most of their marriage the love they had for each other was positive, but at that period of our lives it was directed against the other. I was terrified.

There was a vacancy as an assistant teacher in the village school – someone was needed to work with Miss Bates. It seemed too good an opportunity to miss. It was a local job, it respected Nancy's training and experience – it would stimulate her and relieve her depression. The problem was that I was still too young to start school. So, after Nancy got the job, arrangements had to be made for someone to look after me.

I have no idea why Mrs Neville was chosen. Ingatestone was still a small rural village in the 1940s, so everybody would have known us. Mrs Neville's son, Trevor, was a year or so older than me – he was in the village school too. Word must have got around. As far as I can remember I spent the weekdays with Mrs Neville – Nancy took me there in the mornings and came to fetch me in the afternoons. By this time I had become more withdrawn and shy, and my appetite was even poorer. I think that I had a genuine problem as I gagged on most food – it made me feel physically sick. There were exceptions – Nana sent us some of their sweet rations, so I had developed a taste for sweets and chocolate. Apart from them, my favourite foods at the time were chips, bread and butter and treacle tart. There were no such indulgences in Mrs Neville's house. Even the smell of the mashed potato, softened by margarine, made me feel sick. Mr Neville came home for lunch at midday on his bicycle. He wore an earring – something that I had never seen before on a man. I wondered if he was a pirate. Both Mr and Mrs Neville were kind to me. But Mrs Neville, in particular, was worried about me. One day I heard her talking to the milkman at her doorstep.

'She won't eat anything,' she whispered. 'And she's so shy. She hardly says a word.'

I saw the concerned looks on their faces as they looked over in my direction. I did the only thing I felt that I was good at – I smiled.

Mrs Neville was a kindly woman, with the longer hair that was fashionable at the time pleated back on itself behind her ears and at the nape of her neck in sausage-like waves. Mr Neville's favourite food – or so it seemed to me – was the mashed potato that I hated. I struggled with a mouthful, then tried to hide the rest beneath my knife and fork. In the afternoons Mrs Neville's sister, Kath, came over to listen to the wireless. The two sisters were addicted to *Mrs Dale's Diary*. Just before it started Mrs Neville asked me not to talk when the programme was on. I was so worried that I'd disturb them during the programme that I tried to make my breathing quieter. When Nancy came to pick me up, she always asked if I had been good.

The only time I came to life was when Trevor was there. Trevor had something amazing. Trevor had a rabbit! The rabbit was in a hutch of its own. It was Trevor's job to clean out the hutch and Mrs Neville told him to let me see. 'Let her hold it!' she said and Trevor quietly smiled and handed the rabbit over. I was excited at that and couldn't believe that Trevor had to look after the little animal himself. What a responsibility to have such an important grown-up job! I noticed the little round pellets of dung and wondered what happened to them afterwards. I didn't ask anyone because that would have been rude.

3

Not the Teacher's Pet

IT WAS SOON time for me to start school. I walked down with
Nancy from our prefab and suddenly, as soon as we entered the
building, she became Mrs Williams. She was my mother but,
at the same time, she was Mrs Williams! I certainly received no
privileges. Because my poor appetite was an embarrassment to
Nancy (it was difficult to ask other children to eat their dinner
when her own daughter refused them), I went to Mrs Neville's
for lunch. I probably managed to get a nutritious diet because
of the little bottles of milk we all had to drink at eleven in the
morning. The little crates arrived daily and we all had to follow
the same ritual. The little silver foil tops were punctured with
a straw before we were all handed a bottle. There was cream
at the top of the bottle where it had separated from the rest of
the milk. I drank the milk reluctantly, before handing the silver
foil top back for it to be collected with all the others to make
money for the blind. No, I received no privileges. If anything,
I was disadvantaged. If I put my hand up to answer a question
at the same time as other children, I was seldom chosen to give
the answer. I learnt how to read, write and do arithmetic. I
learnt my tables. I learnt 'kerb drill'. 'Look right, look left, look
right again and, if nothing is coming, quick march.' My school
reports – in Nancy's writing – stated that I was doing well; very
well, in most instances. The exception was PE (drill), but even
that was 'fairly good'. The only stinging comment for me was
the mention of my shyness and my reluctance to 'speak out'.

I didn't like 'drill'. Nancy/Mrs Williams stood before us all,
telling us to 'lift your hands up', 'keep them to the side', 'touch

your toes'... It was better when we were allowed to have free play in the yard. There was a building at the far end of the yard – an ugly concrete building – and we were forbidden to go anywhere near it. One girl told me that it was an air-raid shelter. Another child – probably a boy – insisted that it was an Anderson shelter. I had no idea what either of them meant so, as usual, I kept quiet.

Children are inclined to break rules. The others told me that I wouldn't dare to go in because I was the teacher's daughter. I made a quick dash inside. It was dark and green where moss had grown, and the mould smelt dreadful. But at least I had shown them that I would do it. At the end of playtime, out came Nancy/Mrs Williams again with the brass bell. As it clanged away we all lined up and, when everyone was in a rigidly straight line, we were allowed to go inside. Nancy was never anything but professional. But it had an odd effect on me.

Miss Bates taught the older infants. The school was fundamentally one large room. In its centre was a huge curtain resting on a long horizontal pole; it was pulled to separate the top class from the little ones when necessary. It was kept open for activities that were shared. I had moved up into Miss Bates' class when the curtain was left open for the prayers at the end of the day. Miss Bates and Nancy/Mrs Williams stood out in the front by the coal fires that heated the place – their hands held up together, ready for prayer. Once they had made the gesture, they waited for all the children to follow suit. The prayers began.

Going back to my sweet tooth and the extra sweet rations, I had a tube of Smarties in school one day. I loved licking them and taking them out from time to time to see when the outer colour disappeared. I was generous with my Smarties and began to share them round. But prayer time was not the time to do it. Miss Bates caught me in the act – though how she knew puzzled me as she was supposed to have her eyes shut too!

Prayers were suddenly halted. Miss Bates told me that

what I was doing was disgusting. I had to go out to the front, take my Smartie out of my mouth and place it in the bin. Of course, apart from being shown up and feeling embarrassed and ashamed, I was aware of Nancy's large, limpid brown eyes staring at me. She was another grown-up who didn't have her eyes closed. The prayers began again. I was mortified by what I had done and, when I stayed behind after school as Nancy finished her paperwork, she told me to go into Miss Bates' office and apologise. I knocked on the headmistress' heavy door and heard the words 'Come in!' I went inside to see Miss Bates sitting at her desk with her fountain pen, blotting paper and an attendance book.

'I'm sorry.'

To my surprise, Miss Bates smiled at me.

'That's in the past,' she said. 'It's forgotten.'

Maybe she wasn't so tough after all.

Nancy was more settled by this time, happier with the flatness of the earth and the accents. Some of my enjoyable times were when I walked home with her after school. She was no longer Mrs Williams then. She was my mother, Mummy, Nancy. We used to call into Warder's, the bakers – a small shop with a low ceiling. (I was very interested in it because we had been there from school to see how bread was made. Mr Warder had to get up very early to start the baking. It took a very long time to make bread. The dough started out so small and grew to be so big!) When Nancy had bought her loaf and had a chat, my eyes focused on the little box of Bridgewater Biscuits in front of the counter. I suppose it was the 1940s equivalent of supermarket temptations by the till. I loved Bridgewater Biscuits! They were chocolate-coated, some with a red wrapper and the others with a blue one. I always wanted the dark chocolate one – the red wrapper. If I was allowed to have one, Mr Warder would say to Nancy 'It's unusual for a child to like dark chocolate.' Most children liked milk chocolate!

During the winter we often passed Mr Pinnock who lit the

gas street lights. I was amazed at the nimble way he could climb up the lamp-posts which had little steel rungs on them to help him up and down. There was an ironmonger's shop that sold everything. It was so full of things that it was hard to find anything. But Mr Manning knew where everything was kept – mousetraps, turps, string, glue, Bronco toilet rolls. I loved going into the stationers. Sometimes Nancy needed a new nib or some drawing paper. Paper was very expensive. I was told that I would have a fountain pen when I was older. We passed several pubs on the journey home too. There was the Star, the Bell, and the Spread Eagle where Queen Elizabeth I was supposed to have stayed. Sometimes Nancy bought bread from the other baker's in the village. A lady called Mrs Raven worked there. She had a very pale face with eyes partly hidden by pink tinted spectacles – I'd never seen anything like it before. Her hair was worn back in a bun and she looked very sad but, when she spoke, I could tell that she was very kind. She and Nancy had long conversations.

'Will you be closed on Good Friday, Mrs Raven?'

'Oh yes, you have to show respect.'

'Exactly. Some shops…'

'I know. The least people can do is to close between twelve and three.'

And the two women talked about how things were changing for the worse – it had been the custom to draw the curtains or pull down the shutters on Good Friday. I wondered why it was called *Good* Friday. Everyone seemed to be unhappy about it and I even saw the pain on Mrs Raven's face when she mentioned it.

Sometimes we went to the greengrocers in the village too, and there was a newsagents and a Post Office. From time to time we went into a little tearoom – especially if Nancy had a friend with her. It was solemn there, but exciting too. A lady came over to us with cakes on three tiers of a big china plate. We weren't allowed to touch anything but we could point to the cake we wanted. The lady took the plate away and used a pair of tongs to put our cake on a small china plate. She brought them back to us before we had our tea. China cups and saucers were placed on the crisp white tablecloth and then a teapot was put in the middle of the table. That was a very exciting thing to do.

Back home in the prefab, Lew spent any free time in the evenings making farm animals for me. Wood was hard to come by and expensive. He carved the little creatures out from a pattern and cut them free with a fretsaw. It took him hours and hours – each cow, pig, horse or hen. Every animal was scrupulously painted, with every detail perfect. I was the only child in the whole wide world to have a toy farmyard! The boys in Lew's class had been making a marionette for me in their woodwork classes. When the big day came and it was finished, he brought it home for me. Lew put it on the table and grinned. Both of my parents were watching for my delighted reaction at something *so* special. But it frightened me. It had huge teeth that were painted vertically in extreme opposites of black and white. I knew that they wanted me to smile – so I did. But I felt happier when the little monster was put back in its box. I was scared of it because, apart from the teeth, it looked so real. And, because of the strings, it could dance and move. I can still see Lew's face anticipating my delight. I just managed the quiet smile.

When I was seven I remember Nancy being at the centre of a small crowd of mothers after school. I knew that they were angry. Nancy was trying hard to keep her temper. I later discovered that some of them had complained that I was coming 'top of the class' too often. It was time for me to start in the juniors and my parents made a big decision for me. They moved me to another school. St Anne's School, a private day school, was in Chelmsford. I had to walk to the bus stop in Ingatestone, then travel six miles on the bus on my own before getting off and crossing the main London-Colchester road. It didn't worry me at all.

4

Holidays in Aberdare

THE ADVANTAGE OF having teachers for parents was the shared holidays. No one went abroad then – I was impressed if someone had gone as far as Devon. But there was only one holiday venue for the three of us anyway. Aberdare. It was a long journey and took the best part of a day on the train. First of all, a trunk was sent on as 'advanced luggage'. I was always excited when Lew brought it down and began the task of labelling it clearly. Seasons seemed to be more clearly defined then, so packing was simpler and we had so few clothes anyhow. I had a winter coat and a blazer for summer time. I had a mac. There were two dresses for summer and winter, as well as a couple of cardigans and jumpers. I had best shoes and everyday shoes. Everything I needed for the holidays fitted easily into the trunk as well as my parents' clothes. We didn't go empty-handed either – there was room in the trunk for presents. We travelled down in all the main holidays and sometimes in the half-terms if they were long enough.

With the trunk safely on its way, we made the journey itself. We had to walk the mile down to the station in Ingatestone. The first train took us to Shenfield, where we had to change for the second one that that took us to Liverpool Street Station. I noted the names of the stations: Brentwood, Harold Wood, Gidea Park, Romford, Ilford, Stratford… As soon as I saw the name Stratford, I knew that we had nearly arrived. I could sense that my parents were excited but they couldn't have been happier than I was. I was going *home*. Lew took me by the hand and held me close to him as we went on the underground to Paddington. Out we came from the Tube and up the steps. And then, there it was. The noisy, dirty, loved station! If we had any spare time Lew took me down to the engine to watch as the men shovelled the coal inside. And how I loved to see the steam! I can still see Lew's face as he took me over to watch those men at work. It was much more thrilling than the marionette. He saw joy in my face.

More often than not, though, we just made it in time. There was the frantic checking for the right platform, then the walk down past the first-class carriages until we found one that had spaces. If we didn't have time to do that, we boarded the train and walked down the corridors until we found a compartment with three spare seats. If there were only two, I sat on Lew's lap. If it were even more crowded, I sat on Nancy's lap and Lew stood in the corridor. The seats were stiff and hard – the hairs sometimes chafed my skin. There was a mirror in the compartment with the words GWR – Great Western Railway. West was much better than East. And there were racks above us that looked like long webs of string. We often had a bit of luggage for things gathered together at the last minute. Something to eat maybe or something to drink. An extra cardigan, an umbrella in case it rained…

If we were still travelling in the evening, there would be a man opening the sliding doors that sealed us into the warmth of the compartment. 'First call for evening meal. First call for evening meal,' I heard repeated as the man made his way down the compartments until I couldn't hear him any more. I was quite happy to just sit on the train for hours. One thing that always intrigued me was the communication cord. It had to be pulled if there was an emergency. If anyone pulled it as a joke, there was a big fine to be paid. I wondered what would happen if someone accidentally bumped into it? Or an umbrella got caught in it? I never found out. The communication cord was never pulled on any of our journeys.

The thing that made me hold my breath was the Severn Tunnel. It took over six minutes to travel through it and my ears popped. Nancy showed me how to gulp. Looking back, I don't think that it really scared me much. But both of my parents thought that I would be afraid, so I suppose I was! Once we were out of the tunnel, we were in Wales! There was another change in Cardiff and the next train took us to Abercynon. The last train took us the short distance to Aberdare. I could see the mountains! And there, without fail, at the station to meet us was Daddy Bom. Daddy Bom's lovely smile beckoned me to run up to him and nestle in his arms. We walked home to 4 Elizabeth Street where Nana was waiting with a cup of tea, a meal and the warmest of welcomes.

We sat close to the coal fire in the parlour as we sipped our tea. Its taste was something that I have never been able to reproduce in my adult life. Maybe part of its loveliness is the comfort of the memory. The kettle was boiled on the fire in the kitchen and a little hot water was used to warm the teapot. Then, once the tea had been spooned into the pot, the rest of the boiling water was added. In due course – and Nana seemed to know the exact moment – the tea was poured out into little china cups which rested on saucers of the same design. The pot was put back by the fire and dressed in a knitted cosy. The milk was added to the tea from a little jug, and then the sugar from a bowl – usually two spoonfuls for me. The result tasted like nectar. My parents talked about the journey and recent news, but I just felt happy to be there.

Nana and Daddy Bom's house was a typical miner's terrace. There were two good-sized bedrooms upstairs. The front one overlooked the street and, apart from the enormous bed, there was a huge, deep chest for blankets. There was a wardrobe in the far corner. The back bedroom was about the same size and, again, there was a huge bed. There was a tallboy in this room and a painting of *The Last Supper* by Leonardo da Vinci. In the evenings, when I couldn't sleep, I was fascinated by the names of the disciples and the Roman lettering – I looked at it for hours. I learnt the names of every apostle and wondered what sort of people they were.

Both bedrooms had heavy cream curtains and the floors were warmed by shiny lino. The stairs that led straight down into the kitchen/dining room downstairs were curved at the bottom before reaching a little door that was there to stop any draughts. It had to be held in place with a little hook and catch. And, to ensure that the warmth was kept in even more, a brown curtain hung over the door.

There were two rooms downstairs. The front one that faced the street was the parlour. It wasn't used every day. It was for best. But when *we* were down, Nana usually laid her white tablecloth over the dining room table for us to have our evening meal. As far as she was concerned, we were 'for best'. The room had a sideboard and family photographs rested on its well-polished surface. There was the table, four chairs and a settee that seemed to have been partly home-made (old copies of the *Echo* were hidden under the cushions ready to lay the fires). In the corner was a white cupboard where Nana stored food such as cold meat. In the summer, milk was put there, resting in a bowl of cold water to keep it cool and fresh. The cupboard was close to the open fire that was kept lit all the year round. On each side of the fire were two little 'stools' which served two purposes. The cushioned tops could be lifted so that things such as shoe polish could be stored inside. But, once they were put back in place, they made the most wonderful places to sit. Many a time I scorched my legs from sitting on them, enjoying the luxury of the heat from the glowing coal.

The next room was technically a kitchen and dining room combined. Its focus was the fire. It was a slightly bigger fire than the one in the parlour and, behind its iron grills, the coal constantly burned brightly to keep us warm. On each side of the fire were two little black ovens. This is where Nana cooked all her food. The fire was essential for cooking as well as heating, and the black, charred kettle was constantly boiling. By the fender there was a poker to help get the fire started or to keep it alight when it went low. It was hard work laying the fire. Nana always had a bundle of sticks ready to pile up on top of crushed pages of the *Echo*. Then, the right amount of coal had to go on top – not too much, not too little. If the fire showed any sign of flagging, Daddy Bom held the poker vertically against the grills and pressed a large page of the *Echo* in front of it. This usually did the trick, though sometimes the paper started to singe as he was doing it.

The mantelpiece above the fire had some ornaments, the tea caddy, and sometimes the wild flowers that I picked and gave to Nana. She loved having them – better than any lilies or roses she said. There was a plain wooden table – quite a small one – in the centre of the room beside the window. It was almost always covered with a chenille cloth in deep red. Above the table was the pendulum clock. It had Roman numerals and I learnt how to read them. Sometimes I stood on the table and wound the pendulum up. The key was hidden inside and I felt very important when I did that job. There was another easy chair with upholstered padding – I think Nana had made it and there was a rocking chair by the fire. The sideboard in this room was not as elegant as the one in the parlour.

There was a wireless on the table. Everything stopped in the evening at six o'clock for the news. Apart from the *Echo*, which concentrated on local affairs, this was our main contact with what was happening in the world. I remember it not so much for the news itself (which I hardly understood) as for the notices that preceded it. There always seemed to be an announcement that went something like:

> Will a Mr A Thomas, who is thought to be on holiday in Devon, please return as soon as possible to St Albans, Hertfordshire, where his father, Mr Herbert Thomas, is dangerously ill.

It was all very solemn. I wondered if the relative heard it and managed to get there in time. There was a programme on the wireless that made us all laugh. *Welsh Rarebit* was hilarious. I don't know whether I fully understood the jokes but I simply laughed at the familiar accents and the happiness of seeing everyone else laughing together.

If it rained, Nana couldn't dry the clothes outside, so she had a long piece of cord hanging from the wall by the fire to the other end of the room. The dampest of clothes dried off quickly, as they were never far away from the heat from the fire. Just in front of the drying clothes was the flytrap. It hung from the ceiling and was basically a long roll of glued paper. The flies went towards it and were caught. When it was full of flies it looked very ugly, and I wondered if it was cruel. Nana said that flies brought disease, so it had to be done. Once the trap had done its job it was replaced by another one.

One stone step down from the kitchen/living room was an extension to the house. It was a tiny room – always cold – only protected from the elements by its corrugated iron roof. As an extra measure, Nana had placed on top of it a 'Players' Please' metal advertising board that she had had in her sweet shop when she was young. This little room was called the 'back kitchen'. It had a big, white china sink which Nana called the 'bosh'. And from the bosh came the precious cold running water, always a bit wilder than our cold water in the prefab. Toots lived in the back kitchen. Toots, the black cat, was no pet. She was a hard-working animal. She was sent out to prowl for vermin and sometimes she was let loose in the cellar. Nana rewarded her by cooking up 'lights' (animal offal). It smelt revolting but Toots loved it. I didn't get to know Toots because she was never allowed inside the main part of the house.

The cellar was the one part of that lovely house that frightened me. Daddy Bom took me down there once but I was scared of its cold, dark paving stones, its shadows and the smell of dampness. I was told that I didn't have to go down there again. The most I saw of the cellar after that was when Nana opened the door at the top to reach for one of the jars of pickles or preserves that she used to make. There was a shelf especially for them – high up, almost on a level with the hall which was called the passageway.

The floor of the passageway was lined with shiny lino in bold, whirling designs. There was a narrow piece of furniture where we could hang our coats up, but otherwise the passageway was unfurnished. Laid out neatly on the far side of the passageway near the door was a little line of 'empties'. These were the bottles of pop that had been drunk and were waiting for the arrival of the van that would bring us our next provisions of Corona drinks. Nana had 'money off' the new bottles in exchange for returning the clean, empty bottles. I loved these drinks; my favourites were American Cream Soda, Dandelion & Burdock and Lemonade.

The door out from the back kitchen led to a little area that was open but roofed with more corrugated iron. This was the utility area where the tin bath, the mangle, and the washing board for scrubbing clothes were kept.

Then, down another step, was the tiniest garden you could imagine, one with the blackest of soils. I wondered if the earth there might be coal dust. Whatever it was, Nana managed to grow wonderful things in it. There were pompom dahlias, gladioli and herbs. I remember being given the job of picking a handful of mint for the sauce that went with lamb.

Between the utility area and the garden was the outside toilet – a very small hut. When I used it I pulled the door shut to reach the paper made from little squares torn from the *Echo* hanging on a piece of string on a nail knocked onto the inside of the door. Sometimes I kept the toilet door open. There was a lovely view. Ahead of me was the Graig mountain – *my* mountain. It had a little hut on the top and the road up there was very, very winding. Watching a car – or the red-and-white bus – snaking its way down, delighted me.

Backing onto the garden was a chapel. I liked to watch the people inside on a Sunday – I could only see them as silhouettes. The people sat side by side and then they all stood up at the same time. And that was the moment when I heard the singing. I loved its sound – without knowing why – it was sad but happy at the same time.

31

I never saw Nana using the tin bath. But, once, after he'd been working and came back black, I saw Daddy Bom in it. Nana had to keep on boiling the water in the black kettle before it had enough to partially fill the bath. When Daddy Bom got in, Nana kept on boiling even more water to fill it up and keep it hot. Daddy Bom had to scrub hard. When he came home that day, the coal dust on his face had scared me. It was the contrast between the blackness and his red-rimmed eyes that frightened me. When he was ready to climb out, he put the towel in front of him to hide himself from me. And he smiled. He always had a smile for me. I didn't have to do anything to earn it.

Sometimes, during the day, Nana took me out shopping with her. It was obvious to everyone else – and to *me* – that this gave her great pleasure.

'So you've got your family down, Mrs Williams?' said Glyn Vaughan, the grocer.

'Yes!' Her face shone with pride.

'What can I do for you, Mrs Williams?'

'A quarter of roast pork, please.'

She said the word 'quarter' with that same pride. I reckoned that when she and Daddy Bom were on their own they didn't eat much. Mr Vaughan showed Nana every slice before cutting another one. She stared at it like a detective. Nana couldn't afford to waste good money on meat that was the wrong colour, with too much fat or gristle. Finally, once she was satisfied, the meat was wrapped up in a piece of paper and put into a paper bag that had the name of the shop on the outside – and the price written in pencil.

Then, we went to the market. I loved going there, with all its colour and bustle. It was not a scary sort of noise, and whenever we went to a stall the people were kind to me. A lovely, cheerful roly-poly woman ran the fruit stall. It probably sold vegetables as well but it was only the fruit I noticed. Although my diet was limited, I loved fruit. Apples were a big favourite but, more than anything else, I loved to go to the market in the summer when the fruit stall sold peaches. For me, eating a peach was wonderful. Its slightly hairy skin was like human skin; I loved letting the knife just skim under its surface so that I wouldn't lose any of the goodness of the fruit. I noticed how the flesh was redder and rougher near the stone in the middle. Then there was that wonderful taste. Yes, I loved the market.

If peaches were the attraction in the summer, there was another one at Christmas time. The rounded lady with the rosy cheeks had tangerines – brilliantly coloured with their dimpled skins as shiny as Nana's floors.

4 Elizabeth Street was the house where I felt enclosed in a lavish love. I still have recurring dreams of the house. It is threatened with destruction and I wake up terrified.

5

Cameo Memories of Data

I LOVED MY holidays with Nana and Daddy Bom, but remember less about the time I spent with Data. After we left Aberdare, Data was living alone for the first time in his life – though he still had lodgers. But the memories of visits to the home in which I was born are sparse. I remember them like little cameos. The emotions of the past were probably still raw.

I can't remember the upper storey of the house at all. After going through the front door, the first door to my right was where the lodgers lived. I remember seeing a woman coming out of that door, and stopping to speak to her. There may have been two reception rooms but I only remember one. It was large and comfortably furnished. There was a huge coal fire in the centre of the far wall and a table in the middle of the room.

We spent at least two Christmases with Data. The first time I was excited to see what Father Christmas had brought. My stocking was full. The stocking was a real stocking and it was full of nuts, a tangerine, some paper, a pencil and a couple of tiny toys. I wasn't really surprised that he had been so generous because I had left him a kipper on a plate by the big fire, as well as a glass of milk. He was probably grateful on a night when he was so busy. I remember asking Data and Nancy about all this. Had he really come into the house and had the kipper and the milk? They said that he had. And I knew that it was true because he had written me a letter to say thank you.

During the other Christmas spent with Data I had a doll's house. It was wonderful and I spent a long time opening the front of it with a little hook, and peering inside. It was a perfect model house with two storeys – much bigger than our prefab.

Data had a picture of a baby on the left wall of the main room downstairs. It was a painting not a photograph. The baby was a beautiful little child with curly black hair and she was fast asleep. I wanted to be lifted up so that I could see it better.

'Is that me? Is that *me*?'

I really wanted it to be me.

'Yes, it's you.'

The little white lie made me feel very happy as I was carried upstairs.

On another holiday I remember Data cooking something up in a pan. It looked horrible but I was curious. He melted some fat – probably lard – and added bits and pieces that he mixed all together with a spoon. When the mixture was cooler but still soft, he shaped the food into a ball. Then, before it hardened, he skewered it through the middle and poked a piece of string though the hole and made a knot at one end and left a piece still hanging out of the other end. I went with him into the garden, wondering what would happen next. Data put the top end of the piece of string onto the line so that it hung down. It was for the birds! They needed to be fed too. I watched as they started to come and enjoy it. How did the birds know that it was there?

Data was a devout member of Bethel Baptist Chapel close to his home in Abernant. He had friends there, and one day Nancy and I went with him to visit some of them. We went for tea and cake with the Samuel family. When we had finished eating and drinking, the family entertained us with their music. I especially remember Rhian who was about the same age as me. She played the oboe and we all clapped enthusiastically afterwards. I had a funny mixture of feelings. Rhian was a very good oboe player, so that was nice for her. But I was sad that I wasn't as gifted. I had started to have piano lessons but I recognised that Rhian had something special. She subsequently became a professional musician.

Did I stay with Data just a few times? Maybe. But I might have blocked some of the visits off. I had certainly been seriously affected by that early separation and it's possible that my conscious mind couldn't bear the idea of another one. I sense the pain of the wounds of everyone involved but maybe at last I can honour, own and recover from the emotional grief that it caused me.

6

A Shy Child
in a New School

THIS WAS THE pattern of our lives. Aberdare. The prefab. Work and school. The trunk being sent off. Aberdare – the name that still warms my heart.

I needed a uniform for my new school. Nancy took me up to London to buy it. Everything had to be bought in DH Evans – a leading and expensive store in the heart of the city. A great fuss was made as the items were tried on and agonising decisions were made by Nancy. No mobile phones (no *phones*!) to check it out with Lew back in Ingatestone. The two dresses reached my ankles. But hems could be put up and I would grow into them, I heard them say. The woman in the shop also said to my mother, 'And she'll fill out.' They exchanged a secret smile. I didn't know what all that was about. There was a cardigan. In grey. A skirt in grey. 'It might be better to buy two,' the woman said. The hems could be shortened for the time being so that they'd last. It would be quite a difficult job as they had a slight flare. Hats. I had a winter hat *and* a summer one. A Panama for the summer with the school badge sewn onto its ribbon. The same badge could be taken off in the autumn and sewn onto my velour hat for the winter. There were special socks to buy and a blazer. It was probably the biggest transaction Nancy had ever made. But at least we had a DH Evans bag to take home.

I was taken to a shoe shop in Chelmsford. My feet were put into an X-ray machine to check that the new shoes fitted me.

Start-rite. That was what they really wanted for me – the right start.

Lew had been to visit the school beforehand to check it out. St Anne's was probably the best choice they could have made for me, their shy little daughter. I was as happy there as I would have been anywhere. Although I had recovered from my earlier accident and illnesses, I was not a robust child. I suffered almost continuously from catarrh. Today it would probably have been diagnosed as perennial rhinitis, with episodes of sinus infections. Data sent us herbal catarrh remedies to treat it. I remember Potter's remedies and the Heath & Heather ones – some of them are still available today. Even in the twenty-first century these problems are notoriously difficult to treat. Data advocated steam with a few drops of Friars' Balsam in the boiling water. Little bottles and phials kept on arriving in the post.

These problems caused me so much misery. At their worst they made me slightly deaf and the deafness made me feel unreal. I blew my nose again and again. Every time, after I had got rid of the green or yellow phlegm, I thought that it had all gone. But almost immediately I realised that that was not the case. I repeated the ritual time after time. It could literally take hours out of my day and it affected my sleep.

Another thing that bothered me was nettle rash. I never knew when it was going to come and it was difficult to manage. It happened in Aberdare as well as in Essex. I remember being so badly affected once that I had to stay in bed all day because it was too painful to wear clothes. Nana or Nancy came upstairs regularly to cool me down with hearty applications of calamine lotion.

St Anne's School was very different from the one in the village. I went straight from the 'drill' we had in the yard to eurhythmics. Straight from 'Once Upon a Time…' stories to *From Ur to Rome*. The latter had a black cover, as if to say that the study of classics was a serious business. Art was taught in a liberal fashion for the early 1950s. We went into the hall, put old newspapers on the floor to protect it, and then we sat on the floor with pots of paint. Lew had met the art teacher and liked her (she was an 'independent', he said approvingly); she wore a pretty overall for our classes. A teacher in an overall was very unusual!

Each year I had a different form teacher. One of them, Miss Flower, seemed to have been well named. Her dresses always had floral patterns. I had noticed that women had 'growths' between their shoulders and their waists. No one ever talked about this. I wasn't sure if it was an illness but I reasoned that it couldn't be, because all ladies had them. Some had far bigger growths than others. Miss Flower had two massive growths. Sometimes she read us poetry, and when she did she sighed and put her hand between the two growths.

Another form teacher was Miss Richards. She came to school with her black dog. She couldn't bear to be separated from him, so he attended classes too. When Miss Richards walked back and forth along the lines of desks, Peter the dog followed her as if he were assessing us too. Miss Richards was away for quite a long time when Peter died. When she came back her face looked sad. I remember saying that I was sorry that her dog had died. She did manage a little smile. And she said, 'Thank you'.

The headmistress was a slight, sensitive woman called Miss Martin. When she led assembly, she placed her hand between what I now know to be her breasts – just as Miss Flower did when she read poetry. We had music lessons. I found that teacher a formidable woman. One day she told us all that we had to listen to the wireless at the weekend. We had to read her name in the *Radio Times*. It was all very grand and Lew was very impressed. The programme was on the Third Programme (the name for Radio 3 in those days) – which impressed Lew even more. She was a contralto – another woman with huge breasts between her shoulders and waist!

There was a choir at the school and we all had to have an

audition before we could sing in it. I was terrified when my turn came to sing in front of her. She played a few notes on the piano and then I had to copy the same sounds, but my voice came out as a whisper.

'Reserve!' she said emphatically.

I joined the Brownie pack at the school, so when that happened I had to take a later bus home. I've forgotten the original name of my pack but I remember failing the task of lighting a fire with two matches. I obviously needed lessons from Nana. I did pass other tests and Nancy was more than happy to sew the little badges on the sleeve of the uniform. A few years later, when there were more Brownies, they had to add more packs. I was really surprised when Miss Martin (our headmistress and Brown Owl) asked me to be the leader of one of them. Me, a leader? I was shown a whole range of names to choose from – there were all the usual elves, imps and pixies. But there was one that stood out and I knew that was what I had to choose. *Tylwyth Teg* (the Welsh fairies). I went home and asked my parents how to pronounce it properly. At the time Welsh was considered a dead language in many parts of Wales – something you forgot about if you wanted to 'get on'. So I didn't hear a word of Welsh spoken at home. Miss Martin had greater problems than me in pronouncing *Tylwyth Teg*, but I sometimes think she exaggerated her difficulties to see me smile.

We had French classes. I was surprised again to be given a speaking part in a little play that was put on for the parents. It was basically about the daily life of a large French family who introduced themselves in turn to the audience. I played the part of the youngest son and I can remember my words. *'Je m'appelle Toto. Et je ne suis pas petit!'* The words came easily enough, but the problem was the stamping of my foot that had to accompany the second sentence.

'You are *cross*!' I was told in the practices.

And so it was that I uttered two sentences in French whilst stamping my foot. I remember the delight on my parents' faces as I glimpsed them in the audience. I was so pleased to make them happy.

The big problem for me at St Anne's was gym. The main school was an old building but the gym was a newer addition fifty yards or so away. We had to dress in our horrible rough grey shorts and make our way over there. There was nothing that I could manage to do, however hard I tried. I couldn't climb the ropes. I was terrified of the 'buck' and never had the courage to get my speed up on the springboard. In the gym I was a total failure. One day, in the middle of the lesson, I desperately needed to go to the toilet. It was embarrassing to ask to 'be excused' in that hardy crowd and the toilets were in the main building. Some of the grey in my shorts turned a significantly darker shade. I walked back to the school with the others, my head bowed. A confident pupil said to me brightly,

'Why are your shorts wet, Diana?'

'They got wet in the rain.' It was a fine day.

I found most of the girls bossy and very confident. But there was a girl called Vivien who became my best friend. She was very thin, with straight blonde hair, and came from a Quaker family. Vivien hated gym too. At break-time, when the other girls played lively games on the lower yard that also served as a netball pitch, Vivien and I remained on the top patch where the teacher on duty walked back and forth. We formed a 'secret society'. We were the only members and we shared secrets together. I made the badges – two bits of card tied with a safety pin. We attached them to the inside of our coat lapels. It was a 'secret society', after all. We relaxed the rules to let a girl called Sandra join us. Sandra wore glasses; she had a lazy eye, was a bit awkward and, like us, she hated gym. It was enough to set her apart from the other feisty girls. What is now called bullying was the accepted lot of anyone who stood out from the crowd.

I was a dreamy child at St Anne's. I don't know where my mind went. I suspect that it went quite often to Aberdare. I did well academically but not as well as I had done at the infants' school. I was surrounded by children who, on the whole, came from upper-class families, and they had the confidence that can be a great aid to learning. I didn't always concentrate. One of the girls had silkworms which she sold for a tiny amount of money – a ha'penny or even a farthing. I loved buying them from her and was fascinated by unravelling the tiny, thin threads onto a pencil. It could be done quite easily under the desks. I don't know how she came by the silkworms, but I had never seen anything like them.

7

The King Dies

MY PARENTS HAD a daily paper delivered to the prefab. Comics were beginning to be popular but I wasn't allowed to have one; I had to read the *Children's Newspaper* which was delivered once a week. It really bored me and there were hardly any pictures. It was just intended to present the news to children in the same format as an adult newspaper but in a simpler way. The only thing I remember about the newspaper was a photo of the King of England, George VI. He looked very frail and pale in a photo taken at an airport. He was there to say goodbye to his daughter Princess Elizabeth. My parents had the same photo in their newspaper and they talked about it. They said that he looked ill and sad. I could see that too. Everyone else thought the same thing but, in those days, no one dared speculate. There was great shock when he died. It was as if everyone else became ill. Lew and Nancy said that he had been a good man.

After the pomp of the funeral, people's minds focused on the young Princess Elizabeth who was about to be the Queen. She came back wearing black clothes and a veil, but the mood soon changed. The Coronation was going to be televised so that ordinary people could sit in their own homes and watch the whole spectacle.

We might still have been living in a prefab, but my parents bought a 9" television for the occasion. Nancy was much happier by this time and made sandwiches and drinks for the neighbours who came in to join us. I had a horrible voile dress with a skirt made from pieces of netting – stripes of red, white and blue.

Everyone had a holiday for the Coronation but then it was back to work. Nancy carried on at the village school and Lew's career was thriving. I was eventually allowed to take *Girl* magazine. My parents thought that it was suitable reading as its editor, Marcus Morris, was a clergyman.

At weekends I sometimes went to play with the children next door. They had a sandpit in their garden. The couple next door but one interested me. They were married but had no children. When I asked about this, Nancy said that this was sad. I silently agreed with her. Even when she smiled, the woman's eyes were sad. Her husband had a huge angry scar on his face. I wondered if that might be the reason why they had no children. I always smiled and said 'hullo' when I walked past to cheer them up.

My favourite plaything was the swing that Lew had put up for me on the little bit of common ground beside the prefab. I loved it, especially when I discovered that I could work it by moving the lower part of my legs back and forth.

My dark hair had a little wave in it – but this was not enough. At the weekends or for special occasions, Nancy put my hair in rags so that it would be curly in the morning. Sometimes it worked so well that I had ringlets by the morning! It was a time-consuming procedure. First of all, Nancy put a little bit of the precious sugar (still rationed) in a saucer. Then she added water and combed the sticky concoction through my hair. As soon as it was soaked, there were various mini-partings so that the rags could be swirled round each section. Then, when everything was in place, the divided ends were tied onto my hair so that they wouldn't fall out – it was like having bandages on my head. The rags were very uncomfortable and I tossed and turned at night, knowing that I had to keep them in for the wonderful results. Shortly afterwards, a setting lotion called Amami became available and the sugar was kept for sweetening the tea.

My parents had little social life in those early years. There were no grandparents at hand and no relatives. Babysitters had to be paid and it took a while before they had the means and the courage to leave me with someone else. I remember a Minnie Noakes doing the job – a lovely lady but she *looked* like a Minnie. Then there was a Mrs Chopin. My parents asked me afterwards how the evening had been. For once, I came out with the truth. I didn't like having babysitters. How did I know that my parents would come back? There were no phones in those days, of course. I couldn't quite trust that I wasn't going to be abandoned.

We went to stay overnight with some friends of my parents once. They had three lively children. I couldn't eat lots of the things that were given to me for tea, and I desperately tried to think of an escape. I stashed any food that was fairly solid into my socks and my knickers. Then I flushed them down the toilet. To my alarm, that night I was placed in bed between two of the children. I don't think I slept all night. I was terrified.

We didn't have relatives close enough to help out with babysitting but there were some whom we visited sometimes. And they, in their turn, came to visit us. Nancy's older sister, Peggy, had two children. We made the train journey to Liverpool Street Station and then took the underground to Borehamwood and later Oakwood, near Cockfosters. I saw little of her son who was a couple of years older than me at a time when those years made a big difference. His sister, my cousin Heather, was a bit younger than me but she oozed energy and confidence.

'Go and play with Heather,' said Auntie Peggy.

I went into the bedroom to find Heather jumping up and down on the bed – using it as a trampoline and singing, 'Oh hot diggity, dog ziggity, boom what you do to me, It's so new to me, what you do to me...'

I couldn't make myself join in, so I stood at the edge of the bed and smiled.

Nancy's younger sister Nesta lived in London where she and her husband Bill had a thriving dairy. I shyly watched as the customers came into the shop. Auntie Nesta called everyone 'dear' with a Cockney accent, which was strange as she and Bill spoke Welsh in the little long room behind the shop. On one visit Nesta was breastfeeding her baby son. I had never seen anything like it and wondered what was happening. Nesta just smiled at me. People's behaviour was so odd. I wondered why the baby wasn't drinking from a bottle.

From time to time I went with my parents up to London. We went to see the usual sights, but what I remember most about these visits was the smog. It even *sounded* ugly and it was said with great fear as if it was a disease. We used to sit on the train up to Liverpool Street Station but, once we reached Stratford, Nancy started to wrap me up. My school scarf was wrapped around me about three times so that it covered my mouth and nose. I had to pull my hat down so that I could hardly see. Then my parents started to do the same with their own scarves and hats. When we reached London itself, everyone else was hiding behind layers of scarves and hats. Even though I couldn't see much of their faces, everyone seemed scared. It was yellow, the smog, but not a pretty yellow, like a daffodil. It was the same colour as the infected phlegm that I coughed up into my handkerchief.

Back in Essex, my parents began looking at 'plans' and were very excited when they took me up to the site. We were going to buy a house and its foundations were being laid. Once again, I found adults very difficult to understand. They were smiling and obviously happy to be looking at holes in the ground. The holes disappeared when more bricks were laid down to reach the level of the earth. But I still didn't understand the significance. Thank goodness there were still the holidays in Aberdare.

8

Joy and Sadness
in Aberdare

SLEEPING ARRANGEMENTS AT 4 Elizabeth Street, Aberdare, were simple. My parents slept in one of the bedrooms upstairs and I slept in the other. The mattress was soft so that, when I climbed onto it, it sank in the middle, creating a partial cocoon around me. Maybe it wasn't so partial because covering the mattress were layers and layers of blankets and eiderdowns. It was so cosy and comforting that it probably resembled the security I felt when Data had carried me around with him in a blanket when I was a baby. There was a china chamber pot under each bed so that we wouldn't have to face the journey to the outside toilet at night. It was Nancy's job to empty the pots in the morning. When I was in bed in the front room I heard the sounds of the street. Neighbours' children were allowed to play outside far later than I was.

There was the Italian mother who finally came to her doorstep and called all her flock back in – Paulo, Francesca – they were such pretty names! Then there was the night before the 'ash man' came. That's exactly what he was – an ash man. The dustbins were filled with residues from the coal fires, but the sheep still came down from the mountains – determined to find and eat any food that had been added to the ash. I loved to hear their bleats. It was very clever of them to know what night to come, I thought. Many years later I realised that our occupying the beds meant that Nana and Daddy Bom had to sleep downstairs. Probably, Daddy

Bom was given the settee, because of his poor health. Nana would have spent the nights in the chair. Neither of them complained.

Nana was constantly busy. Concessionary coal was tipped onto the pavement outside from time to time, and she had to carry it all to the back of the house to the little coal house in the utility area. She carried it right through her spotless house – filling her bucket, emptying it at the back, walking back to the pavement to fill it again. And, when that job was done, she set about getting everything clean. No one would guess that coal dust had come anywhere near her home. The passageway was scrubbed and polished, the door was cleaned, the brass on the knocker and the letterbox were polished until I could see my face in its shine, upside down. The doorstep was scrubbed, as well as the pavement outside the house.

In Aberdare my parents often went out in the evenings with friends and came home in the early hours of the morning. Nana stayed up to see if they had enjoyed themselves and was there, as ever, with a cup of tea. She was a good cook and I loved to help her make a fruit pie. My favourite job was using a fork to seal the edges of the pastry with a few drops of milk. The white pie went into one of the ovens by the fire and even the smell was delicious when Nana brought it out. Sometimes we used the whinberries that Daddy Bom and I had collected on the mountain.

We usually had our evening meal in the parlour. Nana spread her white cloth on the table before we ate. She had some little fluted spoons for desserts that I loved. We usually ate some cold meat with vegetables and pickles and bread. Nana was very clever and held the loaf against her body and cut the slices so thinly that it was an art. I liked the bread but I loved the yellow, salty Welsh butter even more. I usually managed a couple of mouthfuls of the meat to please everyone. Dessert was always repetitions on the same theme. Tinned fruit was carefully placed in a glass bowl and shared out. I liked the peaches but they never tasted as good as the fresh ones. My favourite tinned fruit was pears – sometimes we had pear halves and sometimes pear quarters. One tin was ample for us all.

Christmas was different. We had an expensive treat – a chicken. I watched as Nana plucked the bird and cleaned it out. Then she added the sage and onion stuffing before the long hours of waiting for the delicious result. Browned on the top, the chicken looked wonderful. There were two slices of breast for me – clean, white and tasty. My parents had the breast too, though Nana and Daddy Bom had a wing or a leg. None of the chicken was wasted; the leftovers were placed in the white cupboard and we ate the remainder over the next few days. Any fat was saved for cooking. Nana boiled up the bones to make stock and there was always Toots. It was Christmas for her too.

The dining table was right against the window facing the street so that Nana could make the best use of the natural light. In the winter the curtains had to be drawn. When that happened, we missed the curious sight of what was happening outside. 4 Elizabeth Street was right opposite the doctor's surgery. Patients had to queue up outside until the doors were open. We saw them all when the nights were light. Nana and Daddy Bom knew most of the patients. Comments were made about Mr Jones or Mrs Evans. Nana seemed to know what their problems were just by looking at them. By the time we were having our pears or peaches, the patients came out, one at a time, some holding a piece of paper. A few of them looked happy but most of them came out looking sad. I felt that I was suffering with them. Our door was never locked, so if friends or relatives had to go to the doctor's, they often popped in to number 4. Without realising it, our house was offering a counselling service.

I had picked up the fact that the Aberdare I loved was also a place where there was pain. Muriel lived next door with her father and her lovely, gentle friend Enid. Muriel's father, Mr Taylor, was very old and sat by the coal fire. I never saw him anywhere else. He trembled all the time – his hands were never still, he had a weak voice and was very pale. In the manse at the end of the street there was another woman who was married and had no children. I smiled and stopped to say 'hullo' to her. She looked sad. Next door to us on the other side were Dai and Gwen. They had no children either but, when I was a bit older, Gwen told me that she had had a baby once but it died. Her eyes filled with tears. In spite of this Gwen liked to tell jokes – she was a natural comedian. Dai was deaf and it was hard to understand what he said. We often gave up and 'talked' to each other in gestures. We both used to laugh at our efforts. Dai and Gwen's outside toilet faced ours and sometimes Dai and I would leave the doors open so that we could have a 'chat'. Dai and Gwen had a different kind of toilet; it was just a plank of wood with two large round holes carved out of it and it didn't have a flush. Gwen's sister Blod lived next door to Gwen with her husband Danny. Yet another married couple without children! Danny was deaf too. Next to Blod and Danny were Katie and Price. Price had lost a finger and part of his thumb. I tried not to stare but I couldn't help it. I wondered why it didn't bleed. The damaged fingers looked like sausages. Did they hurt? Katie was a big, generous lady and, as she got older, she developed diabetes. I often saw her on the doorstep, leaning on her stick and shaking. Another person with tears in her eyes.

There were a lot of deaf people in Aberdare. I sometimes went to see Mrs Rule after we'd bought some material from the market. She measured me up for a dress and carefully cut the cloth. I had to go several times until she was happy with it. Mrs Rule was deaf. She had a deep pink face and very yellow hair. She chatted away with pins ready for the alterations held in her teeth! (I always thought that she was going to swallow some but she never did.) She talked in a strange way that I couldn't understand very well. Nancy and Nana didn't seem to notice. Mrs Rule always smiled.

Gwyneth and Norman lived in David Price Street. I loved Gwyneth and she always made a fuss of me. Their only daughter, Dorothy, had been beautiful and gentle. She caught a virus and became seriously ill. Before she died, she used to sit out on her parents' window ledge. The family was deeply religious and Dorothy began to have visions and insights in her frailty. She told people who were passing that she was soon going home to be with Jesus. Her words made grown men weep. Data was one of them. There had been a misunderstanding in her family and Dorothy told both parties that Jesus wanted them to make their peace with each other before she went to be with Him. They made their peace. I thought that Dorothy must have been an angel.

Although I could see that Aberdare was a place of suffering, I still had a wonderful time – and so did my parents. They socialised with the 'Gang' – a group of friends. The closest of these for Lew and Nancy were Iris, a lifelong friend, and her husband Stan. The Gang's aim was enjoyment – and why not? Life had been tough for them. Everyone had a lot to drink. There was no awareness of the link between driving and alcohol then, so many perilous journeys were made over the Brecon Beacons and into England on Sundays. Wales was 'dry' on the Sabbath. If the Gang's children went too, we spent many hours outside pubs with pop and crisps.

Iris and Stan often held parties in their detached house which Stan had designed himself. With no near neighbours, it was an ideal setting for wild evenings of singing, dancing and drinking. Although I was so shy, I really enjoyed these parties. Nana and Annie (Iris' mother) were often in the back room providing their own entertainment. They were superb actors and storytellers. They recited long Victorian sagas by heart – 'Little Nell' was one of them, with all the actions. Sometimes I stayed with them but I also ventured into the front room where the piano was. Stan was usually the pianist, though Lew played too. Everyone was so happy. Pint glasses of beer in their hands, the men had a familiar repertoire. 'Gaudeamus Igitur', 'Santa Lucia', the 'Whiffenpoof Song', 'Somewhere at the end of the Rainbow', 'If I were a Blackbird', 'When the Red, Red Robin

(Comes Bob, Bob, Bobbin' Along)', 'Pack up your Troubles' and 'Auf Wiedersehen'. I had my own party-piece. At the time of the Coronation I had learnt a song about the new Queen, 'In a golden coach, there's a heart of gold, riding through old London town'. I was put to sit on the piano and always had a generous applause. Singing about London touched Stan's heart as he was a Cockney, so 'Maybe it's because I'm a Londoner' usually followed.

Nancy and Iris were no singers but they didn't want to be left out of the fun so they usually disappeared upstairs and reappeared wearing anything that could pass as fancy dress suitable for the cancan. In hysterics they scarcely managed the stairs as they flashed their skirts and sang, 'Follow, follow, follow the merry, merry pipes of Pan'. We all laughed and the night usually ended with the crazy conga. Daddy Bom never came to these parties and it took me many years to realise that he probably needed some rest – in a bed.

I didn't mind when I wasn't included in the Gang's activities. I enjoyed watching my parents get ready for their nights out. There was no chance of any personal privacy. Lew had the enamel bowl on the kitchen table, with a few layers of newspaper underneath to protect the wood. Hot water from the kettle on the fire was added to the cold water, and my father washed himself – his face and under his armpits. Before he put his shirt on he did something that was called shaving. He fluffed up the lower part of his face and his neck until it was all covered in a lather that looked like cotton wool. But the Father Christmas look didn't last long.

On the kitchen wall Nana had a piece of fretwork that Lew had made when he was a boy. It was black and its cut-out features showed the figure of Dick Whittington with his cat. On the bottom it had a row of carved curves to hold pipes. And, in the top corner, there was a little square mirror. Looking into that mirror my father took his razor and carefully removed all the lather. I thought that it was a very strange thing to do and had no idea why it was necessary. Once the shaving was over, he combed his hair and whisked some brilliantine on with his fingers so that it was shiny. Lew was a very handsome man and, by the time he was dressed for the night, he looked very smart.

Nancy had fresh water in the bowl for her wash. I was fascinated by what happened next. Her face changed as she applied the make-up. First there was the foundation cream from a tube that made her skin look perfect. Then there was the blue, or sometimes green, powder that she applied to her eyelids, smudging it a little at the edge. It was called eye shadow. Her mascara came in a little case that held the mascara itself in a solid block, with a little brush beside it. She usually spat on the dry mascara and rubbed the brush into the patch until it carried some of the black mascara. Then the brush followed the line of her eyelashes until they were very black and curly. She pencilled in a shape to her eyebrows with a little black pencil. And then it was the lipstick. Nancy made a little pout with her lips as though she were kissing someone before applying her red lipstick. Afterwards she pressed her lips together to set the colour. Bourjois rouge followed – giving her rosy cheeks, before the loose powder sealed it all in. Then her hair had to be combed until it was perfect. Then the perfume. She had a choice. Nancy had two bottles – one in a little red-and-white box called Californian Poppy, and the other in a blue-and-white box called Evening in Paris. She dabbed a drop of one of them behind each ear. I wondered why she put it there. Nancy didn't use the little mirror on the Dick Whittington fretwork piece. She had her own mirror in her handbag. All these luxurious items were carefully placed back before she, too, dressed up in her best clothes and shoes. Nancy wore very high heels. They were not a bit like my own shoes. I waved to them as they went out and I was left in the care of Nana and Daddy Bom.

One evening a week, Nana went up to see her brother Davie. When we were down in Aberdare I went with her. We hurried along the streets, up the steep Monk Street until we came to a fish and chip shop. Nana said it was very clean and took me inside. She ordered a piece of fish for me and, true to character, was very selective before accepting a fillet or a cutlet. She usually chose a hake cutlet for me. I wasn't especially fond of fish but it was worth eating it for the accompanying chips. My supper was wrapped up in paper and we carried on walking up to Uncle Davie's house. There was always a warm welcome for me there. Uncle Davie's wife, Maggie, made a cup of tea, then left Nana and Uncle Davie alone to chat. I stayed with them and, apart from the fish and chips, was quite happy to listen and watch. I simply sat there. I could tell that Davie and Nana were sad when they talked about the 'dust' and 'compo' money. They were happy when they talked about their families. Porthcawl was a happy word too.

I knew that it was rude to stare but I couldn't help looking at Uncle Davie's face. He only had one eye. Where the other eye should have been there was a glass eye – a 'pretend' eye. When he looked in some directions his real eye moved but the other stayed in the same position. I wondered if the pretend eye hurt him. Did he take it out at night?

I loved watching the coal fire. It roared red, then simmered down to a burnt orange colour; when it became darker I thought it would go out but it was poked, more coal was shovelled on – and it revived. All the time, the flames made little patterns which kept on changing. I liked trying to guess what the shapes meant. A giant, a dragon, a vase... When I tired of the fire there was the wallpaper. I followed its lines and waves – it was a repeating pattern – and I tried to see how it all worked together. I loved going to Uncle Davie's house.

Back in 4 Elizabeth Street, Daddy Bom knew my favourite foods and asked me one night if I'd like some toast. He cut a slice of bread and punctured it with a fork as he held it against the iron grills in front of the coal fire. We waited and then he pulled the bread away, always smiling. At first it only turned a pale yellowy-brown, but eventually it was done to perfection and marked with the stripes of the grills. Nana always kept the butter by the fire, so all I had to do was spread it across the bread. They didn't seem to be worried about rationing with me, and I was so happy watching the delicious yellow butter sink into the bread, running down to the plate in the holes made by the fork. When Daddy Bom looked at me and smiled, I knew how much he loved me. He didn't need to say anything.

One night, Daddy Bom pleaded with Nana to let him go to the Bird in Hand pub. He needed a florin – which was a lot of money. Nana said no, but Daddy Bom was good at persuading people. He said that it was hard not to have a drink and buy one for his friends. He put an arm around her and winked at me. He got his florin and went out. When he returned, he was very happy. He gave me that lovely smile of his again and took hold of Nana. He sang a song to her that made no sense to me. 'There ain't a lady living in the land, as I'd swap for me dear old Dutch.' We were all very happy indeed – it was well worth a florin.

Because Daddy Bom was unable to do anything other than light work by this time, I spent a lot of time with him. Sometimes we walked along the tram road to Aberaman where his brother, Lewis John, lived with his wife. When we left the tram road for the main road, there was a little waterfall. Daddy Bom showed me how to cup my hands together to get a drink from the lovely icy water. Even in the summer the water was cold, but it was so much fun to see if I could get a few drops to my mouth. Nothing tasted better – not even American Cream Soda from Corona. There was a pub close by called the Plough. Sometimes Daddy Bom went inside and I stood out on the pavement. I didn't mind at all as he came out to check on me frequently with a glass of pop or a packet of crisps. I loved the crisps, with their little blue twisted sachets of salt hidden inside. I took them out, smiling as if I had found treasure, untwisted them and poured the tasty salt all over the crisps. Lewis John and Sara Ann's house gleamed and smelt of polish – just like Nana's. When I gave Sara Ann the wild flowers that I had picked on the way, she was as pleased as Nana and always gave me a loving, accepting smile.

There were other things to please me in Aberaman. Lewis John's granddaughter was much the same age as me and she often came across to play with me. We would spend the entire afternoon with a little bag of old coats and dresses – jewels were lent for the occasion as Dorothy and I entered the world of Hollywood. She was usually Elizabeth Taylor, and if I remember correctly I was the supporting actress. But we had so much fun!

The other attraction in Aberaman was Tommie, Lewis John and Sara Ann's son. He was lovely, gentle and always smiling. When Tommie played the piano, the whole house whirled. Tommie could play anything – from a song sheet or by ear. I stood at the side of the piano open-mouthed and, when he had finished, Tommie smiled at me in the same way as Daddy Bom. He loved to see me smile and asked me if I had liked the piece. 'What would you like next?' I stayed there, fixed to the spot as Tommie's hands moved like tiny ballerinas over the keys – even the black ones that I found so difficult.

At the end of the day we made the journey home to Aberdare – about two miles. The tram road was flat, which suited Daddy Bom. But it was a long way for me and sometimes I got tired. But we had to keep on walking. There was no choice. When I dawdled behind him, he turned round to face me with his lovely smile and he sang:

If I give you the keys to Heaven,
Madam, will you walk,
Madam, will you talk,
Madam, will you walk and talk with me?

As he sang he held out his hand, waiting for me to place mine in his.

I always sang the reply:

If you give me the keys of Heaven.
Yes, I will walk; yes, I will talk,
Yes, I will walk and talk with thee.

We held hands; he continued to smile and we always made it back to our house.

In the summer holidays Nana and Daddy Bom took me to Porthcawl for a week. My parents were left with the freedom of the house in Aberdare. We stayed in a guest-house owned by a Mr and Mrs Kirkstead. Mrs Kirkstead was from Lancashire and wore an apron over her dress. It was the sort of full-sized apron that was popular at the time – more like a dress without sleeves that had a hole on one side of the waist and a long tie which fitted through to make a knot at the back. Mr Kirkstead smoked a pipe all the time. His moustache was yellow. He was a lovely man. We had the time of our lives in Porthcawl.

I loved walking along the Prom with Nana and Daddy Bom at high tide. I stood against the wall, waiting for the huge waves. Nana was usually sitting in a shelter, but Daddy Bom stood to take me in his arms as I ran back to him just before I was likely to get soaking wet from the sea. We laughed with delight. If I was a bit too slow running away, Nana came out of the shelter and fussed over me, worrying about my wet clothes. But it was summer and it always seemed to be hot. We went to the funfair. Daddy Bom went on the water chute with me, while Nana stood at the bottom waiting to hear our squeals of delight. He held me close as we made the slow journey up the chute and across. We shouted out with laughter as the carriage slid down on the rails quickly and ran into the pool of water that splashed us. There was a ride called Around the World. I loved it. We climbed into little boats that followed a dark canal. I remember Holland most of all, with its girls wearing their traditional hats and clogs and the fields of tulips. (For a long time I really thought that I had travelled round the world.) There were the hoops that had to be thrown over potential prizes, the candyfloss and toffee apples. And, inevitably, we visited a good fish and chip shop.

Back in Aberdare, Nana and Daddy Bom invested in a little house in David Price Street. I think Lew must have helped them financially – it cost fifty pounds. Daddy Bom's health problems were getting worse and the future was uncertain. They must have thought of Data and how he had been helped by the rent from his tenants. I went along with Nana sometimes when she collected the rent. She had a little book especially for this purpose, and always looked very proud as she held it.

'One day, this house will be yours.'

A house for me? I daydreamed about living in that house. Then the visits stopped. As an adult I learnt the reason. A tenant had complained about the condition of the house. Suddenly, Nana and Daddy Bom found themselves caught in the trap of poverty and disadvantage. Daddy Bom wasn't well enough to do any repairs. They had put all their money into buying it and couldn't afford the maintenance. The house was 'condemned' and 'demolished'. They were ashamed.

Every afternoon, Daddy Bom went to 'have a spell' – that is, he went to have a rest upstairs in bed. I thought that this was because of his cough. He must have been desperate to get an hour's sleep in a bed. Up the crooked staircase he went. Nana closed the door at the bottom of the stairs with the hook and pulled the curtain back. So he was locked up there for a while until I heard him knocking on the other side of the door. The first thing he did then was to give me a huge smile. That smile with a secret sadness.

9

Katie Kangaroo
– and others

WHEN SHE WASN'T working, Nana often welcomed visitors. Her father had been a widower before he married her mother so Nana had two sets of relatives. I often had no idea who was who. Katie Kangaroo often came down. She called Nana *bopa* – a Welsh word for auntie. I haven't a clue why she had that name – which was never used in front of her. But she and Nana chattered away for ages over cups of tea. Peggy Pontypridd called over too – her nickname was more obvious. A lovely woman, she usually left the house with a jar of pickles from the shelf on the wall leading down to the cellar. We sometimes went to Pontypridd on the bus to go to the market and visit Peggy. She worked in a big shop. My mother bought a liberty bodice for me there.

Another set of relatives on Nana's side was Elsie and her family from Maesteg. They came over on the bus which made their journey quite long. Once, three generations – Elsie, Phyllis and Angela – visited us; the men were working. My cousin Angela was younger than me. When they arrived Angela had been very sick on the bus and the whole house smelt of it as Nana took her clothes and cleaned them, putting them by the fire so that they would be dry for the return journey. Angela was given some of my clothes while she was waiting and, as she shivered by the roaring coal fire, I had thoughts which made me feel ashamed. I thought it meant that I was bad – like a rotten apple that looks alright on the outside but, when peeled, is full of brown bruises. I was very sorry for my little cousin but the smell of sick was overwhelming in our house and I wondered if I would catch the sickness. Would my own clothes smell of it afterwards too? I managed to smile throughout their stay but hoped that God couldn't see into my heart. Nobody else seemed to have guessed what was going on in my mind.

Nana had one relative who didn't come to the house – we went to *her*. Bessie Briggs managed a clothes shop called Briggs. Bessie always looked very proud when we went into the shop; as she talked she strutted back and forth along the floor of her shop like a peacock. She was another grand lady who had huge bosoms, but she was always kind to me.

Daddy Bom's relatives came too. His brother, Rees, came with his wife Lil. Rees had started out as a miner like his brothers, but Rees was committed to politics – he was a communist. He used to sit on the little stool by the fire in the parlour and talk, talk, talk. Although he was arguing for his cause, Rees was never offensive or angry. He saw his beliefs as the answer to greed. He was always serious and peered from behind his round spectacles. But he was gentle and kind with me. He asked me questions – he was really interested in me. His wife Lil was from Lancashire and they had no children (another couple!). She was very feminine and always smelt of flowers and scent. Daddy Bom's sister, Maggie, came from time to time. We called her 'Maggie bottle of pop' because she lived in Porth near the Corona factory. And, although she was tiny, she had an enormous, heaving bosom and a bubbly personality.

Perhaps the biggest excitement came when Blod – another of Daddy Bom's sisters – came. Auntie Blod had been brought up in Cwmaman (on the outskirts of Aberdare) and had fallen in love with a local boy when she was very young. He was killed in the war. Blod needed a new start, so she emigrated to America and made her home in Harrisburg, Pennsylvania, and raised her family there. At first, when she came to visit,

Blod came over by boat – I couldn't believe that she had spent *weeks* on the ocean waves. Later, she flew – the first person I knew who had been on a plane. Auntie Blod always brought presents for everybody – the doll she gave me was bigger and prettier than anything I had ever seen. I was surprised that Auntie Blod, with her bold make-up and her smart clothes, loved simple things.

We had a short conversation once that is embedded in my mind. I asked her where her favourite place was.

She stopped, as if she needed to get extra breath to tell me.

'Cwmaman,' she said with a sad smile in her American drawl. 'But I could never live there now!'

We both stopped. I think the feelings she had were similar to the feelings I had when I was in Essex. We saw something very deep in each others' eyes – *hiraeth*.

'And what's your favourite song?'

She stopped again. 'The Lord's Prayer,' she said simply.

10

A New House, Data

MY PARENTS HAD worked very hard to buy the new house back in Essex. They loved it but it was to hold bad memories for me. It was a semi-detached brick house with a garage to the side. There were three bedrooms – two double and a smaller third one. My parents had the largest bedroom and I had the smaller one. There was an open fireplace in their bedroom, though it was not lit unless Nancy was ill. I had the extravagance of a single-bar electric fire in my bedroom. There was a little round ventilator inserted into one of my window panes, though I could never remember when it was supposed to be open and when it had to be shut. It got very dirty but it was a small price to pay for the fire. Sometimes, in the winter, Nancy put the electric bar on for ten minutes before I got up so that my vest and liberty bodice were deliciously warm before I put my uniform on.

There was a bathroom upstairs and a separate lavatory. I remember the joy on my parents' faces when they installed a little light in the bathroom that also acted as a heater. We had an immersion heater which produced enough hot water for a bath after twenty minutes. We took it in turns to bath – Lew sometimes used the same water after me or Nancy. Hot water was costly.

Going downstairs, there were two steps before the staircase turned at a right angle to reach the ground floor. We had a lounge with French windows. On the other side of the hall and cloakroom there was a large dining room which was furnished with our heavy post-war utility furniture. Next to the dining room was the kitchen – big enough to hold a small table and chairs. A door led off to the pantry. A novelty feature was the hatch between the dining room and the kitchen. Its little doors were usually closed, but they could be opened like magic for hot food to be delivered straight from the cooker to the table. When the hatch was not being used, it held a box for the RNLI (Royal National Lifeboats Institute) – Data's favourite charity. Outside the back door there was a coal house and another small room for garden equipment.

My parents bought a bureau for the hallway to house all their schoolwork and personal finances. We had a three-piece suite which was upholstered by a local lady called Mrs Horsnall. A kitchen cabinet was chosen for the kitchen. It was a very grand affair and had several sections. The bottom section was for storing food – a bit like two cupboards. Then there was another section at eye level for things that were needed regularly, such as tea. In order to reach these things a door had to be pulled down. This also acted as a work surface. Higher up again were a couple of shelves for even more storage. The cabinet was freestanding, and one day I put too much weight on it and it began to totter towards my body. Lew came to the rescue, halting it by holding his hands firmly against the glass. I was saved, but there was blood all over Lew's hands. He didn't complain. I was safe and that was all that mattered to him.

There was a good-sized garden to the front of the house and a much larger one at the back. The front one had a lawn with borders of shrubs and flowers. I remember peonies and roses. It took time for the back garden to mature, but eventually it had apple and pear trees, a vegetable patch and an array of shrubs and flowers.

All of the housekeeping fell on Nancy in an age when women were expected to do all the domestic work even if they had a job. She got up at six to lay the fire downstairs so that it would be ready to light when we got home. At night-time she had to clean the grate out. It was Nancy who did all the shopping and cooking. And, as if that weren't enough, she had just been appointed headmistress of the village school. The only concession to make her life easier was the employment of a local woman who cleaned twice a week.

The village was changing. When we had first gone there it was rural. Most people worked on the land – mainly in arable farming. There was a small contingent of wealthy landowners who lived away from the main street. Miss Russell glided along the High Street in her purpose-built invalid carriage and always had a regal wave for us (her family owned tea plantations in India). Lord Petre had huge grounds down one of the village's many country lanes.

Our drive of new houses was one of the first to change the character of the village. When we moved in there we had nothing but fields with two grazing ponies behind us. All this land was eventually built on for more housing. The train station in Ingatestone linked the village directly with London, and it was beginning to become a trendy base for commuters.

Data was still working from Abernant for the Hearts of Oak Benefit Society, but he could arrange short-term transfers. He stayed with all of his children for short spells. I was thrilled when he came to stay with us. As Ingatestone was close to London, he was usually allocated to the East End office. If he worked at the weekends I went with him sometimes. We made the journey both ways on the 'Primrose Coach from Bow'. Once we were in London we went along the streets to Data's clients. As we went, Data, who was a superb storyteller, entertained me. *Everything* had a story. He always had a twinkle in his eye. I remember one occasion in particular. We were about to go into a house where the people were nice but they didn't take too much trouble with cleanliness.

'If they offer us a cup of tea, drink it with your left hand!' he said.

We stood at the door – the sturdy moustached man with a trilby hat holding the hand of a tiny girl dressed in school uniform. I was small for my age.

'Ah, Mr Griffiths! Come in. And is this your little granddaughter?'

I smiled.

'Come in. I'll get the book. Will you have a cup of tea?'

I smiled shyly at Data. When he talked to the people in the East End, he stopped sounding like Data – he spoke with a Cockney accent. 'Morning, guv!' The book was signed, money was handed over and then the kettle boiled. I was handed a cup of tea. I wasn't sure whether you could see germs, although the cup didn't look different. But I took the handle in my left hand. So did Data.

We wandered into the street markets afterwards. Data knew how to get a bargain. We looked at a china stall.

'Ten shillings to you, sir.'

'It's not worth ten shillings...'

'Pity my poor wife and children...'

'Nine and six...'

I knew that it was a game because the man selling the things smiled, as if he were enjoying himself. The deal was done and the purchases wrapped up in a piece of newspaper. Everywhere, there was another story. I was so happy!

When he wasn't working at the weekend, Data took me to the seaside to help my 'chronic catarrh'. I had to breathe in the ozone which was supposed to help me. I'm not sure that it ever did but it was good fun. Data found stones and shells. He told me that if I put the shell to my ear I would hear the sound of the sea – even when I was back in Ingatestone! We went into cafés to have cups of tea. We once took a boat trip from Tilbury to Gravesend. Gravesend sounded a miserable place but it was like anywhere else in that flat part of the world. I wasn't sure if I had travelled abroad. And, when these wonderful days were over, we climbed back onto the 'Primrose Coach from Bow'.

'Is this where Dick Whittington lives?'

The reply came in a story. We cuddled up to each other on the coach as the stories continued. Someone went off in search of gold. He was a stowaway called Gwilym. There were tales of gypsies... I leant my head against the warmth of his tweed waistcoat and felt so happy and safe that I wanted the journey to go on for ever.

But I had learnt that journeys have their end. Love disappears. And, when it goes, it hurts.

11

Daddy Bom's Cough

WE STILL WENT down to Aberdare in the school holidays. Daddy Bom's health was worse – he was coughing more. For a while he took a part-time job mowing the tennis lawns with a little electrically-motored gadget. I loved watching him going up and down, with the cut grass being thrown up in the air. I ran along and gave it an extra twirl. It was a good game and Daddy Bom laughed at the pleasure of seeing me happy. I was still very young but I always knew that there was sadness in his smile. I wanted to protect him, even though he was a man and I was a little girl. After he'd finished the work, I sat down on a little bench with him on our way home. He took out his little packet of five Woodbines, lit one and I watched as the ash on the end grew longer and longer. He smoked it right down to the stub. I was worried that he might burn his fingers but, as he cradled that last bit of cigarette in his hands, he never did. After this little break, we carried on home.

Nana had had to work as a school cleaner to make ends meet. Daddy Bom usually went up with her and so did I. Nana had fourteen fires to clear and lay in term time. Even in the holidays there was plenty to do. I remember the school well. Beyond the headmistress' office (which had a fire!), there was the huge school hall. And beyond the hall were the various classrooms. Nana always had a smile for me as she polished and cleaned. In the hall there was a little bundle of hoops and beanbags huddled in the corner. The hoops were made of wood and I remember Daddy Bom showing me how to send them rolling down the room in such a way that, when they lost their speed, they rolled back to me. I played the game for hours. I threw the beanbags into the air and tried to catch them. I usually failed, but it was still fun. When I'd finished playing I had to put the hoops and beanbags back, ready for the school children.

One day I went up to the top part of the yard with Daddy Bom, as he was taking a bucket to fill it with coal and return it to Nana. He carried the filled bucket a little way back before he had to stop to cough. I knew the coughing bouts well – and I hated them. Daddy Bom coughed so violently and collected the phlegm onto his handkerchief until the yellowy-green mucous soaked it. His face changed colour and the veins stuck out, angry and blue on his face. When the bout was over, he smiled at me – that beautiful, sad, sad smile again. I saw, even as he smiled, that he was tired and disappointed – his eyes watered with the strain. He had not even been able to carry a bucketful of coal for Nana.

I went with Nana and Daddy Bom to a hospital near Pontypridd once. Maybe they thought it would be an outing for me – we had to go on the bus. But I wanted to go with them anyway. In the hospital we went to a room where there were a lot of other men who coughed. Most of them had wives with them but I don't think anyone else had a granddaughter. Daddy Bom had to take off most of his clothes so that he was only wearing his vest and long johns. He had to stay like that until it was his turn to go to have an X-ray. Nana held his other clothes, and as we waited I could feel the anger in the air. It was a terrible thing to be hoping that the X-ray would be bad so that they could get some 'compo money'. The X-ray showed that Daddy Bom's cough was not bad enough. I was very cross. Had they ever *heard* it? Had they *seen* how he couldn't even carry a bucket of coal? Had they *seen* the way his handkerchief was filled? No, they hadn't! Going back to Aberdare on the bus, Nana and Daddy Bom did what they always did with me. They laughed and joked and cuddled me.

Daddy Bom spent a lot of time sitting on a little stool that was put on the front doorstep. He smoked his Woodbines there as he chatted to passers-by. I stayed around because I wanted to be there too. I didn't understand most of the conversations but Daddy Bom got annoyed when there was too much talk about 'politics'. He always had the same line. 'There's only one honest man who's ever been to the Houses of Parliament.' The Woodbine was usually still in his mouth. 'One honest man. And that was Guy Fawkes.'

We still went for walks. Daddy Bom knew every path and landmark on the mountain. We found gentle ways of climbing it – up Monk Street, through a gate, then onto the mountain itself where there was heather, ferns and all sorts of trees close together. The coughing slowed us up. I had seen it all before but this one was worse. There was the cough itself, the retching, the change of colour in his face, the blue veins that stuck out on his forehead, the phlegm in the handkerchief, yellow, green, bloody. When the handkerchief was saturated he had to spit on the ground. As he retched, then tried to get his breath back, he leant against a wide tree trunk. But he didn't need to hide himself away from me. I was not frightened. I went up to hold his hand. Once he had gained a bit of strength, we continued our walk. We sat at the top, me resting against him. We looked down at the town of Aberdare and found our house – no bigger than a toy. Then Daddy Bom started crying and big tears fell on me. Neither of us said anything, but somehow I knew that we were both happy to be there.

Back in Ingatestone, life was hard. Lew went down to Aberdare at the weekends. He looked tired and sad. I was never told the reason but I knew that something very bad was happening.

One day, Miss Martin (my headmistress and Brown Owl) called me into her study. I assumed that I had done something wrong. She smiled at me from the other side of the desk, her right hand flat across her breast.

'I've got some sad news for you,' she said gently. 'Your

grandfather has died.' I looked at her, speechless. 'Be a brave Brownie,' she added, with a smile.

She gave the salute. I returned it.

On the bus home, I couldn't understand. Daddy Bom couldn't be dead. He had spent hours with me in the bedroom in Aberdare when I couldn't sleep, showing me how to make animal shadows, teaching me the game of cats' cradles. We had walked to so many places together. There was the sad, beautiful smile. And the coughing. The terrible, terrible coughing. The tears on the mountain. What did dead *mean*?

I got off the bus in a daze and walked back to our house. Nancy opened the door before I had reached it. I saw her anxious smile and her bright brown eyes.

'Did Miss Martin have a little word with you?' she asked me.

'Yes.'

I went indoors and Nancy brought me my favourite tea – baked beans on toast. I just ate them mechanically. There were no tears for my beloved Daddy Bom – just the eating of those orange beans with the sauce sunk into the toast and little, half-melted streaks of golden butter.

He was not mentioned again.

12

Data Comes and Goes

THE JOURNEYS OF the weekends to Aberdare and Daddy Bom's death had taken its toll on Lew. He had probably postponed an operation until after the funeral. He went into a London hospital to have surgery for haemorrhoids. Nancy had sole responsibility for me, the house, and her busy career. Once Lew was out of hospital, it was Nancy's turn to have treatment for her sinusitis at London's Great Portland Street hospital. As an outpatient she had a series of sinus washouts. I went up with her once and we went on to Nesta and Bill's dairy afterwards. During that time Lew had extra responsibilities.

Data came to the rescue and I was delighted. I had the stories, the humour and the warmth again. But, when things settled down a bit, there was friction. I used to go into Data's bedroom for story-time and a cuddle at night, but Lew said that I was getting too old for this. Data and I were both upset and I was the one to initiate a plan. I asked him if he would knock on the bedroom wall after my parents had gone to bed. There was just a partition wall between his room and mine. If I was asleep by that time, it wouldn't matter but, if I were awake, I could creep into his room and we could keep up the stories and cuddles. Quite a few times I heard the little tap on the wall and tiptoed into his room. I stayed there sometimes until I fell asleep. If that happened he gently carried me back to my own room.

One day, Data was in the village talking to Mr Manning – the man who had the hardware shop. They were talking business and I heard Mr Manning say that he had some 'little birds from

Australia that are going to catch on in a big way'. I went over to the counter as he lifted up a little box with small perforated holes. To my surprise and delight, there was a beautiful little bird inside with a blue breast. Mr Manning had invested in cages and birdseed, sandpaper to line the bottom of the cages to make it easier to clean, cuttlefish… Data asked me if I would like a budgie. It was such a pretty little thing – and I had never had a pet. Sometimes, when I had been to the fair with Nana and Daddy Bom, I had won a goldfish – but it always died shortly afterwards. I had had great fun fishing for minnows in Aberdare Park, but they never lasted long either. Of course I wanted a budgie!

Data paid Mr Manning for the bird, the cage, the seed and the cuttlefish. We went home and I had the little box in my hands. My parents were understandably proud of their new home. When we arrived there, Data realised that he had accidentally left the cage in Mr Manning's shop. Bunty (I had already decided on the name of the bird) flew out of the box in her newfound freedom, settled on the window-sill, marking the sparklingly clean ledge with her droppings.

When I went to bed that night I heard angry voices downstairs. When my parents had gone to bed, I crept downstairs to see what had happened. Data was sitting in one of the chairs in the dining room, upright but asleep. His big hands were gently cupped together, and inside that cosy space Bunty was resting. I went back upstairs. The cage was fetched in the morning.

I wasn't surprised when I was told that Data had left and gone back to Aberdare. I knew that there had been a row because he hadn't stayed to say goodbye to me.

I became more and more withdrawn. It's easy to blame, to take sides, to cast the first stone. My parents were trying to protect me by not talking about everything. As an adult I can see that there was difficulty on all sides in the relationships. Lew must have felt jealous and resentful of Data – a 'free spirit' who took the law into his own hands and charmed everybody.

Lew had worked hard. Nancy was caught between the two men she loved. But, as a child, I was devastated by another loss. I locked my feelings inside me.

Then something happened one night in our home that tipped me over the edge. My parents were enjoying greater freedoms – there was more money and availability of goods. They loved socialising and often hosted parties where the guests invariably got very drunk. One of them was a professional man who had taken a great interest in me. He brought little plants around for me to put in my patch of the back garden. He always wanted to know how they had grown since his last visit. I looked forward to him coming but, on that particular night at one of these parties, he betrayed me. I had stayed downstairs for a while, and then had gone up to my bedroom. I wanted to go to the toilet but this man had got there before me, so I waited outside. I watched as he opened the door, still putting his trousers in order. When he saw me, he grabbed hold of me, lifted my upper clothes and fondled my body which was still that of a child. Then his hand went lower. He penetrated me with some of his fingers. At the same time he kissed me, pushing his tongue in my mouth. I hadn't got a clue what was happening and I certainly didn't shout out for help. I was just confused. Eventually, he let go of me and did his trousers up again before lunging downstairs. I went back to my bedroom.

I just kept quiet. I thought that no one would believe me; I wondered if this was the sort of thing that happened to children and I also thought that, somehow, it was my fault. I went to sleep in my little bed and put the experience to the back of my mind. The man continued to be friendly with my parents, though he stopped giving me plants to grow. Maybe he didn't recall much of what had happened. Maybe he thought that it was acceptable.

Shortly after this incident I began to experience a phobia at night. I thought that I was going blind. My parents were unaware of it for a while but photographs of me at the time show a little girl with a pale face and dark shadows under her eyes. I knew that I could see during the day but I thought that the blindness came on at night.

My rituals followed the same pattern. I waited for my parents to go to bed. I waited until I heard them switch off their light. Then, very, very quietly, I roamed the house, putting the light switch on in every individual room, taking care to press it in such a way that it would make no noise. Finally, I went upstairs to my room and started the whole process again until I was exhausted. When my parents discovered what was happening they were horrified, then annoyed. They probably just feared for me and didn't know how to deal with it – but I interpreted it as a rejection. They bought a little night-light for me that hooked over my bed-head. That didn't work because I thought that I could only see within the limits of its pale glare. The landing light was left on for me, but I used the same reasoning. Eventually, Nancy came to sleep with me in the spare bedroom. She was at her wits' end. But so was I. In the end I decided that I wouldn't worry any more about going blind – I would just *go* blind. At least I would get some sympathy. To my surprise I kept my sight, but the problem had not been resolved. There was yet another layer of hurt lying dormant in my unconscious psyche.

We were three unhappy people living in the same house. As an adult I became friendly with Mildred, our GP's wife. When I asked her about this phase in our lives, she said how much time she and her husband had spent discussing our troubled family. One day, she said to him, 'If you mention the Williams family once more this weekend, I'll divorce you.' They went away fishing for a couple of days and left a note on the surgery door to inform all their other patients that there was no doctor available.

It was to this same doctor that my mother took me shortly afterwards. She thought that I was ill. She was an anxious mother – and who wouldn't be with her history, and mine? There was terrible fear then about incurable diseases that were potentially fatal. She was right to be concerned, though

I didn't have anything fatal. The doctor said that I was very anaemic. Diagnosis and treatment was simple but effective. He had a little card with a series of shades of red – from a pale pink to scarlet. It looked much like a colour chart for home decorating. In the centre of each shade was a hole. He pricked my finger and put the blood on something that looked like blotting paper. Then he matched its colour with the shades by putting it against the holes. Yes, my blood was pale. I was given iron tablets and had to go back to the surgery until my blood fitted into the hole of a robust shade of red.

13

The Postman Cycled Past

THE 11+ EXAM was looming ahead of me. Like everyone else, I had to sit the papers on a particular day and the future of my education would be based upon them. Maths was not my strongest subject so Lew tutored me in the evenings. We sat side by side with protractors and compasses and pencils and rulers. He was a kind teacher and patient with my less-than-perfect struggles. The day came for the examinations and I sat the papers. If I passed I would go to a grammar school – in my instance, a prestigious one called Chelmsford County High School for Girls. If I were a 'borderline' candidate I would go to a technical college (known as the Tec.), and if I failed I would go to Moulsham Secondary Modern School. Even the word Moulsham, pronounced in an Essex accent, seemed to be filled with shame and defeat.

Every pupil who had passed the 11+ exams was informed on a set day by the only means possible – post. I was standing in the dining room with my parents that morning when, through the net curtains, we watched the postman cycling straight past our house. None of us moved – it was as if we were suddenly caught in a game of 'statues'. A few minutes later, the postman cycled back and left his bike against our wall as he came to the door.

'You silly buggers,' he said to my parents. 'You *knew* she'd passed. Here's the letter.'

So it was Chelmsford County High School for Girls for me after all.

I had already been travelling into Chelmsford to St Anne's School. The new school meant a slightly longer bus journey, but there was also a mile or so to walk at the other end. I had a new uniform – the greys were replaced by navy. I think that I was the shortest girl in the first form and I still had the body of a child. I was overwhelmed by the size of the school (it had about five hundred pupils, so by today's standards it was small). I didn't know any of the other girls. Vivien, my best friend at St Anne's, was going to the Quaker school in Saffron Walden. I was painfully shy. The worst thing for me was the school dinners. One of the staff – a big, authoritarian woman – watched over us as we ate. We were not allowed to leave any food on our plates. Those of us who did – and I was inevitably one of them – were assigned to special seating at the 'diet table'. It was regarded as a joke.

Many of the girls in my class were not only bigger than me but they were also more confident. They had no problems in speaking their mind and were very posh. But there were some from more modest backgrounds. I felt closer to them and I made a few friends. The girl who became my best friend was Gillian (Gill). She was a lovely, gentle girl who wore glasses. She had long plaits and I think that she felt as uneasy as I did in her new environment.

I struggled through lessons – not so much because I found them difficult as the sheer fact that I was unhappy and not terribly interested in the work. I always managed to get reasonably good reports, but my mind was elsewhere. In Aberdare? Daydreaming? I don't really know, but I have gaps in some very basic general knowledge. It was soon evident that I had no gift for the sciences. I couldn't even light the Bunsen burner properly. My memories of those early years in the new school are minimal and very blurred.

My knowledge of sexual matters was even more minimal. When I was about nine, one of the girls in our village told me about sexual intercourse. On the whole she explained it accurately, though I couldn't believe that adults really *did* this. When I asked her if the Royal family did such things, she replied,

'Oh, no! They do it by injection.'

So I thought that, if you were rich or privileged, you had a different option. I hoped that I would qualify for this one day as the alternative sounded so unlikely and messy. Just after I had gone up to the high school, Nancy got a little booklet from the GP. I remember it well. It was called *The Dawn of Womanhood*. Its cover was blue and white, with the colours merging into each other, and there was the picture of an open-mouthed young woman who seemed to be sighing. Nancy handed it to me and said, 'Hide it under the settee if Daddy comes in.' And then she gave me a secret smile. This information was for girls and women only. I read the booklet and was totally confused by it. There were pictures with arrows pointing to different parts of the body, labelled with long words that I had never heard before. I struggled through it and Nancy asked me if I had understood.

'Yes,' I lied.

Several weeks later we all went for tea at the doctor's house. My parents, as local teachers, were highly regarded in the village, as was the doctor and his wife. Mildred, the GP's wife, had a full-time job. The surgery was held in their house and she was needed to fill bottles with the limited range of medicines that were available – there was no dispensing chemist in Ingatestone at the time. If any patients were distressed, she acted as counsellor and friend. When we arrived at their house only Mildred was there. We had a cup of tea and then Mildred suggested that I might like to go down to the woodshed at the bottom of the garden where Dr Alec was working. I duly did as I was told.

I knocked on the door of the woodshed and the doctor told me to come in.

'So they sent you down here, did they?'

He didn't seem surprised. I had never seen anyone working with wood before and watched with interest as a little block of wood changed shape as chippings spurted everywhere. Engrossed in what he was doing, the doctor asked me if I had read the book that Nancy had given me.

I looked at the floor and said yes.

'Silly little book,' he muttered and, as he put the finishing touches to what he was making, he told me in direct and simple language what the booklet had been trying to tell me. And then he handed the wooden object to me. It was a present – a little pencil holder. There were indents on the main surface so that several pencils could stand up vertically. It was beautiful and I still have it. I walked back up to the house with him, holding my present in one hand. We stopped and he picked up a duck egg.

'Here, have this.'

So I had the pencil case in one hand and the duck egg in the other. Before we arrived back in the house itself he said to me, in his Scots accent, 'And when you grow up and err... be kind to yourself, because no one else will.'

I listened to him seriously and then he opened the French doors. As soon as we stepped inside, Mildred and my parents stopped talking.

As an adult, when I befriended Mildred, I learnt the reason why. The doctor was almost certainly a manic depressive. He was a very fine doctor but he was unable to deal with his own illness. There was no medication for the problem in the 1950s and, even if he had been diagnosed, he would have been struck off. So he struggled on, trying to medicate himself as he continued to practice. Barbiturates helped him sleep at night, amphetamines kept him awake during the day. His behaviour was erratic and he was not always faithful to Mildred. He was a sick and unhappy man.

Back in school, my mother decided that I should have a 'bubble cut perm' and I was allowed to wear some casual shoes rather than lace-ups. Other girls were critical. 'I'm surprised that your parents let you wear those.' It was a very strange world. And the people who lived in it were stranger.

14

Aberdare
but Goodwick too

THERE WAS AN escape from all of this and it still came in the form of holidays in Wales.

Lew had bought his first car, and although it was far more convenient I missed the excitement of the steam trains. There were no motorways and no town and city by-passes. Lew sent off to the AA for a route and the lengthy instructions arrived in the post. They were several pages long. It was very tedious. Firstly, on the little back roads in Essex, we passed all the rural villages. This area was so sparsely populated that instructions went something like this:

> After two miles you will notice a white house to your left. Keep on the same road until you pass a farm on your left. Two hundred yards after the farm, take the right turn at the crossroads.

It took us ages. Hertford, St Albans... Nancy was the navigator and occasionally she dozed off to sleep.

'Nancy, you're supposed to be helping...'

'Sorry, Lew...'

I usually curled up in the back seat and went to sleep. We started the journey very early in the morning and always stopped at Northleach in Gloucestershire to have lunch. I stretched my legs, ate my food, and was ready for the much more interesting second half of the journey. Ross-on-Wye. We were almost in Wales. I watched out for familiar places until

I saw the mountains – the lovely, wonderful mountains. We had almost reached Aberdare itself when Lew was instructed to close the window because of the terrible stench from the Phurnacite plant in Abercwmboi. (He had to wind the window down to indicate that he was turning right, left, slowing down or overtaking, so the window was often open). Nancy felt so sorry for the people who lived there but she was not prepared to suffer the smell. It was very bad – like rotten eggs, but worse. At last we turned up Wind Street and I saw the house that I loved – 4 Elizabeth Street. Nana was always there to welcome us with the roaring coal fires and a cup of tea. She was very proud to have a car parked outside her door.

Things were different in Aberdare without Daddy Bom. No one ever referred to him in front of me. I didn't have anyone to go walking with me any more, so I went up the mountain on my own, tracing the steps that we had made together. Nancy helped Nana in the house but Nana still wanted everyone to have fun. There were still the nights out with the 'Gang'. I still went up with Nana to spend an evening with Uncle Davie and I played with his grandchildren – Margaret, David and Janet. When Nana was not working, Lew looked at all the receipts and the doctor's notes that she had stuffed carefully into envelopes. Because pneumoconiosis had not been listed on the death certificate, Nana wasn't eligible for the 'compo' money. All she had was a ton of coal dumped outside her front door from time to time. Nana didn't grumble – she always seemed cheerful.

She had often been busy before we arrived – climbing ladders, putting new wallpaper in the passageway, keeping the black things black with blacking. Keeping the white things white with whiting. There was still pride in her little bits of brass on the doorstep, letterbox and door handle. They still gleamed. She managed to get everything spotless with none of the modern products that are available today.

Things had changed for Data too. He had sold his house in College Street, Abernant. His older sister, Phoebe, had spent her life as a housekeeper in their native north Pembrokeshire. She had never married, so when she retired she had no home. The solution was obvious to Data. He sold the house in Abernant and bought another in the village of Goodwick – just a few miles from his birthplace. Situated in the main street of the village, Pencaer, 1 Goedwig Villas, was more than adequate for the two siblings. It stood proudly with its three storeys, its bedrooms that seemed to go on for ever and two bathrooms. At the back there was a very steep garden that was quite difficult to climb, let alone tend. It was a short walk away from the sea. It must have been his hope that the house would provide good holiday accommodation for his scattered family. And so it did.

At last I had somewhere to stay with Data where I didn't feel nervous.

His eldest daughter, Peggy, went down a couple of times with her children; Nesta, who was living on a farm in Tregaron, visited (though farming restricted her). Data's son, Owen, went down often with his wife Olga and their two children, Graham and Tara. Although they were younger than me I loved the company of my cousins. I usually went down with Nancy – Lew came down from time to time but he wanted to spend the time with Nana. I'm sure that there was still underlying tension between the two men. It must have been hard for Lew to see the difference between Nana's lot and that of Data. His 'villa' was not only large – it housed some of the antiques that Data had started to collect.

When Graham and Tara were down with us, we spent most days going out to the beautiful beaches in the area – Goodwick itself, Cwm-yr-eglwys, Freshwater, Saundersfoot, Broad Haven, Abermawr... It was wonderful! The three of us messed about in little pools on the sand and paddled. We smiled for the little black-and-white photographs. In one of these, Data and Auntie Phoebe had ventured down to the sea with us as well, dressed in coats and hats, even though it was summer. This rough, wild terrain had reared them but it had never been a place for relaxation. They looked ill at ease.

We never had to worry about the weather either, as Auntie

Phoebe was a wonderful forecaster. She had a piece of seaweed hanging in the huge kitchen and she could tell the weather for the following day by touching and smelling it. My cousins and I walked along the breakwater – it was great fun – a taste of real adventure. We went into the shops in Goodwick – the chemist, the greengrocers, the Post Office and the café. For Graham, Tara and myself, the café was brilliant. We saved up our pocket money and went inside to have glasses of pop. And, if we had any reserve money, that was spent on the jukebox. Our favourites were 'Last Train to San Fernando', Lonnie Donegan's skiffle songs, and Connie Francis crooning 'Among my Souvenirs' and 'Carolina Moon'. We just sang away, tapping our fingers on the table to get the rhythm. We were in our seventh heaven. The one thing that spoiled these days for me was the fact that Owen was so strict with Graham. It hurt me deeply.

I remember one evening when Graham had been sent to bed. Data must have had a record player because Owen had bought a record to play there in the lounge. It was 'Christopher Robin is saying his prayers'. As he listened to the words, Owen smiled at me with tears in his eyes. 'God bless Mummy, I know that's right, And wasn't it fun in the bath tonight...' The words clearly struck a deep chord with the man who had grown up with no memory of his own mother.

When Nancy and I were down on our own, I met some of the very many relatives I had from Data's side of the family. I also had the chance to meet some of Jane's family – the beautiful grandmother I had never known.

Sometimes Data walked up with us to Stop-and-Call (a nearby hamlet) and then we often went on to his native Llanwnda. We literally stopped and called at Stop-and-Call which was at the top of the very steep hill that we had climbed from Goodwick itself. Stop-and-Call was where Auntie Catherine lived and there was always a warm welcome for us. We sat down, had a cup of tea and a biscuit. Auntie Catherine was the widow of Data's brother, William. The two brothers had been close but William had died; he never really recovered after one of his sons had been drowned in the Second World War. The couple had had ten children and I met some of them in the house. There was gentle Owen, chatty Ronnie, sweet Betty and the lovely, warm woman who was called Phoebe Ann.

If we walked on further to Llanwnda we met more of my grandmother Jane's family. Her brother Luke lived there with his wife Maggie and their two children. Their house looked so fragile (it had originally been built of corrugated iron) that I was surprised that it stood up to the winds and storms in such an isolated and exposed place. They were all very friendly and I played with the girls. The one off-putting thing for me was the lavatory. At the far end of the garden was a little hut with a seat inside and two holes. There was no chain to flush.

On the way back from Stop-and-Call we sometimes stopped at Phoebe Ann's house halfway down the hill into Goodwick. Phoebe Ann had married Tommy who had built the house himself. They were lovely and had two lively daughters. Janet was older than me and she had a few tales to tell. She was just old enough to have been employed at the Fishguard Bay Hotel on a temporary basis as a chambermaid when *Moby Dick* was filmed in the area. The film's main star was Gregory Peck and Janet had taken care of him. There were adventures during the shooting – the rubber whale went missing, but the most impressive thing for me was the fact that Janet had Gregory Peck's autograph. Not only that, but he had given her the rubbery scar he had worn during the film to make him look craggy.

Her younger sister, Sylvia, was a year or so younger than me and we had great fun together. The boats that went from Fishguard to Rosslare rested in the harbour between sailings. Pocket money went on strange things! Several times, we walked along the track to the anchored ferry boat and caught the attention of one of the crew.

'Can you show us around, please?'

One of the sailors was always willing as we asked what we

thought were intelligent questions – 'How many people can the ship hold?' 'How long does the journey take?' 'How many crossings are there in a week?'…

The sailors duly answered the questions and showed us the cabins and the decks. We were both tiny for our age but, somehow, at the end of each visit one of us had the aplomb to hand the sailor a sixpence as a tip for his service. And, once we were out of sight and hearing, we broke down into hysterical laughter.

Sarah was Data's older sister. She lived in Cwmcelyn, a cottage in the Dyffryn area of Goodwick. Auntie Sarah was a widow who had her three sons living with her. Her daughters had married but still lived locally. I remember them all. Thomas Henry was a pale, gentle man who had a sad but accepting smile; I liked him. I later discovered that he had been invalided out from active service in the war. The other brothers were twins – Jack and Glyn. I never got to know Jack well and I was scared of Glyn. He had Down's syndrome (called by a different name in those days). No one explained to me why he was the way he was.

We spent a lot of time with Auntie Sarah's daughter, Millie, and her family. Janice was just a year younger than me so we became friends. We sometimes had a meal with Millie and I was horrified by the things they ate. A crab? Seaweed? Nancy loved it all but I played safe with bread and butter.

Nancy and I went over to Letterston to see more of Jane's family. My grandmother's sister, Eliza, was an old woman who lived in her cottage alone – another widow. She sat in a corner of the main room downstairs which was always dark because the walls were solid and the windows were small. There were the inevitable cups of tea and biscuits before the two women talked. All I could see of Auntie Eliza was her white face and hands against her black clothes in the darkness of her cottage. Afterwards, we went across the road to where her daughter Jane (Jane was a family name) lived. This Jane was very beautiful too. She kept a shop – a bit like Mr Manning's shop in Ingatestone. We had to step through the shop itself to get to the living quarters and it was quite an obstacle course as goods spilled out everywhere. Jane was technically open for business when we called so, every now and then, she would disappear to serve someone. We had more tea at Jane's house and biscuits or cakes. My mother was very fond of Jane and the two cousins chatted together for ages. As they talked I couldn't take my eyes off Jane – she was so beautiful and serene. There was a simplicity about her and yet she seemed as sophisticated and elegant as any woman I had seen in Essex – or even in London. She had a very sweet nature and, when Nancy asked Jane the secret of her lovely skin, she took us upstairs. On her dressing table was a little bottle of pink liquid. She let me try it out. It was called Oil of Ulay – which seemed the right sort of name for the beauty secrets of an aunt who kept an Aladdin's cave of a shop.

15

'Arglwydd Iesu'

I MUST HAVE had four or five years of holidays in Goodwick. After the evening meal my cousins Graham and Tara had to go to bed quite early. Nancy sat in the front room with Owen and Olga. I wasn't interested in what they were talking about so I went into the kitchen. And there, with Auntie Phoebe having retired to her room, I had Data to myself. At last! I will never forget those evenings. He was usually working – preparing food for his precious family. Sometimes, as a treat, he made me delicious potato fritters. I watched as his lovely, big warm hands cooked with such delicate sensitivity. There were big chairs in the kitchen, and when he had finished all his work Data and I sat down to talk. I couldn't get enough of it. Wales. The Welsh language. The old traditions. Literature. Poetry. The meaning of life. Faith.

Data had a black Welsh Baptist hymnal and I took it down to look at a few of the lines of one of the hymns. (I had learnt a little Welsh.)

'Arglwydd Iesu, arwain f'enaid, At y Graig sydd uwch na mi.' (Lord Jesus, lead me to the Rock that is higher than me.)

'There *is* a Rock that is higher than us, isn't there?'

And, with moist eyes, he replied. 'Oh yes. And it's always there.'

At the end of the holidays Nancy and I left Goodwick by train. Even though his house wasn't far from the station, Data always booked a taxi – it was his final gesture of hospitality. The pattern was always the same. The taxi took us from his house to the station, then he paid the driver, took out the case from the boot and carried it onto the station platform for us. As soon as the train came in, Data took the case onto the train and put it up on the rack for us. Once he had done this, he said goodbye and got back on the platform. When the whistle blew, he stood there on the platform waving us off with his handkerchief blowing in the air until we lost sight of him and the little white piece of linen.

But, on this occasion – an Easter holiday – it was different. Initially, he did the same but, once he had lifted the case safely onto the rack, he got off the train and looked at us. He was tearful and walked away before the train left. Maybe he knew we would never see each other again.

We returned to Ingatestone. The Whitsun holidays approached but we had made the decision not to go down to Wales. Nancy was a generous soul and she had befriended a widow in our growing residential estate. They had become good friends and I got to know the family. There were two daughters. One was several years older than me but I became particularly friendly with the younger daughter, Susan. The older daughter was getting married on Whit Monday and she had chosen her sister Susan to be her main bridesmaid. But she had chosen two other bridesmaids – one was an old friend and the other one was me! I had never been a bridesmaid before and I was old enough to look fairly adult in my long peach-coloured dress and hair upswept into a bouffant style. We were all excited about it.

The day before the wedding there was a phone call from Nancy's brother Owen. He and his family were down in Goodwick for the holidays. He had bad news for Nancy. I saw her screaming and shouting in disbelief. She was completely inconsolable. Data had died suddenly and unexpectedly in his sleep.

It didn't register with me properly. I felt nothing. I just turned to Nancy and said, 'It's Whit Sunday. It's a lovely day to die.'

Plans had to be made. Lew drove over to bring Peggy

back to us so that the two sisters could go down to Goodwick together on the train the following day. When Peggy arrived in Ingatestone, she was firm with her vulnerable younger sister. She was kind to me and asked me how I felt. She answered her own question.

'I expect that you were like Heather [my cousin],' she said. 'She had a little cry and then she was alright.'

I wish that my response had been as normal as that.

On the following day I went down to the bride's house to get ready. After the short car journey to the church, I followed the bride and the main bridesmaid up the path that led to the Norman church. There was a crowd of villagers assembled to watch us all. In the photographs I was smiling sweetly. When the bride was ready to walk out of the church with her new husband, I followed them down the aisle. I noticed the two sad sisters in the congregation. Desperately trying to smile, they looked out of place with their dark clothes and the necessary black armbands that indicated their state of grief.

Afterwards they left for the station, but Lew and I remained in Ingatestone. With one exception, nothing was said about my loss. At the wedding reception, Susan said to one of the guests, 'Doesn't she look grown-up? And it was hard for her because her grandfather died yesterday.'

I had begun to revise for my O levels. We had a letter from Data that arrived after his death. He had written to tell us that he had been on the bus to see a friend in nearby Dinas. The friend's granddaughter was revising for her O levels too and it made him think of me. There was a new herbal remedy on its way to me for my catarrh.

Daddy Bom had died just before I sat my 11+. Data had died just before I sat my O levels. I had shown no emotion after the losses.

16

Coffee Bars and Justice

I FOUND LIFE at Chelmsford County High School for Girls dull. From the beginning I didn't enjoy my lessons, although I worked hard enough to satisfy everyone and I was in the top stream. But my heart was not there. Adolescence is a notoriously rocky ride and, for me, it was marked by amazing contradictions and inconsistencies.

The one thing that I can remember clearly about the early years said a lot about me. I was asked to decorate one of the window sills. (We had a particularly ugly and dismal classroom in the second year.) To cheer it up a bit, our form teacher chose people once a month to decorate one of the window sills following a theme of their choice. The displays remained there for the month, and at the end there was a competition for the winning display. On this occasion, when I would have been thirteen, Mrs Rees (married to a Welshman) chose the theme of countries. She invited me to do one and I chose Wales. I was pleased, partly because I was so shy but mainly because I wanted to teach everyone about Wales. My parents must have been delighted at my enthusiasm. I had an array of things to make my window sill look lively and informative. I had Daddy Bom's Davy lamp as well as literature and ornaments. I did a lot of research. I spent hours on the task at hand and my window sill, after a month of standing proud, won first prize.

My main friend for the first five years in the school was Gill, a farmer's daughter. I had another friend who was a 'foreigner'. Felicity pined for her mother's native Ilkley, in Yorkshire. We both liked drawing in the margins of our books when we were bored (something that happened frequently). We were regularly reprimanded.

'Don't draw in the margin, Diana!' brought about a sly collaborative smile from Felicity.

'Don't draw in the margins, Felicity!' had the same response from me.

I think that that was my worst misdemeanour there, but I discovered something new about myself. I instinctively defended and befriended anyone in my class who didn't fit in. I liked one girl who was always getting into trouble. One day, she told the first years that they would faint if they put blotting paper in their shoes. Several girls actually did faint – the sick bay was full. She was eventually expelled but I felt sorry for her because she was unhappy. Another girl arrived in Chelmsford from a school in Wales, even though she, herself, was not Welsh. The other girls didn't accept her and the teachers were desperate for her to settle down. I was her friend until her parents decided to move her elsewhere.

It wasn't just the girls; some of our teachers were Welsh. One of them – a sweet woman who was newly qualified – came from Aberdare. The other girls openly mimicked her accent until the day she spoke up. 'I'm proud of my accent,' she said before the lesson began, 'I don't want to hear any of you making fun of it again.' Good for her, I thought. There was another teacher from north Wales who was joked about mercilessly. I didn't like that – it wasn't fair.

This feeling wasn't restricted to the classroom. There was something inside me that made me identify with outsiders, with the losers. It's probably innate but it was certainly something that had grown from my own experience of suffering and loss.

One weekend, I told my friends that I couldn't go out to play with them. I was horrified to see a baby bird fall out of the nest opposite our house. I persuaded Lew to let me look after it, convinced that it would recover. He brought it in and I held it in my hand for hours at a time. Lew found a little syringe and

I let drops of water fall into its tiny beak. We made a nest of cotton wool. On the second day of my nursing care, Lew came up to me and said,

'Diana, I think it has died.'

I looked at the tiny creature in disbelief – and dropped it. Maybe I wasn't ready to face the inevitability of death. I went with Lew as he buried the fledgling.

There was a boy on our drive who couldn't read. His parents were academics and they were very worried about him. When he came to our house I asked him what his favourite song was. It was 'Last Train to San Fernando'. The words are simple and repetitive. I taught him to read. I got my friends on the drive to make some things to sell for Cancer Research.

These years were not without their joys. Whenever there was a rugby match on the television at the weekends, I watched it with Lew. I didn't understand all of the rules but I shouted along with him and we sang so loudly that I wondered if we could be heard at Twickenham. Nancy came into the lounge, smiling, with cups of tea and food. She was just content to see the two of us happy together.

My parents became active members of an established Welsh society in Brentwood. They attended the many social events. I wasn't interested in that but when someone mentioned that there was going to be a new Welsh society in Chelmsford, I joined. At fifteen, I was one of its first members. One of the women started a Welsh conversation class. My parents allowed me to go. One of the teachers in school went to a Welsh chapel in London on Sundays. I managed to get hold of some old O level papers and, with the help of *Teach Yourself Welsh* hidden under my desk in maths lessons, I mastered some of the basics. My efforts were given to the teacher who asked her minister to mark them for me. I decided to change the spelling of my middle name. Instead of Diana Griffiths Williams, I wanted to be known as Diana Gruffydd Williams.

I was a late developer physically. As I waited anxiously to catch up with my peers, I spent my time away from school wearing loose jumpers to hide my flat chest. Sloppy Joe tops were fashionable and they saved my pride.

Nancy was concerned about me and I can understand why. She paid for me to go to Brentwood every Saturday on the bus to have ballroom dancing classes. A friend from the village went with me. I can't remember anything about the lessons at all, but I recall the two of us sitting upstairs on the top deck on the way back. We watched the world go by as we ate our way through an entire packet of Marie biscuits. Not a lot happened in Ingatestone, but when a dance was organised in the village hall Nancy persuaded me to go. I had a very grown-up dress – it was made out of gingham with a hoop sewn into its hem. I duly walked down to the hall and spent the entire evening staring at the ground. The rector was there to keep an eye on proceedings. He talked to me kindly but no one asked me to dance. I didn't exactly look as if I were expecting anyone to take me to the floor. And, of course, I was the local school teachers' daughter.

Nancy had an account at a fashion shop in Ilford called Hélène's. She went up there from time to time and, although she bought clothes for herself, she was generous in buying me my first grown-up dresses. By this time there had been two incidents that led me to believe that I was becoming a 'young woman'.

When I was fourteen or fifteen, I went over to the fair in Goodwick with Nancy. We were watching the Dodgems and waiting for them to finish so that we could have a turn. I had started to wear a bra and I had a V-neck jumper. The V came too low so I pinned it up higher with a little pearl brooch. As we stood at the edge of the rink, the man in charge of the Dodgems looked over at me. He wasn't looking and smiling at a child – I could tell that. I was embarrassed, but Nancy smiled at me. I had passed a rite of passage.

About the same time I went down to Aberdare on my own by train. I can't remember why – either my parents had a social commitment or they needed to finish off some schoolwork. As a child I had occasionally been sent down on my own in charge of the guard. My parents thought I was ready to make the journey alone in charge of myself. Nancy took me to Paddington and saw me onto the train. One of the Welsh teachers from my school happened to be catching the same train home to Neath. The two women chatted together as I went up to a stall to get something to eat and drink for the journey. The man serving me gave me the same look as the one I had had from the Dodgem ride man. I don't think that Nancy noticed but the teacher did – and she gave me that same secret smile.

Away from school my closest friend was Susan – the sister of the person whose bridesmaid I had been. (Susan was a year older than me at a time when that year made a big difference.) Like me, Susan was interested in art and the arts. We went on Saturdays to somewhere exciting and new – I had never seen anything like it. A coffee bar had opened in Brentwood! Susan asked for something called Graves, so I asked for the same thing. It was my first taste of alcohol. Invariably, some boys came up to us but Susan, who had started to smoke, was the attraction. She looked sophisticated – I didn't. I was so disappointed that the boys were interested in my friend – not one of them looked at me. It was as if I weren't there.

Yet, within a year, things changed. Susan and I became very knowledgeable about make-up, perfume and fashion. There was a shop in one of the arcades in Brentwood that stocked the best French perfume, Givenchy, Worth, Rochas... We went into the shop and tried the fragrances on our wrists. We spoke of floral tones or heady ones and, although we seldom had enough money to buy anything, the manageress said that she didn't often have 'customers with such a sophisticated and discerning knowledge of perfume'.

I was learning.

17

A Fiery Celt

ONCE THE O levels were over, I was determined to leave school even though I passed the eight subjects I had sat. I hadn't been happy, and the thought of another two years in the sixth form left me cold. Gill was also going to leave. The problem was that I had no idea of what I wanted to do with my life. Initially, I considered going to art college. I loved drawing and had assembled a presentable portfolio. I applied to the art college in Walthamstow and Lew came with me to the interview. When it was my turn, I went in, showed them my work and they seemed fairly interested. I would probably have been accepted anyhow. But, as soon as I left the room, they saw Lew in the corridor. By that time he had a good reputation in Essex for his work in education. Apart from being head of maths and religious education at various times, he was the first person to be appointed as a careers master in the county. Suddenly, their attitude changed. *Of course* there would be a place for me! As Lew spoke to them, I stomped down the stairs. If I couldn't be accepted on merit alone, I wouldn't go there at all.

So I had to think of something else. I liked French and thought that a bilingual secretarial course at the technical college in Chelmsford would suit me. I enrolled and attended the tutorials. For two days I endured the classes. As everyone practised together on massive typewriters, I was the only one who couldn't get into a rhythm. Then I discovered that the *bilingual* part of the course involved just two tutorials a week. The principal was a Dr Smith – at a time when there were very few PhDs around. I knocked on his office door and announced that I was going to leave.

'Do you think that you've given us a fair chance, Miss Williams?'

'Yes,' I replied – and made my way back to Ingatestone.

Once I was home I locked myself in my room and refused to come out. Nancy left a meal for me outside the door and I only retrieved it when she was gone. I just couldn't face my parents. My life was a mess. I didn't know who I was.

I began searching for a meaning to life. I read books on comparative religions and Christian mysticism. Evelyn Underhill was my favourite, but I had never had a neat faith to cling on to. Nancy had been a Welsh Baptist but, as her school was a Church of England one, she became an Anglican. My father, although he taught religious education, wasn't interested in the institution of the Church. I had been to Sunday school when I was a small child in Essex, but the lessons had left little impression on me. I had been asked to snuff out the candle once and I recall sticking little pictures into a book. That was all. The institution of the Church had not attracted me.

When I was fourteen, I went to confirmation classes. I attended the first sessions but I couldn't take it all on board. Why was there suffering? Why did God let people die? What about the poor? What had it to do with these classes? God was supposed to know everything about us. That was quite a scary idea but, if He knew me, He would know that I wasn't being honest. When I told my parents they were taken aback. I embarrassed Nancy because of her position in a Church of England school. She told me that I should go up to the rectory and explain myself if I was so determined. I don't think she thought that I'd have the courage to do it, but I walked up alone to the rectory, knocked on the door and explained my reasons. My heart was pounding as I spoke to the rector – who couldn't have been kinder. He said that he wished that more young people were as thoughtful as I was. From that night onwards, he was always courteous and showed a personal interest in me. We kept in touch long after I had left Ingatestone and he was the one to write a reference for me when I finally applied to college.

The art college opportunity had gone and I had walked out of the course at the technical college. I was Lew and Nancy's only child and all the old concerns must have resurfaced. They had come here to give me a better start in life – it had been a struggle all the way through and it showed no sign of coming to an end. Because of all the problems in my childhood, I wasn't very spontaneous with my parents and that must have hurt them. There was a distance between us.

But if it was hard for them, it was very tough for me. When I eventually emerged from my bedroom after the confrontation at the technical college, I discussed things with Lew and agreed to do the only thing that seemed to be possible for a sixteen year old. I would return to school and, hopefully, in the sixth form I would discover what I wanted to do with my life. An appointment was made at Chelmsford County High School for Girls for me to see the new headmistress. Lew drove me up there but I insisted on going inside alone.

The new headmistress was called Miss Pattison. She was tiny and wore a fitted suit. Her hair was short, jet-black with white wisps on either side above her ears. She wore lipstick but needed nothing to enhance her thick dark eyebrows and deeply-set eyes. In front of her, at her desk, she had my O level results. She was charming and had no problem about accepting me back at school. Looking at my results, we agreed that French, Latin and art would be good A level choices. She even wondered if I might attempt a fourth subject, but I decided against it. She told me that she was from Yorkshire, so I felt free to be open with her about my love for Wales. We had made a good start. When I went out to Lew in the waiting car, I said that I wasn't allowed to go back. Then I laughed and told him that I was only joking. He laughed back but said that he would have had something to say if I had been refused.

And so I started being a sixth former. There was an unused

building within the school grounds (I think it had been the caretaker's house originally). Miss Pattison had just allocated it to the sixth form, so we had an independent base where we could make coffee or tea and relax between classes. Before long I was really enjoying my subjects. Latin grammar didn't appeal to me much but I did it willingly. It was the literature that I warmed to – poor Dido in Virgil's *Aeneid*! Abandoned. *'Infelix Dido…'* I learned long passages by heart. There was much more relevance about learning French grammar. I enjoyed speaking the language and Nancy ordered the magazine *Elle* for me from the newsagents in the village. I loved the literature. As for art, I was in my element. I'm not a brilliant artist but I enjoyed developing the skills that I had. My main interest was in the history of art. I poured myself into its study, identifying with so many of the painters. Yes, I could understand Toulouse-Lautrec and Van Gogh and Gauguin… Wasn't my soul, with all its inner feelings, somehow linked to theirs? I was unleashing a great passion that I didn't know existed.

Our art teacher took her little A level group for a couple of outings. She seemed almost a friend as we journeyed up to Osterley Park to marvel at the Adam ceilings. An important trip for us was the visit to the Royal Albert Hall to hear the art historian Sir Kenneth Clark lecturing on Michelangelo. After the lecture the audience, which had come from all over the country, was invited to submit an essay for a national competition. The title was 'Michelangelo, painter, sculptor, poet, architect – more than human, angel divine'. I enjoyed writing my essay which was submitted with the others. To my surprise I won first prize. The newspapers took the story and I encountered my five minutes of fame.

At the same time as this surge in artistic and literary interest, some alarming things were happening to my body. For no reason and with nothing specific to trigger it off, I began to sweat and feel dizzy; my heart had loud palpitations and I felt so weak and strange that I thought I was going to die. It happened once, then the second time, then the third time. I had no idea what it was. There was a little library in Ingatestone and I went to see if I could discover what the problem was. There were, of course, very few medical textbooks available to the general public and no information to send away for. Psychiatry was in its infancy and, as I searched the pages of the only relevant book in the library, there was just one disease that seemed to fit my symptoms. 'Dementia praecox is a devastating disease,' it read. 'It often afflicts young people who are highly intelligent. There is no cure.' So I had no future.

The attacks continued but so did my love for my studies. It was as if they went together somehow. I had friends in the sixth form. Felicity was still there – though she was doing different subjects. I became very friendly with two other girls. Margaret Enever was a deliciously eccentric and original girl with extraordinary looks – not conventional at all but interesting. Margaret Fielding was again not the average sixth former. She had beautiful red hair, and every so often she sold it to someone who made wigs. So she went from a very short hairstyle to a long one – apparently unconcerned about its look, either way. She just wanted the money. They both wanted to be called by their surnames only so, apart from Felicity, it was Enever and Fielding. Back in Ingatestone I was still friendly with Susan.

Enever and I went up to London on Saturdays as often as we could. A strange transformation took place on the train to Liverpool Street Station. We found an empty compartment, took out the white lipstick, mascara and perfume, often pouting in the train mirror to check that we had the right kind of sultriness. We were supposed to be making cultural visits – and so they were, because we visited the Tate or the National Gallery. But, afterwards, we found our way to coffee bars in Soho. There were always a lot of foreign boys there. Enever had some German blood in her, so she sought out the Germans. I always chose a French boy, thinking that I could improve my education at the same time. Enever and I agreed on the time to leave for the train home and we went our separate ways. Things were very innocent in those days and all that ever happened was that the boy of my choice kissed me passionately as we sat along the Embankment. Nothing came from any of these encounters – with one exception; I can't even remember their names. But, for an hour or two, I really enjoyed a safe intimacy that I would leave behind later in the afternoon. I discovered that I was good at kissing. One of the boys got impatient with me when I quoted Verlaine at him – he thought that our time was too short to waste on French poetry.

Susan and I also went up to London at the weekends and usually headed for the Lyric Theatre. It was showing *Irma La Douce* – we loved everything about it. We raved over the beautiful, lithe flexibility of Elizabeth Seal and softened to the charm of Keith Michell. We were rather smitten by the photographer – a man called Anthony Armstrong-Jones – Tony Jones to us, even though we never met him! We queued up to get a place in the gods every time and hung about afterwards. I think I saw the musical seventeen times. It's the story about a Parisian prostitute and lost love. It fitted in with my A level work. Paris came alive for me and I loved the songs. I can remember them word-perfect to this day.

In the summer holidays between the lower and upper sixth, I made a bold move. I told Lew and Nancy that I was going to the Eisteddfod in Llanelli on my own. We would already be down in Aberdare, so I just needed a lift to and from the festival which lasts for a week. I was placed with a lovely, homely woman called Mrs Hopkins. I made my own way every day to the field and the pavilion. I drunk in the atmosphere and, once I had gone back to Mrs Hopkins' for tea, I made the journey back to the field for the evening concert. Towards the end of the week I felt faint in one of the concerts and somebody advised me to put my head down in my lap. It did the trick. My parents came to fetch me on the Sunday. Everyone was very friendly and my parents were grateful that I had been kindly treated.

On our journey back to Aberdare, something happened for

the first time. It was more serious than the other attacks. As the wheels of the car turned, I thought that I – Diana, my entire person – had been absorbed into the movement of the wheels. I no longer existed. It was a very frightening experience and I had no idea how to tell anyone about it.

I was tormented. I still did exist because I ate food, drank cups of tea, I replied when people spoke to me. But I was not a real person. Whenever I had another of my attacks, I disappeared again as a human being. I certainly couldn't talk about it to my parents. And I didn't think that my friends would understand either. One day, at school, in the throes of one of these attacks, I knocked on the headmistress' door and let myself in. Miss Pattison couldn't have been kinder – she listened, she offered me one of her Consulate cigarettes and ordered two coffees to be brought in for us. At the end of our session she asked if she could ring my parents and suggest that I see a psychiatrist. I was reluctant but she said that she would be gentle and everything would be confidential. No one else would know. A few days later Miss Pattison told me with regret that my parents had refused to co-operate. I can understand why. At the time anyone with a background of mental illness didn't have a future. If there is still a stigma today, it is nothing like the ignorance that existed then. I would probably not have been considered a suitable candidate for college or university. And I wouldn't get a job.

Nancy, Peggy, Owen and Nesta had all inherited some money from Data by the time I was in my second year in the sixth form. Nancy wanted to spend some of it on letting me achieve a dream. I had seen the film *Moulin Rouge*, studied the paintings of Toulouse-Lautrec, his lithographs and posters. I yearned to see some of the work myself, and I wanted to visit the place where the artist had been born, to absorb its atmosphere. Nancy went with me and Lew went to stay with Nana. How could I travel when I was so ill? My mental state seemed to be related to creativity – that was all I knew. Maybe the holiday would provide a cure.

Foreign tourism was still quite rare, so we needed the help of a travel agent. We flew to Orly airport in Paris where we waited for the flight to Toulouse. It was a real adventure. In Paris we had quite a long wait. I was disappointed that the duty-free area with all the French perfume was cordoned off and didn't realise that we would have access to it on our return. I left Nancy sitting and went up to one of the customs officers and asked why we were barred. Of course I spoke to him in French and was delighted that he understood. He not only understood but accompanied me to the other side of the barrier. Nancy was overwhelmed with pride.

My aplomb fell when we arrived in Toulouse. I assumed that the weather was always sunny in the South of France but we landed in a downpour of heavy rain. We didn't have umbrellas and I didn't know where the taxi rank was. When we finally found it the driver's fare was extortionate. We didn't know what to do. A middle-aged man came up to us. He was going into the centre of Toulouse and offered to share his taxi with us. Nancy sat in the front and, in the back, the man tried to kiss me. It was hard to free myself but, in spite of the rejection, he paid the entire fare. We arrived at the hotel at night and it was still raining. The night porter looked like Fernandel.

The following morning, the sun did shine and we travelled up to Albi by train – me rejoicing in my spoken French and Nancy watching everything that was happening. I did see the Château Malromé and soaked up the atmosphere. We visited the amazing pink cathedral. As it was Easter there were crowds of worshippers in what was an alien culture to us. We bought a box of violets – *Violettes de Toulouse*. The attacks continued but, if I had to die, I would have seen Albi!

Back in Essex the other girls were making plans for their futures. Some of them applied to university and discussed the best choices with the careers mistress. What about me? For a while I nurtured the completely impractical idea of being a shepherdess. There was a little hut on top of the Graig mountain in Aberdare. I could buy it, live there, and when I wasn't shepherding I could make herbal tinctures and sell them. I was just seeking a refuge in past happiness in Aberdare. I got as far as sending off for information about herbal medicine. My Latin teacher was delighted because the application forms were in Latin! I wondered about being an air hostess but I wasn't tall enough. One thing I knew with certainty was that I wouldn't apply to go to university. I wouldn't be able to cope with the stress of a difficult course with my attacks happening so often. They were getting worse and the prognosis for dementia praecox was disastrous. I wasn't long for this world.

In spite of the problems – or maybe because of them – I was still showing an interest in the disadvantaged. We had a course in liberal studies at school. I seldom said anything at all but when we were asked what we thought of the cuts on the railways, I found a voice – a *passionate* voice. I said that they were a disgrace. It was the same story of the cyclical nature of poverty and deprivation. Many of the cuts were happening in areas like Aberdare. Without a reliable train service, most people had no other transport – they couldn't afford cars. This meant that lots of the local people would lose their jobs simply because they couldn't get there. I think I must have sounded like the radical socialist I was becoming and I was met with silence from the other girls. In the end the teacher said that she thought that someone would have responded to me – *she* was impressed by what I had said!

There was a residential school on the outskirts of Ingatestone called Trueloves. It was a home for severely handicapped boys. The first time I went there I tried not to register any shock. But I had never seen such deformity. The boys were mainly in wheelchairs and, with their twisted little bodies, they tried to read books that lay on the huge wooden table. The boys wanted me to take them out for 'walks'; I was determined to please – no health and safety rules and regulations then! As I ran down the road in the grounds pushing the wheelchair, the boys laughed out loud when it was their turn. In the school holidays I spent a few weeks helping out in a school for ESN (educationally subnormal) and maladjusted children (obsolete terms now). Maybe this was telling me that I should be heading for a career in caring for others? But how could I do that when I couldn't cope with myself? I compromised – and it was an excellent decision. I decided to apply to train as a teacher at Trinity College, Carmarthen.

Back at school, apart from Miss Pattison, Miss Pursey (the head of the Latin department) was the only person who sensed that all was not well with me. One day she excused herself from the Latin class because she was feeling ill herself. When she returned I was having an attack.

She said to me, 'Are you alright, Diana? You look like I felt earlier.' She smiled and told me to go and sit outside in the open air. She came out to see how I was shortly afterwards. I couldn't explain to her what was happening but she seemed to know. She couldn't explain her own symptoms either. Not long after I left school she was admitted to hospital where a vast amount of fluid was drained from the malignant growth in her lungs. She died within months.

18

A Mustard-Coloured Coat

I WENT TO Cardiff for an interview to gain a place at Trinity College. I had had a very kind and generous reference from the rector in Ingatestone – the one who had supported me after I declined to go through with confirmation. In a room in Cathedral Road, I was faced with the two vice-principals at the time – a man and a woman. The man looked at my references and noticed that one of my A level subjects was Latin.

'Latin won't be available at Trinity,' he warned me.

'The discipline of a language is never wasted,' I replied with the authority of youth.

'I think we'll find a place for you.'

The female vice-principal admired my coat – it was mustard-coloured and loose-fitting.

'Thank you.'

I received a letter to say that I had been accepted. The first term would begin in September 1963.

Lew went to a lot of trouble to ensure that I had every single book that I needed for my course. My main subjects were English and art. Education and educational psychology were also compulsory subjects.

I arrived in Carmarthen by train. There was a senior student with a large sign waiting on the station to greet freshers and take them up to the college in a minibus. I made my own way. I don't know why I did this – maybe I felt detached from what was happening. I took the bus, got off with my case at the right stop, looked at a list and found my room – which was wonderful! Shelves for my books, a bed, desk, chair, a wardrobe and a washbasin! As much as I liked the room, I showed no emotion at all as I stacked my books on the shelf and unpacked my case. I had been living in Ingatestone. Now I was living in Carmarthen.

Words were hard to describe the way I felt. Sometimes, poetry or art addressed the mood better than prose. The following poem was written at the time and certainly picked up my sense of alienation:

A LITTLE DESPAIR

A little despair
seeps through my whole being
like a venomous spider
that stretches its legs.

My warm, young life
is drained dry,
bone-brittle, bitter-sharp
Dead.
But the parched still exist
thirsty
and always know
that longing taste on the tongue.

When my mind
is tormented in this way
It is then that I feel
that unbearable pain.
The numbness of utter futility
The fear of nothing at all
in particular
And the loneliness of seeing
other people happy.

Unhappiness crawls back up
My body.

My arms can at last,
Relieved,
Relax.

Things are beginning
to appear clearly again,
My eyes focus
on the people around me.

I have been away.
I am now returning
to a world
that I have deserted
for a little while.

In spite of this detachment, I made friends. Kay was in the same unit of eight rooms as me. So was Ann. The three of us became good friends. In the next unit there was a group of girls whom I got to know well – Jean, Mary and Lesley.

The lectures went well – I enjoyed them. I had thought that the attacks would stop when I was living somewhere else. But they were as violent as they had ever been. Sometimes I ran and ran outside the college grounds to see if I could wear them out. It didn't work.

I stood out from the other students in several ways. My essays in English were good. When returning one essay, the head of department at the time (another man who was dying of cancer) asked who I was. We were reading George Bernard Shaw's *Saint Joan* and he got tired of people hesitating, so he always chose me to read the part of Joan. It was flattering but isolating. There was another English lecturer – a pedantic bachelor who discovered that I spoke French. He read *Paris Match* and passed them on to me after lectures; we talked about its contents. I was nineteen when he told me that the calibre of the students had deteriorated as if I were not one myself.

I looked different from the other students. Nancy and I had

been going up to the Kings Road in Chelsea. We loved the buzz of the new trendy shops in the area – Biba and Mary Quant. At the time, a woman in her early forties wouldn't have worn such extreme fashions, but Nancy was very generous in buying a couple of miniskirts for me. There were some very glamorous female students in Carmarthen but I was the first one to wear a miniskirt. I modelled myself on the French singer, Juliette Gréco. I knew her existentialist songs and adopted a similar style and pout. They were part of my being – although I didn't think that I really had any being. My appearance certainly didn't attract the male students. They seemed to be totally indifferent to me.

The factor that marked me out significantly was my behaviour. The toll of the attacks was now visible – I looked pale, tired and sad. I didn't know who I could confide in. We had a warden in our hostel – Sheila Gallagher. She was barely in her thirties but she seemed middle-aged to me. She had a Jaguar, and anyone who had a Jaguar had to understand life. I went down to her room one evening and started to explain what was happening to me. She was very patient and listened. She offered me one of her cigarettes – I think they were Senior Service. Her subject was infant method (teaching us how to teach little children) but she was also a mathematician. She wanted to solve things for me. As the visits became more regular, we were no nearer to understanding anything. Eventually, she suggested that I should go to see the college matron. The matron didn't understand it either. She thought that I should go to see the college doctor. I went down into the town to see the college GP, but I could see that he felt out of his depth too. When he suggested that I should see a psychiatrist, I was scared. I might be expelled. He assured me that I wouldn't, so I agreed. I went down to a clinic in town to see Dr Farr who was the top psychiatrist in the local mental hospital. At last, hope was in sight. He listened to me calmly – and gave me some tablets. I went to the pharmacy to get my Librium. Once I was back in my room at college, I poured out the entire contents from the little glass bottle onto my bed. These would be my salvation.

I took the tablets. The attacks were just as bad. The dosage was increased. The attacks were just as bad. Maybe I tried a different drug. I can't really remember. All I knew was that, in addition to my despair at the bouts themselves, I now knew that the experts couldn't cure me. By this time I was seeing Dr Farr on a regular basis and it seemed that everything had been tried. I wondered if going away for a weekend might help. Somewhere in my head there was still this idea that 'going somewhere else' would do the trick. He agreed that I could try it out; then I worried as I couldn't think of anywhere to go.

I was only nineteen and all my Essex contacts knew my parents. But Miss Pattison – my former headmistress – had been very kind to me. I went to a college kiosk and phoned Chelmsford County High School for Girls. I wanted to speak to Miss Pattison, but I was put through to Miss Johnson – the history teacher with whom I had had little contact. I had been in awe of her because she had a brusque, abrupt manner. But she was very kind on the phone. I explained my predicament. She told me that Miss Pattison was on sick leave. Miss Johnson was a Londoner and she had kept on her city house, staying in a bedsit during the week. I can't remember whether I asked her or if she offered. But it was agreed that I should go to London to spend the weekend with her.

She greeted me warmly when I arrived. She showed me the bedroom where I was to sleep and warned me that she rose at 6am. I discovered the soft jewel in her soul. In an understated way she made me comfortable and welcome. On the Saturday afternoon, as she was marking books, she talked to me openly as if I were a responsible adult. When I began to fall asleep on the settee, she came over and put a blanket over me as if I were a little child. Her sister came over to share Sunday lunch. The imposing Miss Johnson greeted her with a kiss and called her 'duckie'. She introduced me simply as Diana, a former pupil. I didn't know how to repay her for her generosity, so I went out and bought a picture. My fiercely-perceived Miss Johnson's eyes misted over.

On the train back to Carmarthen I realised that I still had the same problem. What would happen next? I suggested to Dr Farr that maybe a weekend in sick bay with increased sedation might work. He agreed. An arrangement was made for me to go to the sick bay on Friday evening when I was given my night-time sedation and, by Monday morning, I thought that I would be refreshed enough to make another start! Because I was being supervised I was allowed to ask the matron for a top-up if the medication didn't work. On the Friday night I took my medication and asked for more in the early hours. But I didn't take them. I saved them up. I took the double dose on the Saturday night but still couldn't sleep. I had the same problem on the Sunday. In the early hours I knocked on the door of the matron who was 'on call' but, as the door opened inwards, I fell inside her room. She was taken aback, and when I saw her with her torch I couldn't stop laughing. When Monday morning came I refused to leave the bed. The matron threw cold water over my face – she used all her gifts of persuasion to get me to get up. But I knew that I couldn't carry on any more. I was worn out. I hid my face under the covers.

An hour or so later the matron came in to see me. 'We're very worried about you,' she said. 'A doctor will be coming down to see you later on this morning.'

Before long a man came into my room. He was tall, thin, pale and wore round-rimmed spectacles. He took his sheepskin coat off and threw it on the unoccupied bed.

'My name is McGill,' he said. 'Are you going to tell me about yourself?'

He sat down on a chair beside me and I couldn't think of anything to say. He must have asked me the questions. At the end of the session he said,

'I'd like you to come and spend a bit of time in my hospital.'

Going to see a psychiatrist as an outpatient was one thing – I could keep it fairly secret. But to go into a mental hospital was another thing. In spite of my desperation, I was horrified.

'I'm not mad.'

'Neither are my other patients.'

St David's Hospital was on the same road as the college – a few hundred yards higher up. People made jokes about it. 'If I go on like this, I'll end up in St David's.' I said that I didn't want to go into hospital.

Dr McGill stood up and put his sheepskin coat back on.

'OK. I'll give you twenty-four hours to change your mind. There's a bed waiting for you.'

And off he went.

Suddenly, I became alert. I would *have* to carry on. I would have to go to lectures. I got dressed and tried to remember where I should be at that time of the day on a Monday. I left the sick bay and stumbled into a lecture room. I was scarcely conscious. I didn't feel real. Who was I? Was I just a figment of my own imagination? Everything around me felt unreal. Then an attack took over again. I was at the end of my tether.

I returned to the sick bay and told the matron that I had changed my mind. She smiled, obviously pleased that I had made the right decision. She asked me to get a few things together and then she accompanied me up to the hospital.

19

Hospital, a Violation

I HAD ALWAYS been shy and needed privacy. I was put on a large main ward with a stark name – FU2 (Female Unit 2). As soon as I had been admitted, little cloth labels were sewn on all my clothes with FU2 marked on them. Diana Williams FU2. A nurse went through my handbag and removed anything that could be dangerous. My mirror went, and so did a small pair of scissors. One of the doctors on call came to give me a physical examination. He told me that I had an eye condition called nystagmus. I told him that Daddy Bom had had it too, thinking that there might be a link. He told me that it was a sign that I might have a brain tumour. I would have to have an EEG (electroencephalogram). I reacted with total indifference.

The results of the EEG didn't reveal a brain tumour but there were irregularities. It was the first of many EEGs. The man who worked the machine – a Mr Long – said later that he had never seen anything like my EEGs. I was a mystery.

Having eliminated serious physical problems, the next stage was to treat my psychiatric symptoms. I went into Dr McGill's office a few times but he needed my parents' permission before he could begin any treatment – so they had to be informed. That did upset me. I didn't want them to know and I feared their reaction.

I soon made friends on the ward. In a strange kind of way I felt more at home there than I had been anywhere for a long time. All these people were sharing and suffering the same kind of torment. I had been protected by my family until then, but I soon learnt about very different habits and situations.

My parents married at Bethel chapel, Abernant, Aberdare, 10 October 1942. My father was granted special leave from the Royal Engineers. My mother was delighted with her beautiful dress. Borrowed, it was sent to her in the post and dutifully returned. Material was very expensive and hard to come by in the war.

I move with my parents to Ingatestone, Essex, in 1946. This photo of me with my father was taken in the little garden of our prefab in 1948 or 1949. By this time I have recovered from a serious accident and two other life-threatening illnesses.

I loved our holidays in Aberdare. Here, I am in the garden of 4 Elizabeth Street with my paternal grandparents (Nana and Daddy Bom). I have borrowed a little of my mother's make-up to give Nana some war-paint! 1950.

I am standing at the front door of 4 Elizabeth Street with my cousin Dorothy. I am the smaller child. I always remember how Nana polished the brass letterbox, door knocker and doorstep until they gleamed. About 1950.

Uncle Davie's grandchildren were more cousins for me to play with in Aberdare. Margaret and David are in the back row and I am with Janet (and her doll!) in the front row. Nana delivered Janet. It was a complicated birth and Nana might well have saved her life. About 1951.

When Data (my maternal grandfather) came to stay with us for a while, I was delighted. He was a great storyteller and we had fun together. Here we are on a Saturday trip to London in 1955.

We still lived in the prefab in Ingatestone, Essex, but things were looking up. I attended a private day school, had ballet lessons, this velvet dress had been specially made for me and (unseen in the photograph) we had a 9" screen television for the Coronation. My mother, Nancy, looks on proudly.

By 1960 I am ready for the bohemian life. My pocket money goes on different things. I bought this silk blouse cheaply (the front collar was singed), I grew my hair, liked big rings and must have had enough money left over to buy a packet of *Gauloises*.

I went to Trinity College, Carmarthen, to train as a teacher in 1963. This photo was taken in Rag Week but my illness was visibly taking its toll. I am distant, pale and unsmiling. Back row, L–R: Kay, Kath, Lesley, Bronwen, Lesley, Ann, me. Front row, L–R: Maureen, Pat, Vilna, Mary.

These line drawings come from 1963 onwards when I was so ill. This one is simply called 'Despair'.

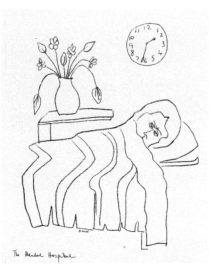

'The mental hospital'.

The Mental Hospital

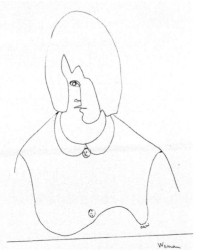

'Glazed eyes don't see'.

Woman

'Escorted walk from Gaskell House,' Manchester, 1967.

Going for a walk

'Who are we?'

'No more'.

I was chosen as a finalist in the 1968 *Vogue* Talent Competition. The prize included lunch and cocktails at Vogue House in London. Here I am talking to *Vogue*'s deputy editor of the time. To my right is Lady Antonia Fraser.

A photo of our immediate families on our wedding day, 15 April 1971. L–R: Nana, my father, Lew, Peter, me, my mother-in-law Pat, my mother Nancy and Peter's father Ralph. The colour slides (a rare luxury) were a wedding gift from a friend.

Peter and I marry at the Register Office in Cardiff. Peter wears a red velvet suit and I wear a pink dress, purple velvet coat with flowers in my hair, of course.

Christmas 1972 is a special celebration for us in 4 Elizabeth Street, Aberdare. There is a new addition to the family – our baby daughter, Meleri. Nana and my mother are thrilled to bits and the little nightdress is airing by the fire. This is one of our last visits to Number 4.

We had very little money in 1976 but I saved up for important things. I took Meleri on the bus to Carmarthen to see 'Uncle Noel' (McGill). He was delighted to meet her – and he had some sweets in the car when he drove us back to the station.

Peter and Meleri in 1981 on holiday in Umag. Now in Istria, Croatia, it was then in the former Yugoslavia. We enjoy the sun, sea and beautiful scenery but are aware of how hard life is for the local people.

In 1983 Meleri was in the *grŵp llefaru* at the Urdd Eisteddfod in Aberafan. I went along too. Meleri wears Coed-y-gof School uniform here. She had started school at Bryntâf which was the first and only Welsh-language primary school in Cardiff until it closed in 1981 to make way for four new primary schools as demand had grown so much.

'The Quartet'. My mother, Nancy, seldom met all her siblings at the same time but this family wedding in 1981 was an exception. L–R: Nesta, Nancy, Owen, Peggy. They were all very strong personalities and, through the 'Quartet', I have seven first cousins and many more relations in north Pembrokeshire.

My father, Lew, was an only child but he and Iris were brought up as brother and sister. She and her family were lifelong friends and remain so. Lew and Iris had a lot of fun together, as this photo shows.

In 1986 I was asked to organise holiday accommodation for children and teachers from a school for physically handicapped children in Nantes. We had a party on their final night in our house for the children, teachers and hosts. Peter entertains with his guitar.

L–R: Eileen, Brenda, me. In the 1980s, my friends and I were trying to deal with a problem logically but we were going round in circles. We gave up and turned to prayer instead. It worked. We met once a week for wonderful sessions which led to outreach ministry.

I completed a two-year part-time course (Clinical Theology Association) in Pastoral Care and Counselling in the late 1980s. Following this, I met with others one Saturday a month for supervision with our tutors, the Rev. David and Gill Bick. After one of these sessions in our house, David is relaxing. Gareth sits on the settee.

Ignatian Spirituality is an essential part of my life. It is surprisingly contemporary. Saunders and Cynthia, John and Mary, Ruth, Margaret and I all did a fifteen-day course on spiritual direction at Llysfasi, north Wales. Here, after a house blessing, from L–R: John, me, Ruth, Margaret. Ruth and Margaret were amongst the first women to be ordained as priests in Wales.

For several years (late 1980s to early 1990s) a group from St Luke's went on a parish retreat to Llangasty (near Brecon). We always came back refreshed. Back row, L–R: Tony, Mary, Gareth, Gill, Diane, Sheila. Front row, L–R: Brenda, me, Marion, Doreen, Hannah, Eileen.

Rachel and Meleri became close friends when they were just two and we got to know the whole family well. Margaret, Rachel and Eleanor arrive at our house for a barbecue in the garden, 1988.

Lew and Nancy were good grandparents to Meleri. She visited them and went on holidays with Granny and Granddad. This is their last visit down to us in Cardiff before Meleri leaves for St Mary's Medical School, Paddington, August 1990.

Apart from his wedding gear, Peter wears casual clothes but here is another exception to the rule. Graduation Day Ceremony in Cardiff.

I have a lot of cousins. Here in Cwmdare, Aberdare, my hospitable cousin Donna entertains us when another cousin, Don, comes over from the United States with his family, 1990s.

Meleri enjoys her arduous medical studies, but it's not all work. She meets Huw, a fellow medical student in London, who comes from Tredegar! 1992.

For many years I have gone on a Quiet Day to Tymawr Convent with a small group. We have valued the input from the Rev. Keith Denerley, enjoyed the beautiful grounds and the gentle sharing of community life. Muriel is on Keith's right. I am to his left with Dorothy.

Meleri and Huw marry at St John's Church, Canton, on 25 April 1998. It was an eventful day and one that I shall never forget.

Four generations. Our first grandchild, Bethan, arrives in January 2002. We take her up twice that year to visit her great-grandmother. Nancy didn't live long enough to know that Bethan would soon be a very literate child, fluently bilingual before starting school. Bethan enjoys drama and literature.

Huw and Meleri's second daughter, Cati (Catrin), arrives in 2005. She is seen here with her dad, Huw, on a holiday to visit friends in Australia in 2010. Huw loves sport and so does Cati. She enjoys rugby, football, netball, hockey, cross country running and athletics.

The *hiraeth* for north Pembrokeshire continues down the generations. Meleri and Gwen after a swim in Whitesands Bay, St Davids, 2017. Gwen likes swimming, singing and horse riding.

A happy reunion. Almost fifty years after we started out as students at Trinity College, Carmarthen, we meet there again for a chapel service, a lovely lunch and a long 'catch-up'. Back row, standing, L–R: Ann, me, Mary, Kay. Front row, sitting, Lesley and Jean.

The cook downstairs was a patient. He was called Rickie the Ram. That one had to be explained to me, and the other patients were kind in the telling, sensing my innocence. There was a woman – recently bereaved – who sang Welsh hymns in the middle of the night in a beautiful contralto voice. I could feel the sadness coming from her heart – an inconsolable lament. A girl who was younger than me was having insulin coma treatment. After the treatment she was very hungry and chips were made especially for her. I was envious. There was an unmarried Irish girl who was pregnant. She had a strong temper and was unstable, but probably not technically mentally ill. Society didn't know what to do with people like her then, so she stayed in St David's until the baby was born and adopted. Some of the older people on other wards had been there throughout their adult life. There was a man whom everyone called Moses. He had an unusual gift – whenever anyone told him their date of birth, he knew on what day of the week it had fallen. He didn't fit into society and people were afraid of him, so they hid him away. There was a woman on my ward who was a brilliant pianist. She played the piano often in the day room but then, suddenly, she cut her wrists. There was blood everywhere and she lay in bed attached to a drip. She was very friendly with another patient. People said that they were lesbians.

Lew came down the first weekend. He was called in to see Dr McGill. Lew was very angry with me and told me that all I had was a complex. If I'd given it enough thought I could have dealt with it myself, he maintained. His pride and hope had been transferred into temper. I felt betrayed. He had no idea how tormented my mind was and how long I'd been hiding it all from him. For once, I responded with anger. Lew didn't know what to do. On the following weekend Nancy came down. She was very upset. When she called in at the college – probably to pick up some clothes for me, Norah Isaac, head of Welsh drama and an eminent figure in Welsh literary life, consoled my mother. '*Paid â becso, Mrs Williams, paid â becso*' (Don't worry). She explained that all would be well, that I was one of the most capable students they had. All would be well.

Nancy tried to smile when she saw me. She, too, went in to see Dr McGill, and when she came out she was very, very upset. She was upset because I was ill, of course, but there was another reason. Dr McGill had asked for my medical notes to be sent down to him. The notes did arrive but there was no reference in them to the accident I had had when I was three. Nancy had to explain why this was to Dr McGill. Before I applied to college, she asked our GP in Ingatestone to destroy the records about this accident. He did this because I seemed to have made a complete recovery. On this occasion and on every other occasion, Nancy could never relate the details without breaking down.

I once asked Lew about it but he said that it was in the past.

Once Lew and Nancy had come down my treatment began. I can only imagine the distress it must have caused my parents. I am sorry about that but I couldn't help the way things were. At first, when I saw Dr McGill, he just wanted me to talk about my background. He told me that I was telling him everything mechanically as if it had happened to someone else. That was part of my problem. At nights I lay awake, rigid. I couldn't cry. My tear ducts were checked. They weren't blocked – but I was. He asked me why I didn't have a boyfriend – 'You haven't got a face like the back of a bus.' I told him that I didn't know.

Eventually he decided to give me abreaction (the 'truth drug'). This treatment was used in the early 1960s to unlock fears and problems that had become deeply hidden in the unconscious mind. I was put in a side room for these treatments and Dr McGill came in to administer the drugs (a combination of stimulants and depressants) that allowed me to 'open up'. I have to confess that I enjoyed the feeling they gave me. It was like being drunk without the drawbacks. Using this treatment, Dr McGill did manage to bring some feelings to the surface but he said afterwards,

'You're only a little girl but you've got the constitution of a horse.'

I didn't know whether that was a compliment or a reproach.

At first Dr McGill thought that my problem was an 'anxiety state' but, as he got to know me better, he said that there was something deeper at the root of it all – a depressive element. I was in hospital for about a month, and when I was discharged I felt cheated. I was still not well. (I later discovered that I had only been discharged because Dr McGill was hoping that I would be well enough to continue my academic course without further treatment. He hadn't 'signed me off'.)

I returned to college. The lecturers were all very kind – some had visited me in hospital. But I felt that I stood out even more from most of the students. Kind though everyone was, I had been a patient in St David's.

During the first long summer holidays, I went back to Ingatestone as my college term ended before my parents' school term. I stayed in Essex until they broke up so that we could all go down together to stay with Nana.

My parents must have been worried sick about me. One thing that troubled Nancy in particular was my lack of a social life. Both of my parents were extraverts who sparkled in company. They knew a local teacher who was engaged to a black man. This mixed-race relationship was very unusual then and Nancy had gone out of her way to welcome them. One evening, the couple were going out to a dance and I was invited to join them. I sat at the bar and had to be persuaded to take to the floor. To my surprise, I found myself actually enjoying the jiving. The car had enough space in the front for three people. On the way back I assumed that I'd sit in the back again but I was invited to sit in the front between the two of them. We had all been drinking and the singing began as we had a very relaxed return journey.

I was at home alone in the house one morning the following week. I liked making my own clothes and, over my nightdress,

I was wearing a long, white dressing gown that I had designed. The black man came to the door and I welcomed him in. I was surprised to see him and told him that my parents were out. He said that he hadn't come to see them – he had come to see me. I didn't understand what he meant. I was shocked. I still didn't understand. I had never seen an erection before – and he was a very big man. What on earth was happening? There was the mystery of the different race and colour. He must have taken his trousers off for me to see him in such intimacy. He took hold of me and got me onto the floor. What was happening? A woman passed by outside. She wouldn't have been able to see anything because we had net curtains. Between her and us was the length of our front garden. I didn't shout. I was frightened. It happened quickly and passionately. I told him that he shouldn't be doing what he was doing as if being rational would have made any difference. He carried on. He murmured that I was beautiful. Was I? Was that my fault?

Afterwards, he sat on my parents' beautifully-upholstered armchair and wept. This was something else that I had never seen. He sobbed and sobbed like someone out of a Shakespearian tragedy. 'I'm sorry, I'm so sorry,' he cried. I found myself stroking his wiry black curly hair to comfort him. Then I asked him if he would like a cup of coffee. But, once he had calmed down, he left.

When he had gone, a strange thing happened. I could remember him coming to the door in the first place but the rest of the episode vanished from my conscious mind. (Later, in my story, I explain how the memory was restored.) So I was left with a dilemma. As usual, I just carried on automatically without emotion. The three of us went down to Aberdare to be with Nana. My mind kept on returning to that odd encounter that I couldn't recall. I could see him in my mind's eye coming to the door. That was all. I was *really* going mad now. I was convinced of it. To make matters worse, I missed a period. The strain of everything eventually caused my body to give up. One day my muscles contracted and I developed tetany. I couldn't close my mouth, and my jaw was stuck in a grimace. The doctor was sent for and he was very sympathetic. He asked someone in the house to get me a prescription immediately and then he spoke to me. Was I under any stress? I told him about the limited memory of the experience and the fact that I had a delayed period. 'Was this your boyfriend?' 'No.' 'You mean you were raped?' 'I don't know what happened.' He took my hand and he was so kind. 'I feel so sorry for you.' The medication freed my frozen body and, within a day or so, I realised that I was not pregnant. Once the tetany was dealt with, the matter was not referred to again.

When we went back to Ingatestone I began to worry that the man would return. I was on my own in the house again once my parents began their school term. I didn't know who to tell. I went to the GP (a new one in the village) and told him of my limited recall. He hesitated, then said, 'I don't think you need worry. He probably realises what a fool he has been.' He was correct about that but the days were long and I was frightened. I eventually confided in Susan's mother. She said that I could spend the days at her house, but she found the responsibility of keeping it to herself too difficult. She phoned my parents. I was in bed. They came upstairs. Lew was furious and asked me what had happened. I don't think he believed me when I said that I couldn't remember. Nancy was very upset. They eventually left me alone and undoubtedly discussed what should be done. From my bedroom the following morning I heard Lew's side of a bitter conversation. It ended with the words 'And don't ever darken my door again.'

The matter was not discussed with me at all. I found out much later that Lew had wanted to take the matter to court. He was eventually advised against that because of the effect it would have on me. I am grateful for that. I understand why so few women make a case for rape. Certainly, I would not have been believed.

20

St David's Again

IN MY SECOND year at college I was put in a different hostel. It was not as attractive as the first one and my room was down a long, dark corridor. My social life was still very limited. The main event of the evening was a trip to the 'hut' where we could help ourselves to a cup of tea from the urn. We could have male student visitors (or visitors from outside the college) twice a week for up to two hours. I had no one to invite.

I was in no mood to be sociable anyhow. I assumed that Dr McGill didn't want to see me again and I was cross. One day, I hid in the hedge beside the road that led from the college to the hospital. When I saw his car coming, I simply ran into the road. He stopped. I went to see him in the hospital later that day. He asked if I had had a good summer holiday. I told him about the incident and my amnesia. He groaned. As an outpatient he wasn't able to get very far, so there was no option but to admit me again.

The Mental Hospital

The flowers are Van Gogh yellow
in the mental home.
The floors gleam with a polish
on which visitors trip.

An army of mothers, sisters and friends
invades the ward
with an anxious smile
and a box of sweets.
They comfort the sick

with nods of understanding
and, comfortless,
grin smugly.
They can cope with the ups and downs,
see-saw, see-saw,
of life in the modern world.

But they can never know
the secret sadness behind those glazed eyes.
The yearning, loathing, despairing
boom of a heart that courses bile.

Clergymen pat the hands of the hopeless few
and tell them of the love of a God
who brings them
sickness and tears...

Night in the hospital is one long journey
through restless sheets and hot dreams.
Breathing is loud and troubled.
A scream. A shout.
Someone is crying in the bitter memory
of something forgotten.
A woman sits on her bed
eating nuts. Sleep does not come easily.

A brilliant light.
The strained, cadaverous face of a nurse,
kind and green and white.
Sleep is a stranger in this land.
Tomorrow I shall walk
around the buildings
if I am allowed.
Buildings.
Walk.
If I tomorrow, Saturday sleep
does not.
Sleep does not come easily
Please God come
Sleep does not
Sleep sleep.

I remained in hospital for about two-and-a-half months. My memories of that time are fragmented and out of sequence. I was very ill. I had abreaction again. A discredited treatment now, it worked for me then. It enabled me to recall the rape and I have remembered it ever since.

Shortly afterwards I was given continuous narcosis. With the help of drugs I was 'put to sleep' for a fortnight. I was just woken up to be fed and to use the bedpan. The prolonged sleep was a total treat for me as I had been unable to sleep for more than four or five hours a night since my disturbed episode when I was eleven. I was so tired and so unwell. When I woke from the continual narcosis, a course of ECT had already begun. I had seen other patients on the ward having the treatment, gripping their jaws onto something that stopped them from biting their mouths. It didn't worry me. I couldn't cope with life – it was too painful. At the end of the eight sessions I was no better. I eventually had a treatment that Dr McGill had not had to resort to for a long time – it was very potent.

Although I had responded to the usual abreaction, he wanted to use something stronger. I had ether abreaction. A mask was put on my face and ether was dropped onto it until I was barely conscious. I have to confess that it made me 'high' and I enjoyed it. It blurred the misery of consciousness. The treatment came to an end.

There were three women on the ward who were sent to Morriston Hospital to have leucotomies. I envied them. They left Carmarthen with their neuroses and worries and, with shaven heads, they returned in a wonderful state of serenity. I pleaded with Dr McGill to let me have a leucotomy. He said that I couldn't have one. I argued that I was as ill as they were. Still the answer was no.

He began to give me rewards for good behaviour. As far as he was concerned good behaviour consisted of stopping nagging him for a leucotomy. I loved those rewards. I was allowed to borrow books from his study and I was allowed to look around the pathology lab – which fascinated me. He couldn't offer me a lot of psychotherapy in the hospital as he was responsible for two wards, so he took me with him when he went to assess new patients in rural Carmarthenshire. I talked in the car as we travelled, and waited there while he went into the houses for the consultations. I dread to think what today's regulations would have made of all this. Nothing untoward happened – he was just a very caring doctor who was doing everything he could to make me well. (There were other patients too who needed a bit of extra help – he 'gave away' one of these girls when she married.) On one occasion he took me to Laugharne. After his meeting with his patient he took me to the Brown's Hotel. This was, of course, the pub where Dylan and Caitlin Thomas drank and he knew that I'd be thrilled. When he asked me what I wanted to drink, I asked for a shandy. But he said, 'You're a brandy girl, Diana!' So I had a brandy – another reward for not asking for a leucotomy.

I was finally discharged in gentle stages. I went to lectures during the day and returned to hospital at night. Then the day came when I felt ready to take my case back to the college and sleep there. Dr McGill passed me as I was making my way back. He wound the window down and smiled. 'Well done, Diana.' Afterwards I was seen as an outpatient.

I can't remember if I had been well enough to keep up with the college work while I was in hospital but, if I had not, I soon made up for lost time. We had a new head of English, Mr Binding, and were given an essay to write on the characters of Simon and Piggy in William Golding's novel, *Lord of the Flies*. I launched into the project enthusiastically. Simon and Piggy were both outsiders – I knew what that felt like. Piggy, the fat boy with glasses, was earnest and desperately wanted to fit in but, however hard he tried, he remained an outsider. Simon, on the other hand, was a lone schizoid. When the essays were returned, Mr Binding made general comments before handing them back. One of them was superb, he said, 'better than I could have done myself.' The essay was mine – I lowered my head as I didn't know how to respond. Of course

I was pleased, but this was another thing that alienated me from the other students. Mr Binding was well aware of my stays in hospital and asked me to baby-sit for his children. Maybe that gesture was more important to me than having written a superb essay.

In my third year at college I had another spell in hospital. It was a shorter stay but it gave me an additional diagnosis. In my college room one day I blacked out and woke to discover that I had wet the bed. I told Dr McGill and another EEG was organised. This time, Mr Long and Dr McGill decided that there was enough consistent evidence to say that I had temporal lobe epilepsy. In addition to the other medication, I began to take anticonvulsants which had terrible side effects. I became deluded and was found wandering around Llanelli market one day by one of the off-duty nurses from St David's. She asked me what I was doing there. I didn't know. This disease had probably originated from my accident at the age of three. I had certainly 'lost' substantial parts of my school curriculum. Did I daydream – or was it something else? Nobody will ever know and, as Dr McGill said himself, 'No one will discover what makes you tick until you're on the pathologist's slab.' An astonishing thought for a very young woman. The days in hospital were monotonous but I was happy with the tedium.

There was a mixed day room where patients from MU2 (Male Unit 2) and FU2 socialised. Perhaps socialise was too grand a word for what happened there. Records were played almost continuously and repeated over and over again. Jim Reeves was the main choice with his 'Put your sweet lips a little closer to the phone' and 'I know that I won't forget you'. Elvis Presley made a close second. Lonely, sad, sick, confused people needed the words like a drug – an assurance that somewhere, somehow, they were loved and loveable. Men held hands with women and women held hands with women. It wasn't about sexuality – just the comfort of human contact.

One of the patients became a close friend. Iris was supposed to have been a lesbian. It is difficult for people today to imagine how attitudes have changed. There was such prejudice and ignorance then. I had met Iris during my first stay in hospital. I wasn't allowed out of the hospital grounds on my own at first but Sister Mock thought of someone responsible enough to go to town with me – and she chose Iris. I have to confess that I was surprised. But, by the time I was hospitalised in my third year, we knew each other well. Iris was the wife of a senior academic at a Canadian university. She was diagnosed as schizoaffective, and every time she became ill her husband put her on a ship back to Wales for treatment. When she was better she was shipped back. Iris was a lovely woman. She and I had such fun in town – we were always laughing together. Trips into Littlewoods were hilarious. We wandered inside to look at clothes and lingerie and when Iris found a bargain, she threw it up into the air for me to see – 'What do you think, Diane?' 'Yes, nice, how much is it?' It was very banal stuff but there was a tremendously close rapport between us. We always ended up in a pub in town. Babycham was a new, trendy drink and Iris usually bought it for me. I knew by then that I could hold my drink very well – so could Iris – but alcohol made her face flush. She had two shades of Creme Puff powder. One was her natural colour, the other a lighter shade to make her appear sober for our return to the hospital.

After I was discharged from hospital in my third year, Iris was lonely. I often got back from lectures to find her in my room, drunk, with a bottle in her hand, asleep on my settee. Our friendship was so warm and fulfilling that I doubted my own sexuality. One day, she said that she was going back to Canada – to give her marriage another go. I later heard that she had committed suicide.

In spite of everything, I knew that I had chosen the right place to be living and studying. I had friends. Some of the staff became like friends to me as well – Norah Isaac had a soft spot for me because I was trying to learn Welsh; there was Sheila Gallagher too and Irene James. One of the English lecturers invited me home and he and his wife offered me tea and sympathy. I was also surprised to discover that people respected me. The head of the art department said that he depended on me to help him out when help was needed. 'What would I do without you, Diana?' he said one day. I smiled at him.

The chapel was at the heart of this Church in Wales college. Although services were not compulsory, nearly everybody attended them. We had to get up early enough to have breakfast and go to chapel before lectures began. Sometimes, students were invited to take an evening service (yes, there were evening services as well!). I took two of these. The principal at the time, a Lancastrian, complimented me on my approach. I sang in the choir and took part in a special memorial service after the death of President Kennedy. We practised and practised so that we could do our best at singing the wonderful Fauré's *Requiem* and Pergolesi's *Stabat Mater*.

I organised an art society in the college. One of its aims was to invite local artists to give a talk in the upstairs library. I think I asked the college lecturers to speak first and that worked well. I don't know who put me in touch with another artist from Carmarthenshire. He was a good painter but, when he turned up to speak, he was drunk. Any serious discussion was lost as he slurred his speech and rambled from one topic to another. The head of the art department and the fabric printing lecturer were there and, when I started to giggle, they found it hard not to follow suit.

I kept in touch with this artist who was one of the few men to show an interest in me in my college years. He came to my room one evening before he was due to leave for Kenya – he had been appointed head of art at Nairobi High School for Girls. Instead of any romance that night, he was suffering from the terrible after-effects of all the vaccinations he'd just had. Shivering and in no fit state to leave my room, I had to report the presence of my lodger.

'I've got a man in my room.'

'Well, you shouldn't have, Diana.'

'I know, but he's just had injections to go to Nairobi.'

I was so worried that I can't remember the outcome. The college probably arranged for a taxi to take him home.

There was another young man who had failed his exams as a theological student. He seemed to be really interested in me but, before long, he wanted to climb into bed with me. I wasn't prepared for that, so we split up.

The third man was Alan. I had met him in St David's Hospital where he, too, was a patient. He'd had a breakdown when his second marriage failed. At the time divorce proceedings had to go through court in a very public way. His wife had made the same meal every evening for some weeks and he had asked her if there could be a bit of variety. There was obviously an underlying problem but he was very upset that the court had reduced their marital breakdown to a fight over 'egg and chips'. We spent a lot of time together and it seemed to help him. In fact, it helped him so much that Sister Mock (whose husband was in charge of the male ward) suggested that we should meet in an empty consulting room in the evenings. If those evenings helped Alan, they also taught me a lot about the frailty of human beings and their relationships. I began to understand how major grievances can often grow from something very trivial. I think and hope that my times with Alan taught me a little bit about humility.

Unsurprisingly, when Alan no longer needed my support we became a couple. Alan was more than twenty years older than me – handsome with a shock of curly white hair. He worked as a painter/decorator, but was a very able artist in his own right. He wrote poems for me, he carved me a love spoon. He said that he would always be gentle with me after my bad experiences – and he kept his word. We walked around

Carmarthen together – he treated me like a queen as he took me to meals at the new Chinese restaurant.

In my final year I had to choose the titles for my two theses. I was taking a special advanced main course in English as well as main art. The topics I selected said a lot about me – my art thesis was a visual presentation of TS Eliot's *The Waste Land*. I went through the long poem and selected lines or passages that fitted in with drawings or paintings. There was plenty of room for Toulouse-Lautrecs in such disjointed verse! I matched the lines to the graphics and wrote a short summary of the visual work and its artist.

For my English thesis I chose a comparison between TS Eliot's plays and Greek tragedy. In the thesis I used the word 'paranoid'. It was such an obscure word then that my tutor asked me if I knew what it meant. I would probably be asked in my viva! Both vivas went very well. My friend Lesley and I had seen nightdresses in town with Egyptian motifs on them. They were simple cotton shifts with slits at the sides and we both bought one but I felt that they were wasted as nightwear. I wore mine for my English viva and was complimented for extending the Classics mode into my clothing!

Ready as I was with my theses, I hadn't joined the other students in applying for a job. I simply couldn't imagine leaving Carmarthen and Dr McGill. I thought that, if I did nothing, the situation would resolve itself. When Dr McGill realised what was happening – or failing to happen – he witnessed me filling in an application form and posted it himself. I had no idea where I wanted to go – I didn't want to go anywhere. Ideally, I had thought of staying in Wales (I had taken a bilingual course which qualified me to teach Welsh as a second language). But all those desirable jobs had gone. Kay had applied to a school in Manchester, and so had the newly-married Ann. Perhaps Manchester would be the best bet. I was so late in applying that I got one of the least attractive jobs in the city's primary schools. St James' Primary School in Collyhurst was a real baptism of fire.

I made a final gesture towards staying a bit longer in Carmarthen. I was unwell after the exams, though my fear of moving on was part of the problem. Dr McGill refused to admit me to hospital again. He arranged for me to work as an assistant occupational therapist. I lived in the nurses' quarters. I received a letter through the post. I had passed my college exams with double distinctions.

21

Fallow Field

KAY HAD A large flat in the Fallowfield area of Manchester, so I went to live with her. I had a bedroom and we shared all the other facilities. 'Fallow field' – the name came to symbolise everything that I felt for my time in Manchester during 1966–67. As Kay received visits in the flat in the evenings from her boyfriend of the time, I felt very lonely. Ann was getting used to married life. Every morning I had to make two bus journeys each way to get to and from the school. When I stood in the bus queue I could hardly see more than one person ahead of me because of the fog. Other than the fog, it always seemed to be raining. When a bus came, it was usually too crowded for me to get on board – I just shifted up the queue a bit. By the time I reached Manchester Piccadilly, I noted miserably that this Piccadilly was nothing like the one I knew in London. Then there was the second bus and a short walk afterwards to the school where I had a class of about thirty six year olds to teach.

The school hadn't been able to attract a headmaster, so one of the male teachers was the most senior member of staff. Some of the teachers were very capable and caring people. There was a lovely lady called Mrs Eckersley who was a magistrate. She was very kind to me and helped me identify the parents who couldn't be trusted – there were quite a lot of them. Alice, one of the other teachers, was a gentle person. Although she was older than me, it was her first teaching job too – she had been a pianist. Alice was a dreamy musician and, like me, wondered what on earth had hit her. The woman in charge of the nursery department was tiny – four feet something. She wore boots and woolly socks but she had more control over her flock than anyone else. There was another girl who had just left college, and she and I took it in turns to get flu and colds as our immune systems got used to the constant contact with children. Once, when she and Mrs Eckersley were both ill at the same time, I had the whole of the infant school – about 120 children – on my own. We had to go into the Assembly Hall – the only place large enough to accommodate us. No supply teacher came near the place.

I just got used to the deprivation. I can't remember any social workers coming to attend to the welfare of the children. There were a few bright children in my class and I remember their names – Irene Connolly and Marie Jacques. I hope and pray that they were able to get out of the misery and make a decent life for themselves. I had a little boy who was gradually going blind from a disorder which, today, in different circumstances, would be treated. Another child with epilepsy had a seizure in the classroom. There was no one to help me. I put him to rest on a beanbag in the corner and wrote a letter to his mother to let her know what had happened. He came back to school the following day and throughout the entire week. He also had an ear infection at the same time; one problem triggered off the other. On the Friday his mother came to see me. I had been naïve enough to think that everyone was literate. She pushed the letter into my chest and asked what it was about. I told her and she shrugged. It was better for her child to be in school than to stay at home on his own. Another misconception – not every child had two parents.

Most of the children had free dinners but, on one occasion, they all needed to bring some money to school – I can't remember the reason. Several children came empty-handed. I wrote a note to Mrs Eckersley as I didn't know how to deal with the situation. 'Don't trust this particular family or that one' was the written reply. 'They're bad debtors.' The brother of one of my children (aged nine) ran away to Blackpool with a girl. The police brought them back. A little girl had been absent for a few days and I asked if she were feeling better. She looked at me vaguely. 'Me Mam's been washing me dress.' I looked at the dress – pretty, made of voile, but totally unsuitable for the Manchester weather. When another child had been away for about a week, I actually had a letter of explanation. Written on the back of a football coupon, it informed me that 'H. as nt been cmin to school cos we av nt been gettin up.' At least it showed some consideration.

It was quite common for a child to run out of the classroom. When this happened I had to run after them to retrieve them. In the meantime, the others were playing havoc, if not running away themselves. I was comforted by the fact that this happened in classes other than my own. It was bedlam.

I felt a lot of empathy towards one little child. These days I am sure that he would be diagnosed as autistic. Then, he was just a silent child whose exercise books remained blank. When I went to look at the children's books, I always stopped by his desk in the hope that I was communicating in some way. His large, brown limpid eyes didn't seem to register anything, but he rewarded me eventually. In his empty book he scribbled a long line in pencil. I complimented him on it. And he smiled. Just a little smile – but a smile, nevertheless.

I never had a break at dinnertime. We all had to be on duty, as the children struggled to get through a meal without violence erupting. They were not allowed to have knives in case they stabbed each other, so we had to cut up their meat. Apart from eating in the hall, we all congregated there for assembly and, on one occasion, for the harvest service. Dear Alice had tried to teach them where to take a breath in the well-known hymn 'We plough the fields'. She explained that they should sing 'We plough the fields', take a breath, 'and scatter the good seed on the land'. We had a visitor for the event – a Reverend Blowers. Alice began to play the piano for the hymn. The children, who failed to work as a team in any other circumstances, were united in their efforts. They sang 'We plough the fields and scatter.' They didn't just take a breath then; they uniformly slowed down the pace, making blowing movements with their lips to the embarrassed cleric. The acting headmaster swore at the children and made them start all over again.

One of the male teachers offered me a lift home one night. I went with him over to the car which would not start. He fiddled with the controls for a moment, then went out to inspect the engine. It had disappeared. *He* swore as well.

An HMI (Her Majesty's Inspector) came round to the school to assess me. In his smart suit he paid me a great compliment, 'You're doing very well in an extremely difficult school, Miss Williams.' And then he left quickly. If my health had been strong I think I might have stayed – a younger version of Mrs Eckersley, maybe.

It was easy to blame the school but I would probably have had a breakdown wherever I had been. I had registered with a GP who was happy to prescribe me with my alarmingly potent drugs by the hundreds. Maybe he thought that, with such medication, I was a lost cause anyway. This gave me the opportunity to 'take an extra tablet' when things were tough. In the evenings I went to the nearest pub and drank brandy. Soon, I couldn't be bothered to go to the pub. I bought bottles and drank back in the flat on my own. I often phoned the Samaritans. I occasionally took myself to casualty, having taken mild overdoses, which were nothing more than cries for help. I was always discharged, often after I had had my stomach pumped. I was frightened. Kay and I were not good for each other as flatmates then, as she had a tendency towards depression. In despair, I spent a night at Ann and Ray's house in a more attractive part of Manchester. I haven't a clue what terrors were filling my mind, but they forced me to climb into the marital bed. Ann and Ray just laughed – and let me stay.

I don't know how it came about that I landed up in hospital again. It doesn't really matter. I vaguely remember hiding in a corner of the flat one night with a coat over me, moaning. Maybe that was the final straw. I don't know.

I was admitted to Gaskell House – the psychiatric wing of Manchester Royal Infirmary at the time. A pleasant young Scots psychiatrist took care of me. I was given a bed in a room with three other women. The psychiatrist had to assess me before presenting my case to the consultant. The process took a month!

Gaskell House was a very bad experience for me. Of course there is a link between mind and body but, at the time, they were experimenting with the connection. Each patient had a nurse who was responsible for checking bodily functions. I was followed to the lavatory, though at least my nurse didn't come inside with me. I had to keep my urine for analysis. I was asked if I had had a bowel movement. If I said yes, I was asked about its texture. I was followed around the hospital. Once, I hid in a cupboard to have a bit of peace. We had to get up at 6am and make our beds in army fashion. Our efforts were inspected and, if they were not up to the mark, we had to improve a crease here or an angle there. It was not a warm building and the room for relaxation was freezing with no heating. This was where the little television was, but few of us ventured into the room at all. One of the patients was a convict serving time at Strangeways. The facilities in prison were not adequate for his psychiatric treatment, so he came to Gaskell House. He pleaded to be allowed to go back to jail.

After the month's assessment, which included physical tests including an EEG, I was asked to go into a large room with a motley crew of professionals watching me. I was asked questions. Notes were made. I was not compliant. I was then asked to sit outside. They let me back into the room again when they had discussed me and come to their conclusions. Everything was so clinical. I was given the double diagnosis again – depressive illness and temporal lobe epilepsy. New drugs were given to me. One of them was called Surmontil. I was surmounting nothing. We had to take exercise. They tried to get us ballroom dancing. One of the patients was suffering from a major depressive breakdown. An only child, he had been pressurised to train as a doctor. He was admitted after he had lost control during his final exams. There was an attempt to match us up. We shuffled around the room and he apologised to me. I apologised to him.

The person who made my stay tolerable was Betty. Betty had been a lecturer and was in the same little room as me. Our personalities and interests were alike and we probably had similar diagnoses because, apart from my anticonvulsants, we were taking the same antidepressants. It was our job to go to the local shop around the corner to purchase the newspapers for the other patients. We were both little more than zombies from the medication, and the task was not as simple as it seemed. People didn't give us the right money, so we had to remember what change was due to whom. Some people wanted extras – sweets or cigarettes. I'm not sure that cigarettes were allowed, so we may have been breaking hospital rules. We usually ended up laughing in the shop. They knew where we were from and that made it funnier. Going for longish walks in a crocodile line with a nurse was part of our therapy. Betty and I stuck together. As a treat on one of these walks, we were allowed to go into a café. A lovely, but very disturbed lady began offering dog biscuits to the other customers. We moved on.

Just before Christmas we were taken to a carol service in the main infirmary. I'll never forget the sight – us in our mental woundedness and others from the main infirmary on stretchers covered with red blankets. That same Christmastime, one of the patients in Gaskell House – a woman who was a very devout Roman Catholic – knelt down in the room where we were given our evening medication. She began to sing 'O come all ye faithful' in Latin. Everybody looked at her but I knew the Latin words too and knelt down beside her. '*Venite adoremus.*' The words had never sounded so poignant.

Betty and I were both discharged about the same time – neither of us feeling well. I was told that I had two options. I could either be admitted to Prestwich – a mental institution where I would probably have had to stay for a very long time – or I could go back to live with my parents. I went back to live in Essex. I was advised to lead a gentle life, avoiding active involvement in either politics or religion.

22

Ballet, a Tracheotomy

IT WAS A difficult time for all of us back in Ingatestone. My parents wanted to keep my illness a secret as there was such a stigma. That cut me off from being open with people. The doctors at Gaskell House had given me a sealed envelope to give to my GP. I'm afraid that I opened it and resealed it. 'This highly intelligent and creative young woman,' it said... 'depressive psychosis... temporal lobe epilepsy... too severely depersonalised to respond to psychotherapy.' At least I knew.

I was seen as an outpatient at the nearest psychiatric hospital – Severalls, near Colchester. Soon I was given another course of ECT – as an outpatient. A woman with a little woolly hat arrived in a van to pick me up and take me home. She collected a couple of other people on the way and there was that same rapport between me and the others that I had experienced at St David's. We didn't have to explain ourselves – we just knew how the other felt. It was like being in a forlorn club where our only comfort was that we belonged to it. I don't know whether the ECT helped – I think it did.

But what was I going to do with my life? If I made another application for a teaching post I would have to have a medical. My psychiatric problems wouldn't be visible of course but I couldn't withhold them. I was unable to lie. Dr McGill had told me that I was very honest. Maybe there are times when honesty doesn't pay but I felt that I had to tell the truth and, anyway, I didn't feel that I had overcome my illness.

I enrolled to do a course in beauty therapy in Bond Street, London, and travelled up every day for six weeks. We had

135

exams at the end of the course – practical and theory – and although I passed with distinction, I wondered how I'd be able to use these new qualifications. I saw an advertisement for a lectureship in a London technical college – in fashion and beauty therapy. I had no official fashion certificates but I had always had a distinctive and lively interest in fashion. I designed and made my own clothes – I had my own style. I applied and got an interview. The panel was very impressed and more or less offered me the job on the spot. Before I left I told them about my medical history. Their faces fell and I received a letter a couple of days later telling me that my application had been unsuccessful.

I was looking through Lew's copy of the *TES* (*Times Educational Supplement*) one day when I noticed an advertisement for a job teaching in a private school. I wouldn't have the same rigorous medical checks there. I wouldn't have to lie. The post was as an academic teacher to children at a residential ballet and drama school based in a mansion in Tring, Hertfordshire. I plucked up the courage to apply, had an interview and was appointed. My time there was a strange experience. The children I taught were mostly primary school age. In many ways it was all very quaint. The children wore full-length cloaks as part of their uniform and they had to curtsey to the staff! They had half of the day doing vocational training and the other half doing their academic subjects. As their vocational education was in the mornings, this was the only time that I had free. I had no private transport. Tring was a very small town then – there was a single row of shops. I had nothing to do except go to the café and order the same thing every morning – milky coffee and a couple of rounds of toast.

The children seemed to warm to me. Some of them had famous parents, some of them were exceptionally gifted, and some were there because of ambitious parents. It was hard trying to fit all the work into the time that was allocated to me. A highlight for me – and for the children – came at the end of the day when I read them a chapter from a book. I suppose it was like a replacement for the traditional parent's bedtime story. *The Secret Garden* appealed to them all and I managed to produce a convincing Yorkshire accent when needed. When I'd finished there was a plea, 'Another chapter, Miss Williams. PLEASE! Another chapter! Another chapter.' I never had time for another chapter but that added to the overall pleasure in the long run.

In the evenings the staff took turns to be on duty. It is said that Nell Gwynne's ghost haunts the place (Charles II was supposed to have met her there) and from time to time I had a knock on the staff room door. A child was convinced that she had seen the spirit wandering. This meant that I had to search through the secret passageways with a torch and then assure them that I had seen no one lurking about.

When some of the children went on tour for *The Nutcracker Suite*, I was asked to go with them to Southampton. It was an amazing but very tiring experience. There were two teachers – one from the vocational department – and myself. We had to look after the children in the mornings when I tried to teach them things like arithmetic! We had to check that they had eaten the hotel food. It was a rundown hotel on the outskirts of the city, so we had a long trek by bus for the afternoon rehearsals. Whenever the children were not rehearsing or performing in a matinée, they had to mend their costumes – the ballet took a heavy toll on the fabric. When they were on stage, I had to wait in the wings with the second costumes for the children who had to change quickly. A perk for me was when John Gilpin came offstage and passed me with a smile. 'HULLO, teacher!', he said, grinning. Once the evening performance was over we had to trek back with the children to the hotel. It was so late by that time that the place was in darkness. We had to make them a cup of Ovaltine before checking that they were tucked up safely in bed. It was arduous and far from any romantic ideas about stage life.

I got in touch again with Alan, my old friend from Carmarthen. I'd heard that he was working as a head waiter in a Cotswold town hotel. He had a car and it was only an hour's drive away. He came to see me and took me back to the hotel where I was given a beautiful room. For the first time, we became lovers. We talked about marriage. He loved me – he *adored* me. I could do no wrong in his sight. But I was unsure of things. Part of my motive for getting in touch again was because I was lonely. I liked him very much – but I wasn't sure if I loved him. I realised that, as his wife, I would be put on a pedestal. At the same time, Alan was concerned that our different backgrounds would be a barrier. I wasn't so sure about that but the fact that he had doubts made it easier when I said that we should part.

In the school I got on as well with the staff as I did with the children. But I knew that I was struggling with my old health problems again. The head of the academic staff picked it up and said that, if I needed a holiday, I could have one on full pay. I was grateful, but I needed more than a holiday. I had been going to outpatient appointments at the nearest psychiatric hospital – Beacon House, in a village called Stone, near Aylesbury. I gave in my notice at the school and just about managed to serve it through. The children and the staff bade me a tearful farewell. I took the bus to the hospital.

Another hospital, another psychiatrist, another set of theories. It was an open hospital with extensive grounds. I made friends with the other women on my ward, some of whom were very disturbed. There was a lovely, elegant lady there and we got on very well. She was tall and slim, with beautiful long auburn hair that she wore in a low chignon. She had been an actress. (Her son Rupert was also a patient on the male ward.) During the days I spent a lot of time with these women. But when I was free to go out in the grounds, I mixed with the male patients too. I decided to help a male patient who had an extremely severe obsessive-compulsive disorder. He was rather a sweet man who had been in hospital for years. When he walked along the pavement he couldn't let his feet go anywhere near a crack. If he stepped less than six inches or so from a crack, he had to go backwards and repeat the ritual. I went for walks with him and assured him that nothing bad would happen to him if his feet went near a crack. He improved a bit and, although the obsession remained, he cut down the amount of space needed between his feet and the cracks. He said that I had helped him more than any of the doctors.

I became friendly with an Irish lady who was very disturbed. She had had surgery for a heart condition. The surgery had been successful but it had left her with mental impairment. She liked me so much that she delved into my wardrobe in the morning and wore my clothes. We were not the same size.

I was there to receive help myself, but it didn't seem to come. I think part of the problem was that I didn't fit neatly into any category and I struggled to get a rapport with my psychiatrist. My mind was so muddled and tormented that memories are vague. About the only comfort I had was going to the little café in the grounds to have a milky coffee. Most people stared into space – others were aggressive and suffering from hallucinations and delusions. I decided that I wouldn't go to occupational therapy to make baskets.

I tried to get in touch with Alan again. Maybe I'd made the wrong decision about him. When I got through to the hotel, a woman told me that he had left. He had been homesick and missed his children. Dear, sweet Alan.

I hope he caught up with them and enjoyed their company. A couple of months passed, new drugs were tried and I was in a black hole.

My parents came one weekend to take me to see a film in Aylesbury. Heartbreaking though it must have been for them, I was out of my mind. The actors came out of the screen and followed me. They seemed to be coming towards my body. I could hardly keep my balance. As if that weren't enough, my skin broke out again in very angry urticaria and angioedema. When some sixth-form pupils came to visit my ward, they spoke to everybody except me. There was only one solution. I felt sorry for my parents and, as an only child, I must have disappointed them. If I disappeared they could adopt a child and just forget about me. I was ugly, hideous and wicked.

I began saving up my sedation. If I couldn't sleep by about 1am, I was allowed to go to the night nurse and have an extra dose. I didn't take those extra doses. When I had accumulated enough I felt very calm. I was making the right decision. I wrote a letter to my parents. I wrote a letter to my psychiatrist. On the night itself I planned the best way to do the deed. I was in a four-bedded ward, so I had to make sure that the other three had no suspicions. When I went for my evening sedation I showed no signs of agitation. I ensured that I had plenty of water at my bedside. I waited for the other patients to go to sleep. The night nurse usually looked in on us at about midnight to check that everybody had settled down for the night. I waited for that. Then I filled my left hand with as many tablets as I could hold. I swallowed them down with the water and, as soon as I felt drowsy, I lay down in a normal sleeping position with the blanket up to my head.

I only have other people's comments as to what happened next. Apparently, one of the other patients noticed that my face had gone purple in the morning. A member of staff was summoned and an ambulance took me immediately to nearby Stoke Mandeville Hospital. One of the male nurses came with me in the ambulance. My heart stopped beating and it had to be massaged to get it restarted. When I arrived at Stoke Mandeville my breathing was laboured. Someone told me that I had contracted pneumonia. I'm not sure about this, although I did have to have an emergency tracheotomy. I woke up some time later. I've been told different things about the length of my coma – anything from three days to three weeks.

When I eventually surfaced I had no idea where I was or what had happened. Children with Down syndrome features were cycling towards my head. But, at the same time, I saw my parents. They seemed delighted to see me and they smiled. I think that this process of waking and sleeping continued for a while, but eventually I noticed a large woman in a dark blue uniform above me. I tried to pull out the drips and lines that were attached to my body. She put them back. I tried to talk but couldn't as I had the tube in my throat. The woman gave me a piece of paper and a pen. I couldn't write. But I did manage a scrawl. 'Where am I?' The woman said, 'You're in hospital.' Why didn't she write back to me? Gradually the muddle subsided and I remembered what had happened. I had to stay there for a while until I was physically strong enough to return to the psychiatric hospital. There was a young woman about my own age in an iron lung next to me. She wanted to get married and desperately wanted to live.

Shortly after I had returned to the psychiatric hospital, I was transferred to St John's Hospital for Diseases of the Skin in London. For a week they tried everything available at the time to find out the cause of my allergies. I had to have a cold bath, but the cold didn't trigger the symptoms. I had to have a very hot bath. I had to lift weights to see if exercise was the problem. Every antihistamine was tried. I returned to the psychiatric hospital without them or me being any the wiser.

However, my mood changed radically. One of the women on my ward had been discharged. She rang me up via the ward kiosk phone, saying that she was desperate. I found some excuse to get out of the hospital and went to visit her. An Irish Catholic, she had six children and a husband who was trying to make ends meet by supplementing his day job by taxiing at night. She should have had some help. It's a very dangerous time after a hospital discharge. I helped her that day practically with the children, and reported the situation to the hospital. Where were the social workers? Did she have a follow-up appointment? (Several years later, I made a BBC broadcast about that very problem – continuity after hospital discharge.) I felt that there were great flaws in the way that the hospital was being run. I made detailed notes of all these weaknesses, with ideas on how to rectify them. Once I was satisfied that I had covered everything, I went up to the office where the head physician was based. I had no appointment. I just knocked on his door. I went through the list of the problems, then followed each one with the solution. He listened to me seriously, and before I was discharged some of my ideas had been put into action.

23

Escapades

WHAT WAS GOING to happen to me next? These high moods were short-lived and I went back into depression. The hospital had not really helped me. One day my psychiatrist said that he wanted me to go to a hospital in London that specialised in hopeless cases. Maybe I exaggerate, but that was the feeling I had. I had to go for an interview to the Maudsley Hospital to see if I was bad enough to be admitted. I passed that strange exam. I was transferred.

Once again, I had a new set of things to deal with – a new ward, new staff, new ideas. It was – and is – a leading teaching hospital. It has helped so many people but it didn't work for me. In the six months that I remained there, the only positive things to happen had nothing to do with my treatment.

The late 1960s was a crucial and innovative time for psychiatry. Dr William Sargant had been a consultant at the Maudsley and his approach relied heavily on physical treatments. But there were new people coming up with radically different theories – people like RD Laing, who claimed that it wasn't the schizophrenic who was sick but the people around the 'sick' person who were forcing 'the patient' into behaving abnormally.

I shared my psychiatrist with two other women on the ward. None of us found him easy – he was young and needed time to mature himself. He was always sarcastic to me – a strange therapy. We had a lively and lovely ward sister called Sister Winiki. She was Polish and very eccentric. Sometimes I felt that she ran the hospital. I remember running to her one day to tell her that a patient was lighting a fire in the communal bathroom. She rushed to the scene with two buckets of water – one for herself and one for me. We managed to put the fire out, even though a lot of the water had soaked me to the skin. We ended up laughing. 'Sank you, my darlink!'

As an inpatient I tried to think of a future. I wanted to fall in love. Maybe that would cure me. The rules on the ward were very relaxed, so I went one day to a marriage bureau situated in Central London. I told the woman in charge about myself and my interests. She asked the obvious question – 'Why is an attractive young girl coming to a marriage bureau?' 'Because I haven't found the right person yet.' I was only twenty-four, but a lot of my contemporaries were engaged, if not married. The woman put me on her books and I was introduced to someone – a lovely man. We went out together a few times. He was gentle and kind, though picking me up from the Maudsley was hardly an auspicious start. A couple of months later and after a lovely meal, he walked me back to the hospital and told me that it would be better if we split up. He had only contacted the bureau after the break-up of a deep relationship. He needed to deal with that before committing himself to anybody else.

Still as an inpatient, I had a letter forwarded to me. I had been selected as a finalist in the annual *Vogue* talent contest. I had an invitation to go to Vogue House with the other finalists for lunch with the senior staff of the magazine and associated personalities. I left the Maudsley and made my way across London to the illustrious headquarters where I mingled with everyone over a drink. The features editor told me that she had particularly enjoyed my entry. We had had to write six essays – one on ourselves, another on fashion, one on beauty and the remainder consisted of a series of reviews – theatre, films and books. When we sat down for the meal I found myself sitting next to Lady Antonia Fraser. Later, when we were being shown around the offices, the director of Condé Nast publications pointed to a blown-up photograph of Catherine

Deneuve. 'She's wonderful, isn't she, Deneuve? Ageless.' I agreed wholeheartedly. When it was time for us all to leave, I took the bus back to the Maudsley.

Shortly afterwards I had another letter forwarded to me which held a strange ironic twist. I had been invited to give a talk at a conference in Church House, Westminster, on psychiatric care. I had previously visited the headquarters of the National Association for Mental Health (now Mind) and I was on their 'books'. Until then, patients had never had a say on their care. I agreed to do the talk and had no nerves as I stood by the microphone with a full auditorium before me.

Something had to be done about the food, I said. More fresh fruit was needed. No patient should be discharged without a follow-up appointment. Life could seem almost back to normal in a hospital setting but, with the responsibilities that came with going home, there were often setbacks. It was a far better option than a repeat admission.

I can't remember all the points I made but the organiser said that she heard a lot of 'hear, hears' in the audience. When the other guest speakers had finished, we all had a meal in a huge elegant room. I was on the VIP table. Dr Farr, my first psychiatrist in Carmarthen, came up to congratulate me. He had been in the audience. Life is very strange.

After the meal I was invited to the Guildhall for a reception. A woman working in television wanted me to do some programmes for ITV. They never materialised, which is probably just as well. I was carrying a heavy enough stigma as it was. I did do an interview for *Woman's Hour* under a pseudonym. Sue MacGregor asked me about my experiences and my feelings about the different approaches – she had just interviewed William Sargant and David Cooper and told me how sane I seemed.

I also wrote a full-length novel when I was in hospital. Although I was still young, I had a wealth of life experiences. After an unsuccessful attempt to get it published through an agent, an old college lecturer helped me. He asked me to send him a copy and enjoyed reading it so much that he got it published (in a Welsh-language translation) through the Welsh Books Council for which he then worked. There are various theories about the connection between creativity and 'madness'. I had written that novel when I was an inpatient at the Maudsley Hospital.

I was still in hospital when they wanted me to try a part-time job to see how I managed. I heard about a newly-formed pyramid business selling beauty products. I went to their headquarters, was approved of, and duly bought the little business bag with its products inside. The idea was that I should go from door to door, asking women if they would like a free professional make-up. They were supposed to be so impressed by the products that they bought some. I went around the streets of Camberwell, which was a very mixed community, and began my job. I didn't worry about the middle-class women, but I felt so sorry for the less privileged ones who thought it was exciting to have a professional make-up at home. They reached for their purses and I could see that they couldn't really afford the products. I was clearly no businesswoman.

The final and most significant thing to happen to me when I was at the Maudsley came as a total surprise. I was still in touch with the beautiful red-haired actress whom I had met at the previous hospital. But it was not she who visited me one day on the ward. It was her son, Rupert. (As noted, Rupert had been a patient at the psychiatric hospital near Aylesbury when I, too, was there.) Rupert was notorious for being outrageous. He arrived to see me, wearing a felt hat and a smoking jacket from Portobello Market. He was extremely handsome and very charismatic. He had been given a serious diagnosis but, in spite of this, or maybe because of this, he was one of the most brilliantly intuitive and intelligent people I have ever met. He was about five years younger than me but he spoke about philosophy and life with a convincing authority. I was pleased to see him but didn't realise that he had found me attractive.

He couldn't stop kissing me and I certainly didn't object. He told Sister Winiki that we were going out. She smiled at us indulgently.

There was a park opposite the hospital. I have no idea how long we were there. I was oblivious to everything except the fact that I had instantly fallen head over heels in love with this unusual man. And it was clearly mutual. We lay on the grass, kissing and caressing. I didn't want him to go. He didn't want to go. In the end he had to leave, promising that he would sort things out for us. The love letters that arrived for me almost every day were so passionate. He invited me to stay at his parents' home. I had the advantage of already knowing his mother. He must have discharged himself from hospital near Aylesbury but that seemed a trivial matter. I discharged myself from the Maudsley too. I can't remember how I travelled to see him that weekend. I must have taken the train. The home was wonderfully eccentric. They generated their own electricity, the light switches were placed so high that I had to stand on a chair to reach them, his grandmother lived in a cottage in their grounds and when she showed me a photograph of her deceased husband, he just *happened* to be in the company of Picasso, Diaghilev and others. Rupert was an only child and, when his parents failed to persuade us to go along to a rugby club dance with them, we were left alone.

That night we became very ardent lovers. It was the late 1960s and a common progression – no one wasted much time. The next stage was finding somewhere to live. Rupert came to Ingatestone and met my parents. He was able to charm them and convince them that he would look after me. When he left I went down to the station with him to see him onto the train. Once he was on the train he wound the window down so that we could kiss. We weren't prepared to let go of each other and we kept the train waiting. The guard blew his whistle. He had to blow it again. I felt so happy – happier than I had ever felt in my life – except when I had been with my grandparents. This, of course, was an entirely different relationship. My heart was racing; I could think of nothing else but Rupert. He was in my thoughts all day and he wafted in and out of my dreams at night. I went over and over all the things we had said to each other, all the things that I wanted to say. I went through all the intimacies we had shared; I couldn't bear being separated from him. If they had any misgivings, my parents didn't show them; they must have been delighted to see me so happy. Rupert found a flat for us (it was a bedsit – one room with a bed and a 'kitchen' in the corner of the same room that was just curtained off to hide a basic cooker). We shared the other facilities with the rest of the tenants.

We were an interesting lot – the landlord was black and had violent rows with his Irish girlfriend; there were a couple of other black people at a time when there was still a lot of racial prejudice; there was an upper middle-class English girl who had married a black American to get him out of the war in Vietnam, and in the next room to us was a lovely Irish girl who was a prostitute. Everyone was taking drugs. We needed to have some income to pay for the flat but Rupert had already seen to that. He had signed both of us up as models at Camberwell Art College. It was an ideal job for me. I had nothing to do but pose for the art students and it was quite well paid. Rupert was reading books by Kahlil Gibran – they amazed me with their beautiful insights. I was writing poems. I had joined Plaid Cymru before I met Rupert and was still committed to it. Rupert told me that politics had its place but it also had its limitations. There was something *beyond*.

We were both on spiritual journeys but they were taking us in different directions. Rupert became interested in paganism, the Arthurian legends, druidism. Love really is blind – I was failing to see the problems in our relationship. Rupert ignored social and moral boundaries. He asked me to marry him, but marriage for him would have been the locking of hands on a hill in the presence of a couple of friends.

There was also the question of the drugs. I was still taking my medication and my psychiatrist (thankfully, a different one) warned me against taking anything illegal as they would make a dangerous, if not lethal cocktail. When we sat in a circle smoking a joint, I put the joint in my mouth but I never inhaled – I was simply too scared. But I am fairly convinced that some LSD was put into my coffee one day – I went from peeling potatoes to having violent hallucinations in seconds. They were violently different from anything I had experienced before. Everything went red and I remember throwing the kitchen knife into the air. I was mumbling about Satan and saints. Rupert was not law abiding and I began to worry that we would both get into trouble with the police. When someone told me that they had seen Rupert with another woman, I was very hurt. To Rupert's way of thinking, it didn't matter; he was not obligated to me. We struggled through the next month or so; I was still very much in love with him and, although not committed to me, he still loved me. It was a mutual decision to split up. It should have happened earlier but I thought that things might improve.

I had a lovely set of earthenware coffee cups and saucers that I had bought with my first salary in 1966. Rupert wanted them but I said that they were mine. That is my main memory of that troubled day when we parted ways – an argument over coffee cups.

I kept the crockery but didn't know where I was going to take it. I'm sure that my parents would have welcomed me back but I felt that I couldn't return there. Lew wrote me a long and carefully worded letter supporting me and saying that I was loved. I spent some time at Mildred's house (the wife of our first GP in Ingatestone). She was lovely and understood the complications of a disastrous and complicated relationship. She told me about her life and we became good friends. But I couldn't stay with her as she was also friendly with my parents. I didn't feel able to continue with my modelling in case I bumped into Rupert.

My friends in Plaid Cymru came to the rescue. One of them had a large flat in outer London and he offered me a roof over my head. I slept on his settee. He was engaged and always behaved perfectly. I had no income so I bought a copy of the local newspaper. There was only one job that I thought I could manage – I was in a state of turmoil but didn't want to return to hospital. An usherette was needed in a local cinema; it showed films that were risqué, so it was a members-only venue. I went for an interview and got the job. My tasks involved checking that everyone coming into the building had a valid membership card, showing people into the cinema, walking down the aisle with soft drinks and ice creams in the intervals, and ensuring that everybody left at the end of the showings. Even in my fragile state, I could manage that. The only perk of the job was that I was entitled to free soft drinks and ice creams. During my time there I lived on little else but Pepsi cola and choc-ices.

The manager of the cinema was an interesting man. He seemed to spend a lot of his time in his office reading literary classics. When I was there it was *Ulysses* by James Joyce so, when the wretched films were being shown, he called me in to discuss them with him. He said that I was wasted in the job but he was riveted by our unlikely discussions.

My salary was very basic but it enabled me to do several things. Firstly, I was able to give my friend a bit of money to pay for my keep. Secondly, mainly living on my diet of cola and ice cream, I was able to supplement it with bottles of brandy that took the edge off the anguish I felt. The more I drank, the more my capacity to tolerate alcohol increased. Inevitably, I was extremely vulnerable at the time. I have no idea how many partners I had in London – most of them little more than 'one-night stands'. I was confusing sex with love. I can't even remember who some of them were. Lonely men, hungry men, lost men, excited men. It was, of course, a recipe for disaster.

I went to Wales for the Eisteddfod and met someone who had been at college with me – a poet and a writer. Fairly predictably, we began a relationship. As there was no real commitment back in London any more, I decided to stay in

Wales and found a bedsit in Cardiff. It was another relationship that didn't last but there was more substance to it than the earlier ones. It was followed by a couple more relationships of some depth but none of them lasted. My illness was too formidable an intrusion.

I had to get a job and, once again, I looked for something that was undemanding. I helped a writer and publisher for a while. Then I worked as a secretary/clerk for a firm of money lenders. When I had been living in London, my catarrh/ sinusitis/perennial rhinitis had developed into something more frightening. The breathlessness was so similar to the panic attacks that I didn't seek out help for a long time. A few months into my job in Cardiff, the breathlessness was so bad that I had to go to see the GP. He gave me a Ventolin spray but no diagnosis. My bedsit became like a prison. I had to ring up my employers and tell them that I was ill. Then I had a very bad bout of bronchitis. The antibiotics didn't work and I knew that my employers were losing patience with me. I wondered why I had ever thought that supporting money lenders was an ethical thing to do anyway.

So I was unemployed and too ill to fend for myself properly. I didn't have the strength or motivation to get any welfare help. I had a gas fire in the bedsit but I often didn't have the money to pay for the power. When I was cold I went to bed. There was a little shop on the other side of the road – I struggled over there and bought whatever I could afford. My cupboard was almost bare in every sense. The coughing went on and on. I was scared. When my parents and Nana came to visit me, I put on a show of normality.

24

A New Start in Wales

THE PROBLEM WITH being in a new city is making contacts and finding friends. Before I had become physically ill, I had gone to poetry readings that were held once a week in a pub in town. They were good fun – I read some of my own work and listened to others. There was someone there who wrote poems, songs and played the guitar. His name was Peter and he was unusual – but then we *all* were in that place. Peter's poems were esoteric, his songs lovely and his guitar skills superb, even though he couldn't read music. He was tall and very thin with dark curly hair and a beard that had a red tinge. He was working as a research technician with sewage sludge. This was a short-term arrangement to carry him through until he finished his PhD thesis on polymer chemistry. I didn't really know what polymer chemistry was. He had been very kind and friendly to me at the readings and invited me over to his flat if I ever wanted to visit.

I didn't think that I'd ever take up the offer but I continued to have one illness after another. I was very low on the August Bank Holiday. Bank holidays are very difficult for the sick and the lonely. It was quite a long walk over to Peter's flat. Neither of us had a phone so I didn't even know if he would be in. I knocked on the door. Peter smiled when he opened the door and let me in. He was sharing his rented flat with another PhD student and it wasn't easy stepping over all the paperwork on the floor without disrupting it. He made me a cup of tea and he asked me how I was.

Before long we were going out with each other. It was an

odd courtship, with my ups and downs and Peter's work. The first time we ventured out of Cardiff we went to Bath where Peter had some friends. We had a good time. But, once we were back in Cardiff, I passed out on the station platform. We made our way to the Cardiff Royal Infirmary. I had glandular fever and tonsillitis – a test for any new relationship.

We certainly didn't have the sciences in common. Maybe part of the attraction was our common vulnerability. Peter's life had not been easy either. His mother had died when he was a young boy. As a Christian Scientist she had refused pain relief and his memories of her were mainly her cries of agony. Peter had been told that if he prayed for her to get well, she would. When she died Peter thought that it was his fault. He was unable to tell his father and he soon had a new step-mother. His father married Peter's mother's sister, so his step-mother was also his aunt. The newly-married couple were infatuated with each other. Some time after Peter and I met, I went to meet them and Peter warned me that they were unusual. His father was a talented artist and an excellent cartoonist who had worked as the publicity manager for the *Western Mail* before taking early retirement. His wife was lively and forthright.

Peter also had broken relationships behind him – and he had had a breakdown of sorts. There is something very attractive about mutual vulnerability. I soon found out how kind Peter was, very kind. He wrote a song for me that he performed in one of the poetry sessions:

> The moon is drifting down
> On her dusty dressing gown
> And the happiness I see
> Is not couched in misery
> So the feathers of a bird
> Hold more notes than I could ever hope for.
>
> If I held my sway
> In this raining day

Then one deed that I'd do
Is to climb down from my tower
Forgetful of the hour
And cast away my fickle crown forever.
The only reason this song's in-between us
Is because I don't want to die
Or let my spirit fly
Until it's yours and mine together.

We had known each other for about six months when we married. I didn't want a big wedding, so we had a short ceremony at the Register Office in Cardiff. My parents and Peter's came. Nana, by this time frail, was delighted to come and, although the walk challenged her arthritis, she was determined not to miss a moment. Iris and Stan from Aberdare had been very close friends and they asked to be part of the day. A small crowd of friends waited outside the Register Office to wish us well – Geoff and Fran, Bob Thomas, Peter Finch, Doug and Mila... Still very tiny (a size 8), I was dressed in a long, pink dress under a purple velvet coat. I had pink roses in my hair. Peter wore a red velvet suit, and to complete the outfit (Peter normally doesn't care about clothes and appearance) he wore a pink shirt and a tie that complemented the shirt and suit. Someone said that the bridegroom looked pretty! Afterwards we went back to the Park Hotel – Nana was still walking! We had chosen the Park because it was quite up-market and I hoped that it would compensate for the simple ceremony. It did the trick but, Peter's father, true to form, chose fish and chips as his main course. Peter and I spent our wedding night successfully dissuading someone from attempting suicide. Peter went to work the following day.

On the following Saturday we had a party at the Central Hotel. It was a relaxed and happy occasion. Relatives from Aberdare hired a minibus, old friends made the journey, and there were lots of poets and artists there too. It was such an unusual mix of people that, when an intoxicated stranger came in from the street, no one really noticed.

Six weeks later we finally managed to have a holiday. We went over to Killarney by boat and train. I nudged Peter on the Irish train to draw his attention to the headlines on the newspaper that was being read by a nun. Unmarried politician Bernadette Devlin was pregnant! We loved Killarney and stayed in a small guest house on the outskirts of the town. We drank a lot of Guinness, went to ceilidhs and thoroughly enjoyed ourselves.

Back in Cardiff we had to make practical arrangements. Peter was still working on his PhD thesis but I persuaded him to apply for a teaching post. He wasn't sure about this but he soon proved to be an inspiring and versatile teacher. We'd been living in a shabby flat in Cardiff and Peter's new job was at Bedwellte Grammar School. We had no car, no phone, no contacts. The nearest town to the school was Bargoed, so I went there on the bus to see if I could find some accommodation. It would have been very difficult for Peter to travel on buses from Cardiff every day.

Bargoed was a typical Valleys town, though it was one that I didn't know at all. I bought a local newspaper and found nothing. I wandered past every shop, looking in the windows for adverts on postcards. Still nothing. Then I did a very sensible thing. I went in to have a cup of coffee in an Italian café. Mr Rossi was a lovely, obliging man. I told him of our plight. There was a lady he knew – a Mrs Romanik – one of his customers. She lived in the nearby village of Deri. She was German (she turned out to be half-Danish and half-Russian but her main language was German). She and her husband (an Ukranian Pole who had come over to work in the coal mines) lived in a terraced house in the village. Mrs Romanik had bought a little cottage for her widowed mother but, when the old lady came over from Germany, she couldn't settle. As far as he knew it was furnished and still empty. I had no choice but to get on another bus to Deri. Mr Rossi knew all the bus times. I smiled and thanked him. Italian café owners *do* know everything!

The bus took me to Deri and I began looking for the address that Mr Rossi had given me. When I found it a gregarious woman, Elfrieda Romanik, came to the door and I told her my story. She took me down to the little cottage which was furnished in a quaint Bavarian style. She had let it once before but said that the people were confidence tricksters. She didn't want to take the risk again. I think her heart softened when I said that Peter was going to teach at Bedwellte Grammar School. We struck a deal and I took the buses back to Cardiff.

When I got back to Cardiff, Peter, of course, knew nothing of the transaction. We had no phone. Peter's brain is impressively brilliant and wide reaching but he is not an organiser. He'd been happy to leave things to me. I was relieved that we were moving to a better home – a more convenient one. It was a tiny house but sweet and attractive. Downstairs, there was a main living room and a kitchen. There was a winding staircase which took us to the first floor. Upstairs, there was a largish bedroom, a tiny bedroom and a bathroom – and outside there was a little patch of garden. Peter had only been in the school a few days when a colleague offered him a lift both ways.

I was pregnant. I had kept in touch with Dr McGill and, when I went down to Carmarthen shortly before getting married, I asked him about the possibility of having children – something that I would never have believed possible. He looked at his copy of MIMS (a database of prescription and generic drugs) and checked all my medication. As I was having a good spell and was taking nothing that would harm a baby in my womb, he suggested that I should try to conceive fairly quickly.

Amidst the excitement of the pregnancy was the fear. I used to go to the telephone kiosk and tell the ever-patient Dr McGill about my worries. I registered with the local GP and waited eagerly for the antenatal check-ups. Times have changed so much that it is difficult to believe how unprepared I was. As an only child, brought up away from my extended family, I had never held a baby before. Peter hadn't either. I bought a Dr Spock book and read it page by page. There were no other books available and no antenatal classes.

A good opportunity came my way – it alleviated my anxiety for a while. The head of the English department in the school liked Peter and called at our house one day after school. Until a new permanent post was advertised and filled, he was short-staffed. Could I help out? I was delighted, and worked at the school until I was seven months pregnant. I taught some A level English – not easy to inspire seventeen- and eighteen-year-old boys with Wordsworth – but I did it with pleasure. I also helped out teaching French to the third years. Earning a bit of money helped and the work took my mind away from worrying too much. Just before I left the school there was a dance at the end of the term. I had great energy as I took part in the 'Gay Gordons'. I wore a long, red floral dress that I had bought at Portobello Market in London. It had a very full skirt and was the ideal maternity dress for the only social occasion I went to throughout the pregnancy.

Back home I was getting everything ready. About three weeks before my due date of delivery, I read the *Guardian*. A medical researcher had published his findings. Women who took anticonvulsants during pregnancy were more likely to have babies with deformities. It was back to the phone kiosk and Dr McGill again. I don't know if the worry affected me. Maybe it would have happened anyway. When I was almost thirty-eight weeks pregnant, I went to the toilet and wondered what was happening to me. I had read about 'waters breaking'. Was this what was happening? I struggled out with a towel wrapped around me and called down to Peter before lying on the bed, too scared to move. I pointed to the soaking towel.

'We'd better call the ambulance!'

'Yes, we'd better call the ambulance.'

As we were indoors, we hadn't been aware of the snow that was by that time falling heavily. We lived up a steep hill on the edge of the mountain. Peter ran out into the village. There were three public phone kiosks but two were out of order. He eventually got through and the ambulance was on its way! When he returned, Peter's hair was covered in the snow that was showing no sign of stopping. The ambulance men knew exactly what to do. But they said that, if we had called them any later, they wouldn't have been able to make the hill. Peter came in the ambulance with me, and he sat as I lay down listening to the sound that ambulances make when they are in a rush. We had to get to Caerffili Miners' Hospital as soon as possible!

Once I was admitted a nurse examined me and said that I would have a long time ahead of me before the birth. The snow was still falling heavily. Husbands weren't allowed to stay for the deliveries. The nurse thought that Peter would be better off having a good night's sleep at home. But, of course, he had no means of getting home. It was too late for the buses and, anyway, the snow would have put them out of action. The ambulance driver did a mercy mission. He drove Peter home but didn't attempt the hill.

I was put in a side room. Although I welcomed the privacy, I had no clue what to expect. I was having contractions – at least, I supposed that's what they were. When did I ring the alarm for the nurse? The pain was still bearable and I was very reserved. Rather than ringing the alarm, I made a few discreet moans in the hope that the nurse would hear. She did and examined me. Still a long time to go, she said, but, as she had nothing else to do, she stayed in the room with me for company. We chatted and she admired the rings I was wearing. She looked at me closely, then said, 'You're a fascinating person!' And then she began to tell me her problems! She was worried about one of her children. I listened and showed interest but the pains were getting worse. She examined me again and this time I was whisked into the delivery room. I asked for pethidine but she said it was too late. I was offered gas and air. For a few minutes I thought that my body was splitting into two.

'Push. Push. Here it comes. The head. You've got a little girl, Mrs Morgan!'

There was none of the immediate bonding that is encouraged these days. The cord was cut and my baby was taken away to be cleaned up and weighed. When they brought her back for me to see, I couldn't believe my eyes. She was a miracle. Such tiny fingers and hands, little toes; she was perfect and she had a shock of black hair. It was not yet 6am so I had to wait before I could let anyone know. As soon as the ward came to life, I asked if they could bring me the telephone that could be wheeled around the ward. (The nearest thing anyone had to a mobile phone.) I didn't have the right money but I knew that I could reverse the charges! I wanted every one to know about my little girl. And every one was thrilled. The sad thing was that I couldn't let Peter know. But, when he went down to the village at 8.30, there was good news for him. He was a dad.

25

Teething Problems, Nana

I WAS IN a small ward with three other women. Our babies were with us during the day and wheeled out at night into a ward where they were all cared for by night staff. Although my baby was small, she didn't need to be in an incubator. On her first day, the nurse came past me and told me that I wasn't holding her correctly. I couldn't feed her myself because of my medication. I stayed in hospital for ten days so that I, like the others, had bed rest. The bottles were made up for us. There was a chart at the end of the bed and it recorded how much milk the baby had drunk. Three ounces was the target. When I had to feed her, I hoped and prayed that there wouldn't be a drop left in the bottle. And, all the time, I couldn't stop looking at my little daughter who was so beautiful.

Because of the heavy snow it was difficult for Peter to visit. Lew was determined to make the journey on the second or third day, so he picked Peter up en route. Father and grandfather arrived, excited and having celebrated the birth first with a drink. Lew was moved to tears. He'd missed out on seeing me – he wasn't going to miss out on his granddaughter. Peter and Lew both held her in their arms – very gently, afraid that they would crush her. This little child was going to be loved. We went over the names we had thought of – there were no prenatal scans, so we had an array of names for a boy or a girl. We liked the name Rhiannon but thought that it would be difficult for people outside Wales to pronounce. We liked the name Llinos (a linnet). But that name would be difficult to pronounce too. And we liked the name Meleri – easier to pronounce. So we gave her *all* the names we liked. Rhiannon Meleri Llinos Morgan was a long name for a little baby – we decided to call her Meleri.

When we were discharged Meleri was wrapped up warmly in a shawl. It was still very cold. She slept in a Moses basket lent to us by the head of the English department at Bedwellte. I was full of conflicting emotions. I was overwhelmed with love for her, but awed at being plunged into new, unfamiliar skills and tasks. I had a dozen terry-towelling nappies and Nancy bought me twelve more. She came down to help out for a week when I came out of hospital and I appreciated that. But she was a worrier. My midwife had told me that I should demand feed a small baby. Nancy went into the launderette in Bargoed one evening to do the washing for us. By a strange coincidence, the only other midwife in the area was there at the same time. Demand feed a small baby? Oh no, that was asking for trouble! I didn't know who to believe. I had two buckets for soaking the nappies – one each for the two different stages of soiling. The biggest asset was the disposable nappy liners. I had no washing machine or tumble dryer, so once the nappies had been washed they had to be dried. I was dependent on the Deri weather. If we had rain they had to be draped over the storage heaters. Then there was the sterilisation of the bottles. Everything went into a Milton container and Peter and I were obsessive about getting it right.

I didn't know anyone in Deri well. The main social centres were the pubs. Peter had gone to these in the evenings or at weekends, but I had stayed away. There was just a small Co-op in the village and a sub-post office. I had to take Meleri to be weighed in the school building. Although it was heated by a coal fire, it still felt cold. When I went for more detailed check-ups, I had to take the bus to the health centre in Fochriw. Prams were not allowed on the bus so I had to use a carrycot. Apart from the health centre, there was just one shop in Fochriw and that looked like a Nissen hut. Its roof was leaking. I had to wait there for the bus home. On one occasion the bus was filled with elderly men – most of whom coughed. There were still notices on buses that said that spitting was not allowed. No one stood up for me and the carrycot was incredibly heavy. I had to go into Bargoed for the chemists and any baby shopping. Again, I had to get the carrycot on the bus, carry it around, then put my shopping inside the carrycot before returning home. Mr Rossi's café was invaluable again. He always commented on the baby and spoke to her. He was *Italian*, after all!

We had a record player and I played an LP of Nana Mouskouri songs to help me relax when I fed Meleri. I was on my own all day. I was getting little sleep at night. Even though Peter was very involved in caring for our baby, it was no great surprise that I became depressed. I thought that I was a useless mother. I didn't deserve such a lovely baby. What a disappointment I must be to Peter! I will never know if I'd have felt so wretched with an easier social situation. Because of the shame I felt at the way I was feeling, I couldn't face our GP. I dropped a letter for him under his door. He happened to live in a large detached house opposite us. He visited me several times, and after writing profuse notes he arranged for me to go into hospital in a side ward – *with* Meleri. He was an excellent GP who had wanted to be a surgeon but he was another victim of the prejudice and ignorance that existed about mental illness. He was a manic depressive. To have admitted that would have meant the end of his career. So he struggled on. My depression coincided with his hypomania. We ended up in the same hospital at the same time.

I was given another course of ECT. I looked after Meleri for most of the time and it was only when I was having the treatment or recovering from it that the nurses took over. I left as soon as the ECT was finished. Back in Deri we had to make decisions. I was finding life impossible – I had no friends, we didn't have a phone, a car or suitable shops.

We decided to go back to Cardiff. This time it was Peter who went in search of accommodation. He got hold of the first edition of the *Echo* – flats were taken within minutes. He managed to get us a large but shabby flat above a shop in Victoria Park. I was able to take my baby out to the park and we walked past a line of shops that served all our needs. One woman who worked in the fresh fish shop always came out to smile at Meleri and ask how we were. The importance of small gestures! It made so much difference to me.

If the depression had lifted, my physical health remained a problem. I had a cervical ulcer that had to be cauterised. This meant a short stay in Llandough Hospital and I begged Peter not to visit me. I wanted him to use his strength to focus on Meleri for those few days. The surgery was straightforward and a doctor, noticing that I had no visitors, took off his white coat at the end of his shift – and visited me! I went back home. At the time it was the norm for women to have a career break to look after their children at home. This is what I was doing but I had no choices. My physical health was dismal. One of our GPs came to visit me and was convinced that I was seriously anaemic.

'We'll soon get your mummy well!' he told Meleri cheerfully.

Some blood was taken but the results were normal – I was just very frail. I worried that Peter was coming home to all of this every evening after work. He had changed schools and was working as second in the physics department at Bassaleg School. Once again, he was able to have a lift.

We needed some extra money but I was very limited as to what I could do. When I was back in the sixth form at school I had discovered that, although I was naturally very quiet, I could be incisive, vocal and determined about things that meant a lot to me. It was the same trait that helped me out then. I read the *Guardian* and noticed that there hadn't been any arts reviews from Wales for a while. I wrote to the arts editor and asked him if he needed a correspondent. He wrote back and invited me to submit a review of the next major exhibition. As a result I wrote for the *Guardian* for about four years. I had £6 for each item that was published – quite good money. I took the pre-school Meleri with me to the National Museum or other local venues – and I took her with me afterwards as I phoned in the copy from the telephone kiosk up the road.

The editor of *Welsh Nation* asked me to write theatre reviews. It was a small magazine running on a budget so, although I wasn't paid, I had free tickets and a chance to meet the cast in the manager's room over a drink in the interval. I reviewed everything – from gang shows to musicals, from the excellent amateur Orbit productions to Marlene Dietrich. I was amazed at Dietrich's performance. With the minimum of effort, she managed to control the audience with one hand and the orchestra with the other. As soon as she opened her mouth to sing in that unique way of hers, the middle-aged men in the audience went completely berserk – standing on their seats, throwing things onto the stage. It was a chance to see the bewildering way in which a celebrity can magnetise crowd behaviour.

I went for an interview to teach art at night school. This would be possible as Peter could look after Meleri one evening a week. As I waited I noticed several other people with portfolios, so I thought that my chances of getting a job would be marginal. In the space of fifteen minutes or so, I devised an entire syllabus for an art appreciation class. My plan worked, and I was appointed to teach adults at Cardiff High School one evening a week. The salary was welcome and I enjoyed doing it. The students were so responsive and enthusiastic. Because of an earlier link, I was able to take them to London to meet Josef Herman at his studio. Some of them went later to the Uffizi Gallery in Florence! They sent me a postcard 'from your devoted pupils'.

The rent of the flat was so high that we were never able to save much. But, in 1974, we had enough money to put a deposit down on a first-floor flat in a Victorian house in Canton. It was leasehold (which caused us problems) but it was located in a lovely, quiet street that led up to St John's

Church. There was a full-sized bedroom and a small bedroom, a living room, a lovely well-equipped kitchen (even though we still didn't have a washing machine), a bathroom and separate toilet. Via a fire escape, we had access to a shared garden which was a patch of concrete. It was a good place to live but the mortgage repayments took most of our cash. Apart from the bare necessities, we had very little money left at all. I saved up to go to Carmarthen on the bus with Meleri from time to time to see old friends like Dr McGill and Sheila Gallagher. Such outings were treats.

Not long after we moved into the flat, Peter was offered the post of head of physics at Bassaleg School. He had completed his PhD and was not only a popular teacher but a highly respected one. (The retiring head of the department said that one of the things he would miss most were the interesting ideas that 'Dr Morgan' had.) A head of physics post would have provided us with a stable, good income. But there was a complication. At the same time, Peter was offered a university job in the chemistry department on a temporary contract basis. There was no guaranteed long-term security at the university and he would have a drop in wages. But Peter and I both knew where his heart lay. He took the university post. He was – and *is* – an academic.

Hard though things were, I began to have some success with my writing – a couple of my short stories were broadcast and I featured in a few radio slots. I was still reviewing for the *Guardian* and also the *Western Mail*. I contributed to its features page – my beauty therapy background helped me and I received free samples from cosmetic firms – a great luxury. My parents were generous – they gave us a three-piece suite but, apart from that, I went up and down Cowbridge Road searching the second-hand and junk shops for furniture and carpets. I got wonderful bargains and I still have some of the items – the oak desk for £3, the huge over-mantle mirror for £5, the Singer treadle sewing machine for £2.50... The traders got to know and respect me and told me when they were expecting items from somewhere posh like Cyncoed. The concreted garden was a bit depressing, but I got hold of an old bed, upturned it and cut out the springs – it made an excellent 'bed' for colourful, jolly plants like nasturtiums.

Our next-door neighbour was a delightful elderly widow. She was sad that she was too frail to be of practical help but her friendship and wisdom offered us more than she could ever have imagined. Mrs Stenner had lost her only son, Jeffrey, in the war. After she had been informed of his death she received a letter from him stating that, 'the only thing that keeps me going through this war is the thought of coming home to you, Mother, with your smile and your pearl necklace.' From that moment on, Mrs Stenner was determined to carry on wearing her pearls – and her smile. She was in her eighties but she still had wonderful serenity. She used to go to the outside toilet at the end of the garden using her Zimmer frame because she couldn't manage the stairs. I was concerned about this but she said cheerily, 'If I'm in trouble, my dear, I'll leave my bottle of Domestos in the window to let you know.' There never was a Domestos emergency but she gave us so much. Whenever Meleri had a haircut, Mrs Stenner wanted to see it. 'Turn round, my dear, for me to see how it falls!' Or, when she had a new dress, Mrs Stenner wanted to feel the material, admire it all. For a little girl who had no grandparents at hand most of the time, it was wonderful.

An extended Italian family lived next door to Mrs Stenner. They became friends too. Maria was three years older than Meleri but they played together. I have photos of them sitting by the thriving bed of nasturtiums.

In 1974 we decided to go on holiday to the National Eisteddfod which was held in Carmarthen that year – I still loved the place. It was quite an experience as we stayed in a basically equipped caravan. It was very small and Peter is six foot tall; he found it very constraining. There was a central table with benches on either side. These had to be folded down in quite a complicated manner to make a bed for the night.

On the whole, the weather was miserable and the sound of the rain on the roof was like gunshots. When the sun did shine, I pushed two-year-old Meleri around in her pushchair. She had a pretty checked dress and a broderie anglaise sunhat. I wore a long dress and a milkmaid's hat from Laura Ashley! Someone came up to us and asked us what part of Brittany we were from.

The following August we decided to go to the Eisteddfod again for our summer holiday. This time it was held in north Wales. We didn't want to risk a caravan again, so I applied for us to be put on the guest accommodation list. The job of the committee was to match applicants to local people who offered accommodation. By May, we still hadn't heard from them. I rang the office and was sure that, for some reason or other, we'd been overlooked. I didn't expect the letter that we received a couple of days later. We had been invited to stay at the home of Sir Clough Williams-Ellis and his wife Lady Amabel! Clough Williams-Ellis was the architect who had created the magical Portmeirion. We went up by train and made our way to the village of Llanfrothen where Sir Clough and Lady Amabel lived at Plas Brondanw. Peter Finch, the poet, had a stall at the Eisteddfod and was looking for somewhere to stay, so we checked it out with our hosts and invited him to join us too. There was plenty of room. It was an amazing experience. The rooms we had were on the top floor, with views of Snowdon. Lady Amabel rang a bell to invite anyone who was in their home to tea. The furniture was unusual, antique – and fun. We were able to wander around the generous larger-than-life grounds with its little follies and summer houses in the distinctive Portmeirion pastel colours and, when we finally went to visit the famous village itself, Sir Clough gave us a slip of paper to allow the 'Morgan family' free entrance. When we left, Lady Amabel gave Meleri a little book that she had written on gypsy folk tales.

I always rang my parents every week and was looking forward to telling them about our holiday. I went down to the kiosk in Llanfrothen one evening and told Lew about it all. He responded, but when I'd finished speaking he said in a slow, cautious tone,

'I don't want to spoil your holidays. And I don't want you to finish them early. But I have to let you know that your grandmother has died.'

Nana! I can't remember what I said on the phone except that I was sorry. I didn't cry. It was the way I seemed to respond to bereavements. Nana was well into her eighties. She had carried on living in Aberdare until a couple of years before her death. She had made a good recovery from a stroke and wanted to remain at home. Lew and Nancy arranged for the coal fires to be replaced by the convenience of a gas cooker and fire. They bought her a 'magic' Ewbank cleaner. But there came a time when she could no longer manage. As well as the aftermath of the stroke, she had severe arthritis. She went up to live with Lew and Nancy in Ingatestone. All was well for a while but then she broke her pelvis. After surgery she was confused. She returned to my parents' home and a neighbour, who happened to be a trained nurse, came in to look after her while my parents were working.

The Nana I had known and loved so many years ago had disappeared well before her actual death. I talked to her when I went up to Ingatestone and sang her favourite song to her – 'Ar Lan y Môr'. She smiled at Meleri and remained cheerful to the end. But the lack of dignity that her different illnesses reduced her to was so sad to see.

Her funeral was held in the Chapel of Rest in Trecynon, Aberdare, and she was buried in Aberdare cemetery with Daddy Bom and her own parents. Lew was devastated. Nancy was so worried that she would be upset and unable to support him that she took a prescribed Valium. As a result, she couldn't stop laughing. I think that Nana might have smiled at that herself. The house – my lovely 4 Elizabeth Street – had to be sold. Lew was so upset that he couldn't stay inside. He had been born there and, after a few minutes in the house, he came out onto the pavement to have a cigarette. It was one of the few times when I saw him vulnerable and dependent. I made all the arrangements to sell the house.

Back in Cardiff, Meleri was going in the mornings to a local Welsh nursery school. She was taken there with the other children in a white van driven by a woman called Blod. When she was just three, she made a close friend – Rachel. They were inseparable and remain the best of friends today. Peter and I had decided that we wanted Meleri to be educated through the medium of Welsh. It was a bold move for us – Peter understands a lot of Welsh but has difficulty in speaking it, and I was a Welsh learner. Just before she was due to start school, I had second thoughts about our decision and decided to go to see the headmaster. I needed to be assured that Meleri wouldn't be at a disadvantage because she came from an English-speaking home. What would happen if she didn't feel well and couldn't express herself?

Tom Evans was an enormous man with a generous heart. He answered my questions but my mind was decided for me by an incident that happened when I was in his office. There was a knock at the door and, after booming out *'Dere i mewn!'* (Come in!), a little boy came into the room with a milk tooth in his hand. He wanted to show it to Mr Evans. Tom Evans looked at the tooth with interest, knew the child's name, and showed such kindness before telling him to go back to his classroom that I knew the right decision had been made. I hoped that we would eventually become a Welsh-speaking family at home, but it never happened. Apart from the fact that Meleri's Welsh was soon better than ours, English represented security – and our daughter was to need as much of that as possible in the ensuing years.

26

A Devastating Loss

FROM THE TIME when our GP thought that I was anaemic I had continued to be physically unwell, often with chest infections. I still had a Ventolin spray but no diagnosis. One day, when Meleri was still in her pushchair, I was so wheezy that I walked into the casualty department of St David's Hospital in Canton. I was whisked into a cubicle and took Meleri with me. I smiled at her and she seemed quite interested in what was going on. I can't remember what medication I was given but, as a result of the visit, I was given an urgent referral to the asthma clinic in Llandough Hospital. It took a long time for the consultant to stabilise the condition. I had difficulty walking more than a hundred yards. I still had the Ventolin spray but I was also given another prophylactic one. I was also prescribed aminophylline which is a very powerful drug. If I developed an upper respiratory infection, I learnt how to assess it from the colour and texture of my sputum. If I was too breathless to inhale the sprays, I needed a short course of steroids.

Because it was obviously a bad time to get pregnant, I went to the local family planning clinic. With such an array of drugs in my system (I was still taking antidepressants, sedatives and anticonvulsants as well), I was not surprised when I missed a period. But something intuitive inside me made me ring up for an appointment to see the GP. Confirming a pregnancy was a far more difficult procedure than it is now. A urine specimen had to be sent to the hospital and the results were sent back to the doctor. I had to wait a few days. When I rang the surgery

I was told that the pregnancy test was positive. Peter and I smiled at each other.

It took minutes for the reality and seriousness of the situation to hit me. Dates suggested that I was only five or six weeks into the pregnancy but, again, my instinct told me that it was further advanced. I went back to the GP. I don't think she believed me but, when she examined me, I was right. I was into my second trimester. I thought of all the drugs with which I had unwittingly fed the foetus. Asthma sprays, aminophylline, anticonvulsants, antidepressants, steroids, antibiotics... Looking after Meleri – who was an easy child – had pushed me to my limits. An appointment was quickly made for me to see a consultant gynaecologist. I was in a state of shock by the time I saw him as an outpatient and, when he heard my past and current medical history, he was angry. I burst into tears. I thought that he was cross with me but he was angry at the situation. A committed Christian, he listed the reasons for a termination. They were long. I had felt no movements, my physical health was probably too fragile to sustain pregnancy and childbirth; I had had postnatal depression after the first pregnancy; I already had a small child to bring up. Then there was the matter of the medication that I had been taking. He said that he didn't have any option but to terminate the pregnancy. I was devastated. Even though my brain told me that it made sense, my heart was broken. Peter, who was waiting outside, was called in. We had to sign a form of consent. The consultant said that he would perform a tubal ligature at the same time to ensure that there would be no further pregnancies. Again, I can see now how another child would have been too much for me to cope with, but I was nevertheless totally crushed.

Where did I search in my desperation? Religion? I had gone to the Welsh Baptist chapel sometimes with Data in Goodwick. I didn't understand all the Welsh but I sensed the fervour. When I was a member of the Chelmsford Welsh Society, I looked forward to a *Gymanfa Ganu* (community hymn singing) more than any of the social events. At Trinity

College, Carmarthen, I went to chapel regularly and had taken a couple of services. I spent hours in the chapel on my own struggling with the Almighty God who allows suffering. When we moved into our flat, I'd gone to the nearby St John's Church where I was moved beyond measure by the three-hour service on Good Friday. Now, with this particular operation ahead of me, I wanted to be baptised. The gentle vicar, Dewi Davies, was very kind and arranged a simple, private service for me. I had met a few of the parishioners and one lady amongst them was learning Welsh. So Ruth and her husband John became my godparents. I hoped that I would be well enough for the confirmation service.

There was no time or energy for us to get too upset. Peter performed in pubs sometimes with his friend, the banjo player Peter Casey. It was Peter who offered to let my Peter and Meleri stay with him and his daughter while I was in hospital. We bought a little red case for Meleri; I hoped that it would make it seem like fun – a holiday. Mrs Stenner next door suggested that I should give Meleri something precious of mine to look after – I gave her my rings.

When I was admitted I was too weak for the surgery, so I had to be 'built up' over the next couple of weeks. The thought of what was happening to me and the baby affected me so much that I simply shut my conscious mind off. It was too painful. Finally, I was wheeled down to the theatre, and returned too weak to lift a cup of water. I asked about the baby but no one would tell me anything except for the fact that I needed to 'put it behind me'. When I was strong enough to go onto a bigger ward, Peter came to visit me with Meleri. The first thing she did was to show me the rings that she had polished. She wanted to climb onto the bed to have a *'cwtsh'* (cuddle), but I wasn't strong enough to hold her. I hid my feelings when they were with me but, once they had gone, I sobbed and sobbed. I was totally inconsolable. No one and nothing could ease the grief. As I became a little stronger, I wrote and illustrated a book for Meleri, still in denial about what had happened. There was no bereavement counselling, nothing to acknowledge the existence of the baby – and it must have been equally hard for Peter. We had no close relatives at hand. I didn't even want to *tell* my parents because I felt that I couldn't deal with their reaction as well as my own. Although they found out eventually, nothing much was said.

I remained in hospital for several weeks and, one day, I was taken down in a wheelchair to see a psychiatrist. I honestly think that my mood was one of grief rather than depression, but I had a past history. I only saw that particular psychiatrist once but he referred me to another one to see when I was discharged. That was one of the best things that could have happened. Dr David Shaw helped me tremendously. I was also given a referral to a psychotherapist. Psychotherapy is a drawn out business and, although the relationship between therapist and client is notoriously explosive, I learnt a lot.

So everything was in place to make my life easier, and when I arrived home I thought that things would settle down. However, one day, a few weeks after the surgery, I almost blacked out when I had spasms of severe pain. They resembled contractions and I contacted the GP. I was prescribed ergometrine. Everything was so vague and confused in my mind. I assume that part of the placenta had remained inside and my body was trying to get rid of it. I was advised to have complete rest for three weeks. Anyone who has a little child knows that this is impossible. Peter had already lost so much time from work. I was at my wits' end.

Ruth and John, my godparents, took us in to their home for those three weeks. Peter was able to go to work and Meleri went to her nursery school in the mornings. To help us out, some of the other mothers in the nursery offered to have Meleri for a couple of hours in the afternoons. The mother of one of her little friends rang me up when Meleri was with her. Anxiously, she said that Meleri was sitting on a chair and had refused to leave it until she was brought back to me.

It was a terrible ordeal for all of us. If it hadn't been for

Ruth and John, I don't know what we would have done. Peter and I were both able to give their girls some tuition later and I hope that that rebalanced the debt. We hadn't seen a lot of my in-laws but my mother-in-law came down for about ten days to help – I think she actually enjoyed it. I managed the confirmation service – Dewi Davies held my arm as I made my frail, slow steps to the altar.

The following year, Meleri was ready to start at her primary school, Bryntâf, as a full-time pupil. I'll never forget the kindness of the headmaster. Many mothers wonder how they will fill their time when their children start school but I still had health problems. I continued to have such heavy monthly bleeding that I needed two D&Cs (dilation and curettage). They were minor operations but it was further disruption to the wobbly structure of our lives.

Although I had taken the decision to be confirmed into the Church in Wales, Meleri showed an interest in going to Salem, the local Welsh Presbyterian chapel. She went with her friend Rachel, but I went along too as I thought that she was too young to be there without a parent. Rachel's mother, Margaret, and I became involved in chapel life and I even taught in the Sunday school.

In 1979 our flat had become too small for us. Peter needed space for a study and Meleri's bedroom was tiny. We searched and searched for a house. We didn't have a lot of money and it was hard to sell the flat. We saw plenty of places that we liked but couldn't afford. It was hard to get mortgages in the 1970s. We finally moved to a large house in Lansdowne Road. It was within our means because of its location (a busy road at the front and the railway at the end of the back garden). It was not in a good state of repair. The advantages were the garden and the space. We didn't have the money to make many of the alterations that were needed, but my parents were very generous and helped us out. Peter surprised me by laying a concrete floor. As I knew that we were unlikely to have a smart home, I was able to be creative. Murals appeared; I decorated the edge of a large mirror and I painted the bath. It was an old bath with stains where water had dripped down over the years. We couldn't afford a replacement so I got hold of non-toxic paints and designed a little 'Giverny' on the enamel with water lilies and blue sea. One of Meleri's friends said that it was the most beautiful thing she had ever seen.

I wondered if I could find a part-time job that would fit in with Meleri's school hours and managed to get a couple of afternoons teaching art in a local private school. We needed some extra income and I enjoyed teaching the girls. Rachel's mother had Meleri whenever there were 'time gaps'.

I missed going to Aberdare but there was nowhere to stay after Nana's death. Stan, our old family friend in Aberdare, had died and shortly afterwards his daughter Anne got married. Anne was Meleri's godmother and she chose my little six year old to be her chief bridesmaid. The wedding was set for the day before New Year's Eve. Iris already had family members staying with her, so we needed somewhere to stay the night. We chose a B&B which was little more than an adapted large house. The weather was bitterly cold and we arrived to find that the central heating had broken down. My parents were in one room, and Peter, Meleri and I in another. The plan had been to have a relaxed night before the wedding but we were so cold that we just went to bed. I'd been lent a fur coat to wear (yes, I'm afraid that in those unenlightened days it was real fur), but it served an important extra purpose for those few days. It made a wonderfully warm bedcover as we shivered and cuddled up together. After the service the following day, we made our way up the steep hill to the Aberdare Golf Club for the evening reception.

Everyone ate, drank and was merry until Iris received a phone call. None of us had realised that it was snowing heavily. The minibus driver had intended to make several journeys to and from the golf club to transport everybody home. But he said that, in view of the severe weather conditions, he'd be able to make just one journey. He was on his way.

Suddenly, the atmosphere changed. Everyone began to make their claim for a place on the minibus. Stan's sister and her husband had diabetes and heart problems. They had seats. As a mother with a young child, Meleri and I had seats. There were ongoing quibbles between the other guests, many of whom were 'under the doctor'. Meleri and I got on board and arrived back at the freezing B&B. The only thing we could do to keep comfortable was to go to bed. I left the key under the mat outside for everybody else. In due course, Peter and my parents got back too after an eventful walk. Nancy had persuaded a friend to lend her a mink hat. She lost it in her efforts to get down the hill. It had to be searched for in the darkness and in a snow drift. It was eventually found.

27

Born a Cripple?

As Christmas approached in 1979, life seemed to be more settled. We were looking forward to Christmas and I decided to go to the second-hand shops in search of a dining room table. In the flat we had only had room for a small table, but in our new house we could have a proper traditional dinner on a full-sized table. I found a lovely drop-leaf table made of gleaming, solid wood. I got a good deal on it and it was going to be delivered. I was in a good mood as I returned home. I waited for the green man to light up on the pelican crossing on Cowbridge Road, near the post office in Canton. All the shops were decorated. It was just after five o'clock in the evening and already quite dark. The green man shone and I began to cross the road.

Then I wondered if I had died. I could see the lights from the shops but they were all jumbled. I didn't know where I was. I didn't know *if* I was. I realised that I was lying on the road. I could taste salt by my mouth and, when I lifted my hand to touch it, it felt as though teeth had come through my skin to the surface. Most of the pain was coming from my legs. I looked over at my right leg which was at such a strange angle that I thought it might be severed from my body. I ached all over. Yet I felt a sense of detachment as though this had happened to someone else.

A crowd of people had gathered around me and I heard someone ask 'Is she dead?' In what seemed like an 'audience' gathered around me, I noticed Mario – one of our Italian friends. He hadn't realised that I was the victim and when I called out to him, he came up to me, shaken. I remembered that his aunt was seriously ill and asked him how she was. Remembering that Peter was picking Meleri up from a Christmas party, I asked Mario to let Peter know. 'Tell them I'm alright,' I said. He promised he would pass on the message, then a shopkeeper came out with a blanket to cover me. The police and an ambulance arrived. I suppose the whole episode lasted little more than five or ten minutes. For me, it was a long sequence of disconnected images.

When I arrived at the hospital on a stretcher, the team began their work. A nurse cut my boots off my leg with scissors and I remember being horrified. My leather boots had cost a fortune! I chatted with the anaesthetist about the amount of hydrocortisone I would need during the surgery. I asked if I could go home later that evening. Peter and Meleri arrived with a friend. I must have frightened them but I just smiled and asked how the party had been. I promised them that I would soon be home. I couldn't bear the fact that I was causing more problems and troubles for my little family. I was taken down to the theatre. A doctor told me that my right leg was badly smashed up. 'But hopefully we'll get you walking again.'

I woke up on a ward. I was told that I had a double fracture of my right tibia and fibula, a double fracture of my jaw, severe bruising of my left leg and a dislocated elbow. My right leg was encased in a heavy plaster from my foot to my thigh and my left leg was covered in bandages. I had stitches on my chin after facial surgery. A nurse showed me an account of the accident in the newspaper. I still felt detached from it.

I was moved to a side ward. There were Christmas decorations up everywhere. Nurses wore inverted bedpans on their heads, covered in mistletoe and holly. The whole thing felt completely unreal and mad. I was allowed home for Christmas, though it was not the celebration we had planned. I had to have the bed downstairs, and a commode. It was an effort to do the most basic of things. Peter had to do all the shopping and cooking. Nancy came down, then Lew. He told me that he had wept when Nancy told him the extent of my injuries.

After the Christmas holidays I had to go to the fracture clinic at the infirmary every week by ambulance. A lovely young doctor recognised me as I was waiting and asked how I was. He commiserated with me – the plaster was a very heavy one. I walked slowly with the aid of two crutches. The bones began to heal but they were out of alignment so I was told that I needed further surgery.

Under general anaesthetic once more, they rebroke the bones and reset the plaster. I came home. After that, a further X-ray showed that the bones were still out of alignment. Rather than having a third operation, the orthopaedic surgeon decided to insert a wedge in my plaster. A type of saw was used to get through the plaster to my skin and the wedge was inserted and jerked into position. More plaster had to be applied to secure the wedge, so my plaster was even heavier. I remained in this plaster for six months. It was very painful but, one day, the pain was excruciating. I asked for an ambulance. The pain came from the area around my heel, and when the plaster there was cut away it revealed an ulcer that had not been able to heal. It was treated and more plaster was applied. It was a long, hard journey for all of us. Peter did some home tutoring in the evenings to supplement his income.

When the six months was up, I assumed that my right leg would look as it had done before the accident. I was shocked – it looked more like a matchstick than a leg. The hairs had had nowhere to grow so they had formed little circles. The leg had lost its shape. There was a bow as the result of the imperfect alignment. The skin was so dry that it flaked off in huge patches. I was not as far as I thought along the road to recovery. Physiotherapy followed twice a week. A young man, a welder, went in the community ambulance at the same time as me, and we joked together at the exercises that we were subjected to. Before long, I was asked to experiment with just one crutch but it took time to build up confidence. I was terrified of crossing a road. I graduated from the crutch to a stick. My urticaria recurred.

The long legal process began. The driver who had knocked me over had been drunk, was speeding, had no licence or insurance, and the van was faulty. He had been identified because he was the only one trying to drive away from the scene of his crime. I had to see all the specialists who were treating me for my problems. In addition, I had to see all the specialists who were representing the driver. The stress of this was very hard. They all disagreed with each other.

When the day came for the case to be heard, I was taken into the court room in a wheelchair. The driver had chosen a solicitor with a reputation for taking on criminals. I was handed a very vague map which I believe was designed to confuse me. I was asked where I was standing at the time. I put a cross in the wrong place which gave the solicitor great pleasure. He even stated that alcohol could increase the alertness of a driver. I burst into tears – something that seldom happens. Rosa, one of our Italian friends, had accompanied me to the court. She was a very forceful character and had had a lot of experience as an interpreter for the police. She told the magistrates that the farce had to stop. They agreed. The man was found guilty on all counts. He was fined £200 (it may have been £250) and he was banned from driving for a couple of years. He walked away from the court smiling. Strangely enough, I didn't feel angry with him, although I refused to shake his hand.

All the health assessments continued, and after a couple of years I eventually settled on the first compensation payment I was offered – £8,000. I wanted to put the whole episode behind me. I broke the habit of occasionally depending on a stick to walk in an unexpected way.

Meleri came home from school one Friday, tired and pale. This was not too unusual and I tried to coax her into having something to eat. She refused, so I tried to get her to drink something. She just wanted to lie down. I lay beside her. She had a tummy ache. All of a sudden, she said 'Help me!' That alarmed me and I rang Peter. Then I rang the surgery. The GP came out. He was a new young doctor with the practice, and he came straightaway to examine her. Peter came home from work.

'I think this little girl has appendicitis,' he said, and asked if he could use our phone.

He rang the hospital and asked them if they had a bed. It was an emergency. We went to Llandough in a taxi. I had gathered a few things together and bundled them up, and phoned Ruth to ask her if she could look after our cat. As soon as we arrived at the hospital, Meleri was put in a crisp white bed and examined. She was so pale and quiet. Before they took her down to the theatre, I pushed her little soft toy into the bed beside her. Freddo the frog was a great favourite of hers, loved for his ugliness. If I couldn't go into the theatre with her, she had something familiar to hand at least. Peter and I went into a day room. Some of the mothers had been sleeping in the hospital for weeks with their sick children – some of whom had leukaemia. They were exhausted – but the love of parents doesn't give up.

Every time we heard movement in the ward I went up to see if Meleri was back. She seemed to have been away for a very long time. What goes through the mind at a time like this? I always imagine the worst, and become very quiet. Peter, on the other hand, chats. Eventually, the surgeon returned to the ward. There was no sign of Meleri but he smiled at me. 'She had a very long appendix,' he said. Apparently, it wasn't far from rupturing but, thank God, the operation was straightforward and successful. When she was finally wheeled back onto the ward, Meleri was not the only one to have bandages. Some kind soul had given Freddo a wristband and a piece of lint was stuck to the area around his appendix. The convalescence period was quite long – frog and owner remained in hospital for about ten days and missed quite a lot of school.

In my concern for my daughter, I forgot about my stick.

I was able to get an article published on the plight of the other mothers who, at the time, had no accommodation. A bungalow was built for them some time later. I had made a small contribution to their cause.

There had to be some light in what seemed like an everlasting tunnel of despair and it came when we started going abroad for a week in the summer holidays. At first, we were foot passengers on Brittany Ferries going to Saint-Malo. Two summers after my accident, we decided to go to Austria. It was a package holiday so that we could make the break as active as we wanted. Peter and Meleri could go together on the coach trips if I was too tired. In the evenings, I was all too ready to go to bed when Meleri settled down. Peter was able to enjoy the company of the others. He told some of them about my accident, and the following day a kindly woman came up to me and said,

'How dreadful! I thought you had been *born* a cripple.'

28

What did my GP say?

ONCE I WAS walking more steadily, life seemed to be easier. I felt that I had a future. Meleri was happy and doing well at school. She enjoyed being a Brownie. She still went to Salem. School trips took her to Llangrannog and the Urdd Eisteddfod. She had piano lessons and then went on to violin lessons and the junior orchestra. Margaret ferried the girls around in her car. I was asked to be a member of the PTA (Parents/Teachers Association). Peter was getting papers published, even though he was still on a temporary contract at the university. His circle of friends had grown as people were attracted by his friendly and helpful nature.

We used some of my compensation money to pay for a wonderful holiday in Italy. For once, I didn't need to depend on a contribution from my parents. Based in Baveno on Lago Maggiore, I delighted in using the Italian that I had learnt. We walked, swam, enjoyed everything about it all. It was a much needed treat – a great luxury for us.

The following year we went to Yugoslavia (when it still *was* Yugoslavia). Few tourists had travelled to the country at the time and we visited it with a sense of adventure. We flew to Pula airport and travelled up to Poreč by coach. There was a jeep that took us further up to the little town of Umag. I was struck by its beauty but also by the hard lifestyle of its people. When I made up picnics for lunch, the rough bread from the shop was weighed and wrapped up frugally in a piece of paper. The only medication I saw available in the same shop was aspirin and quinine. There was no sign of a pharmacist. We loved the warm, blue sea and the palm trees. We played mini-golf and kept the scores on a little ticket marked in Serbo-Croat. I was quite pleased with myself as I had learnt some Serbo-Croat in preparation for the holiday.

There was a little train that ran locally. Its destination one way was the town centre, and in the other direction it terminated at a popular nudist beach. One day, as we were waiting for the train, an elderly lady, dressed in black and carrying a Bible, was obviously about to go in the wrong direction. Peter pushed me in front of her and I found myself setting her on the right track.

We took a coach to visit the amazing caves in Postojna. We went down in a little train, and were given warm cloaks as the temperature was so much colder underground. The train took us to a point where there were blind fish in an illuminated tank. As we got off the train we were asked to go into groups according to our native language. Once we had been shepherded into the English-speaking group, a guide started the route around the caves – but I realised that this would involve climbing. As I was unsure of myself after the accident, I told Peter and Meleri that I wouldn't risk it. I would wait for them and join them on the train back to the surface. I have always had a poor sense of direction and managed to get myself lost. I was in a state of panic – these were the biggest caves in Europe and the train we had taken was the last of the day – we were well into the afternoon. I walked in the dark and was probably worse off than if I had gone with the crowd. My aim was to find the blind fish again. I couldn't see them but I heard footsteps. I cried out 'Dobro jutro!' and a male attendant approached me and carried out a one-way conversation in Serbo-Croat. But we did return to the blind fish safely!

When we were ready to go home after the holiday, we went back to Poreč in a jeep and by coach again to Pula airport. It was very hot – as it had been throughout our week's stay. There was a delay. Pula airport was not then equipped with facilities for food and drinks. Returning travellers are notoriously impatient and demanding. Someone somehow got hold of some food for us all. It was a very foolish decision on my part to have chosen chicken. Once we had landed safely at Gatwick, we boarded the train home. I was aware that it had been a long day for Meleri, and we occupied her by filling in the questionnaire on the back of the travel catalogue. We had to tick different aspects of the holiday (accommodation, service, food, hotel, etc.) with a grade. The choice ranged from excellent to very poor. We all agreed that the food was very good. Within a few hours of us reaching home, I was ill.

I had dreadful vomiting and diarrhoea that persisted. I was soon so weak that I couldn't stand. I remained in bed and we called the doctor. I had contracted dysentery. I was told to stay in bed, drink as much liquid as I could, and I was given medication. I had to have separate towels and crockery. I couldn't believe that something else had happened to me. We never got round to sending off that questionnaire!

I remained in bed for what seemed like a very long time and was visited often by GPs. I was still dehydrated but beginning to recover when Steve Glascoe – the GP who had diagnosed Meleri's appendicitis – came to see me. He wondered if acupuncture might help and he happened to have his needles with him. I was keen to have anything that might help, and agreed. The needles were inserted and had to stay in for five or ten minutes. Dr Glascoe and I chatted as we waited. Then, completely unexpectedly, he said to me,

'I think you're a healer.'

I was astonished.

'Why do you think that?'

'Some people just are.'

He took the needles out and left. I don't know whether the acupuncture helped or not, but I did improve. What was the meaning of that very brief conversation? My own doctor had seen me in such a vulnerable state. He knew very little about me. Yet he had sounded so certain. I put it to the back of my mind and concentrated on getting better.

The following year, after the failed D&C operations, I had a hysterectomy. A healer? Surely not! I had a longish convalescence ahead of me after yet another major operation.

29

'Watch and Pray'

AFTER SO MANY ordeals, I no longer had the stamina to teach. Peter was very busy with his work and he was also co-writing a science textbook. He had very little spare time.

Meleri moved on to her comprehensive school in 1983. I needed to do something to stimulate myself. I am a Francophile and there was a brand-new course being offered at the university which appealed to me. It was a two-year part-time diploma course in French Studies. I enrolled knowing that, if I couldn't manage the two evenings a week, it wouldn't be the end of the world. No one was employing me. The course was a challenge and the standards were very high – grammar, literature, history and politics. I wondered if there was something else I could do during the day. I signed up to learn Italian at a local adult centre in Canton. I picked up Italian fairly easily because of my French and Latin. I was delighted to eventually gain a distinction in my French Studies course, as well as winning an essay prize. I had an A in O level Italian. Apart from the satisfaction of doing the work well, it had been a long time since I had been able to stay with something consistently without the interruption of serious illness (if I missed a couple of weeks, it was easy to catch up). My morale and sense of dignity were restored.

But however satisfying the studying was, I knew that I was searching for something at a deeper level. I had been to St John's and Salem but I had never made a long-term commitment. I don't know who told me about St Luke's Church in Canton. All I remember is that, when I went there for the first time, I felt excited and experienced a sense of mystery that held me fast. Had I found a spiritual home at last? It was Holy Week – the week leading up to Easter. I loved the liturgy. There was something so poignant and real about that week. The grimness of all that had happened prior to Jesus' arrest was picked up in the readings and in the simple, repetitive songs sung by the small choir.

I sensed the deep spirituality of the priest, Graham Horwood. St Luke's is a High Anglican church with the associated 'bells and smells'. The incense and ritual helped me to reach beyond myself into the mysteries that we cannot fully understand. On Maundy Thursday I was overwhelmed by the tragic beauty of the enactment of all that happened on that terrible night. During the service the priest and his assistant washed the feet of twelve people in the congregation – just as Jesus had done. At the end of the service everyone processed in the darkness to another area of the church where, seen by the light of a few candles, a mass of beautiful flowers had been arranged. This represented the Garden of Gethsemane of course, and we were encouraged to stay there and pray. The choir repeated the simple Taizé chant 'Watch and pray... Watch and pray... Watch and pray.' I was hypnotised. On the following day, Good Friday, there was another long and moving service and there was a vigil mass the following night. It began in the dark but a bonfire was lit in the little space between the church and the hall. We all lit our own candles from the bigger fire and went into the church. The mood was beginning to change. Easter began at the end of this service and the church was filled the following day for the main Easter service. There was light everywhere and it really felt like a day of great rejoicing. I was deeply moved by it all. Looking back, I suppose I felt that I had entered the place that I'd been reading about in Evelyn Underhill's book *Mysticism* all those years ago when I was sixteen.

My commitment was challenged almost immediately. I contracted a bad bout of bronchitis. I wondered if the incense had caused it – a sad thing for me if, after searching for so long, I had been given a taste of something that I would be denied. I recovered and went back to St Luke's.

In some ways the church was intimidating for a new member. Everything seemed to be running so well that I doubted that I had an active contribution to make. There were a lot of talented people there – flowers were beautifully arranged, readers were excellent, rituals were performed effortlessly... But that was where I wanted to be even if I were only an onlooker. An August festival was held in the summer, with lovely flower arrangements – but it was the guest speakers who inspired me. One of them, Archimandrite Barnabas, was from the Orthodox Church and he spoke in that wonderful mystical way that is at the heart of the best of the Orthodox tradition. I was totally riveted. I could have listened to him all day long. It was as if my soul were on fire. I hope that I didn't neglect Peter and Meleri too much in those mountain-top years – I had been locked in deep dark valleys for so long.

Meleri was growing up. She had given up her piano and violin classes to concentrate on the flute. She played it well, and before long was a member of the transitional orchestra and then the youth orchestras. Her friend Rachel played the oboe and I was still indebted to Margaret and her car.

We wanted to move again. Part of my compensation money went into helping us buy a new house. Peter was still working at the university on a temporary contract basis. My financial input over the years had been negligible and it was ironic that it took a serious accident to improve that! We didn't make money on our old house but we broke even. We viewed about fifty properties and my patience was running out. We wanted a house where we could stay and we couldn't find one. I was prepared to compromise but Peter wasn't. It paid off.

One day, on his way to work, Peter noticed a little crew of surveyors going out from a local estate agent's office. He followed them to a quiet little street in Canton where they began taking photographs. He phoned me straightaway and told me to call at the estate agency. That's what I did, and as a result we moved to the Edwardian house where we still live.

Lovely though it was, the mortgage repayments cut deeply into Peter's earnings in 1984. We had never profited from high interest rates. Once again, there was very little money left over for anything but the essentials. The previous owner had also been the first – he was in his nineties when he died. The little galley kitchen just had a sink with a basic unit, a gas cooker and a mangle. The lovely Edwardian bath was deeply-stained and there was a limit to what we could afford to upgrade. But we soon discovered that we had some lovely neighbours – many of them have become friends. One of them was going to sing in the chorus of Handel's *Messiah* and asked if anyone in the street had a score. She was offered four! We were a cultured and devout street into the bargain!

Before long Meleri was approaching her O levels, though the system had changed and she was in the first academic year to sit GCSEs. She was gifted in the sciences and she and Peter totally lost me when they talked about it all. Peter was still employed by the university but no longer in the chemistry department. He was involved in a scheme called graduate enterprise. He and other colleagues travelled around different colleges and universities in Wales, encouraging graduates to start up businesses that were related to the subjects they had studied. If the venue was in north Wales, he had to do a fair amount of travelling, sometimes staying overnight.

I was so glad that I had my life at church. I began to make friends there – it was an exciting period in the history of the church with Bible studies and prayer groups. There was a woman in the church who was extremely gifted in almost everything she did. Brenda excelled at the flower arranging, sang in the choir, organised the music, knew the liturgy inside out, was an excellent cook for parish events; she was a good reader and leader of prayers. In those pre-computer days, as a trained shorthand typist, she was an ideal parish secretary. I felt very much in awe of her but she seemed to like my company. Another person who became a very close friend was Eileen. Eileen had come to church when she was widowed and we became soul mates. She was bubbly and lively, good fun to be with but she also had a very deep, intuitive spirituality.

One day, Brenda came over to our house and we chatted. I think that I've always been ready to listen to people and, although she had probably come over because I had been low in spirits, I asked Brenda how she was. She *told* me.

Then, she said simply, 'I think you have a ministry of healing.'

She was the second person to say that to me so I felt that I had to take notice. There is a tradition of a healing ministry in Christianity, even though it's often avoided and misunderstood. I didn't know where to start! Where could I go to find out? Our priest, Graham Horwood, had a ministry of healing – something that was rare in the Anglican Church, particularly in the 1980s. I went down to see him at the vicarage and I hoped that he would actively encourage me (or discourage me) so that I would know where I stood. I wanted direction. He listened very carefully to what I said, then just suggested that when I next went to visit someone who was ill, I should ask if they would like me to say a little prayer. That was all. Just see where God was leading me! He lent me a book on the healing ministry – a rare thing to get hold of then. People in the healing ministry were regarded on the whole as being a bit odd. The book was written by a charismatic Catholic priest, and I found it off-putting.

I discovered that there was a church in Marylebone, London, that had become involved in the healing ministry – they were using their crypt as a healing centre. I wrote to the secretary and asked for leaflets. They were so precious that I had to copy them in longhand and return most of them. I learnt how the healing ministry had been lively in the Early Church (how could it have been otherwise when one of Jesus' orders to his disciples was to lay hands on the sick?).

It gradually went out of mainstream worship – there was the big problem of people who didn't get healed. It was people like William Temple in the twentieth century who tried hard to restore it to its rightful place. He met with a lot of resistance. Gradually people like Morris Maddocks were reintroducing the idea of 'wholeness' – healing isn't restricted to physical healing. It was a lot for me to absorb, and my first steps into the ministry were cautious.

30

A Channel

I WENT TO see Val, a parishioner and friend, a couple of times when she was ill. She was a lovely lady. Her cancer was terminal. I was about to ask her if she would like me to say a prayer when a relative burst into the room. I could see that God has a sense of humour. Val, whose appetite had been badly affected by her illness, had requested a hot Clark's pie. The relative had rushed out to buy one and heated it up. I left Val to enjoy her pie. The next time I called, I asked Val if she would like me to 'say a little prayer with her'. She was pleased, and as I laid my hands on her I just hoped and prayed that the words were fitting. She told me later that she had felt warmth transferring from me to herself. She was very grateful and said that she felt better in herself. I visited Val a couple more times at home and she always appreciated these prayer times. Then I heard that she had been admitted to the local hospice and assumed that I wouldn't see her again. I enquired about her health at church, and a few weeks later Brenda told me that Val still wanted visitors. So we settled on a time and Brenda drove me over to Penarth. Val was very weak and barely conscious, but she knew that we were there. It seemed insensitive to stay for more than a few minutes, so before we left I prayed with her, Brenda holding her arm gently one side and me holding the other side. I have no idea what was said but I'm sure that it included the word 'peace'.

The following day was a Sunday, and for many weeks I had listened to Val's name being read out on the list of people who were sick. It was missing. After the names of the sick people were read, the names of anyone who had recently died were read. Val's name was among them. A strange thing happened when I heard her name. I had an image in my head of Val – but a Val who was healthy and vibrant, smiling and at peace. I hadn't known Val when she was well. The experience was profound and it preoccupied me all the way through the service. Could I tell anybody? Was I hallucinating? When I spoke to Brenda after the service, I was reluctant to mention it but it was Brenda who said,

'When Val's name was read, I had a lovely image of her.'

Nobody could be more sensible than Brenda – I told her my experience. They were identical even though neither of us had known Val when she was younger. It was a confirmation for me that the prayers had been worthwhile. Unbeknown to us or him, our priest had been to anoint Val just after we left.

In spite of all this encouragement it was a hard start to a ministry. I began to wonder if I had done something wrong. Maybe I should have prayed harder, more frequently? I knew logically that Val had always been grateful – and so had her family. There was the wonderful confirmation from the 'picture' that Brenda and I had shared.

I was reluctant to tell people about all this. Would Peter take me seriously? And what about David Shaw, my psychiatrist? I had nothing to fear from either of them. When I broke the news to Peter he carried on pouring the tea and just muttered 'I'm not surprised.' We drank our tea and talked about something else. When I told David Shaw, his face beamed with delight and he said 'Haven't you been well-trained!'

I was often on a spiritual 'high' in those days. It was as if I was drunk on the love of Jesus. Did it somehow link with my diagnosis of temporal lobe epilepsy? This disease often causes similar experiences. When I mentioned this to David Shaw, he just said that, whatever the cause, it didn't invalidate the experience. I was still sleeping badly and had restless nights. But something had changed within me.

I woke very early one morning on a high. I wondered what

it was about and prayed that I would be shown. A very vivid image of a friend came to mind. John Jones was our bank manager. We were certainly not the sort of clients who were pampered because of our bank balance. Quite the opposite – I had got to know him because the bank had continued to take payments out of our account when they should have stopped. Seventy-five pounds was a lot of money to have lost and I was determined to put things right. I think he liked my fiery determination. He asked me about myself and was very interested to know that I spoke French. He was struggling with French lessons himself and asked if I'd help him. A true but unlikely story – that was why I knew John quite well. It was his face that appeared inside my head. It wasn't the same as a hallucination. I wondered if all was well with him. When I got up I decided to call in to the bank. When I asked to speak to him, a member of his staff said,

'Haven't you heard?'

'No. What?'

'Mr Jones has been taken into hospital. He's had a heart attack. He's in intensive care.'

I walked out of the bank in a daze. There was no doubt that I had been given the picture for a reason. I went home and wrote him a letter. I can't remember what I said but I felt an urgency to post it. I know that I told him that he would recover. The letter went into the post-box, then I immediately worried about having been so rash. The following day, John rang me from his hospital bed and said that it was the most beautiful letter that he had ever received. It encouraged him and he was beginning to feel better already.

What makes mysterious things like this happen? In the Epistles, there are lists of the gifts of the Spirit, and among these are the gifts of knowledge, healing, wisdom, discernment and prophecy. Maybe some of these gifts had intermingled through me and worked together for John's good. A few years later, a friend in the healing ministry told me that I had the 'gift of knowledge'. This can enable me to have insight into something in a particular way. It can't be explained rationally. It can be compared to telepathy or ESP (extrasensory perception) but this is only a similarity. Very often people with such gifts claim them as their own. They believe that they are the ones with the power and this can easily lead to abuse of the gift. The knowledge that sometimes works through me is not something I have gained, and certainly not acquired by merit. Indeed, it doesn't belong to me at all. I am merely a channel through which any gifts might flow. I have to try to let go of my ego as it is a great deceiver. Even then, I don't always get it right.

It would have been very neat if my depressions had suddenly disappeared during these exciting years. It would have been even neater if my physical health had miraculously recovered. It didn't happen. For every short spurt of euphoria, there were far longer journeys into darker places. Brenda said that, at such times, I was unreachable. I am particularly sorry that Peter and Meleri had to bear the negativity of this. The positive thing was that, apart from one very short hospital admission of six days, I managed to stay out of hospital.

My parents retired in 1979 and went to live in Llandrindod Wells, Powys. Apart from one of Nancy's former colleagues, they had no connections with the area at all. I was concerned that they wouldn't settle down but they surprised me and many others by beginning a new active stage of their lives. So many things had happened when I was a child to put a strain on my relationship with them, but they certainly made up for that with Meleri. She often went to stay with them and was initially invited to take a friend up with her as well. There were boat trips on the lake, walks on the hills, the playgrounds, the waterfalls... Lew and Nancy took her away on holidays with them too, and I have plenty of photographs showing the great pleasure on their faces.

Back in Cardiff, Meleri was soon in the sixth form at school. She had good friends, was a proficient musician, specialising in the flute. As well as the county orchestras, the school orchestra performed a lot and went on tour. On one occasion Meleri went with them on a performing trip to Austria. Alun Guy was their talented teacher and the trip had been well prepared. We had even received advice on the best insect repellent! There was nothing for us, as parents, to worry about! We all confidently waved them goodbye. Two buses were supposed to take them all from Cardiff to the ferry, but one of them caught fire on the way and had to be replaced. As one half of the orchestra waited for their replacement bus, the other half carried on up the M4. The second coach missed the ferry, so there were parents (in those pre-mobile phone days) who had calls from kiosks, with one child on the Continent and the other in England. The children and staff stayed in a hotel; we were told later that there was a vendetta between its management and that of the hotel over the road. Chairs were thrown across the street. To cap it all, the coach driver was drinking too much and the Welsh teachers sacked him. The replacement bus was local, so there were language problems. With all the hitches, they missed performing at some of the venues. But, were they all alright?

It was a nail-biting time waiting with Margaret at the school to welcome them home. All the parents had heard conflicting stories. The travellers all arrived back, smiling – they had had a wonderful time. It had been worth it! I was a stage further on that difficult road of 'letting go'.

***

The healing ministry can't really be taught – it is a gift, but nevertheless I wanted to find other ways of learning how to help people. I went on a course in pastoral care and counselling. It was a part-time two-year course and it covered an impressive range of topics which involved a great deal of soul-searching. Without being aware of your inner self, mixed motives and the complexities of the mind, it's difficult to help others without projecting on to others. It was easier for me in many ways because my background had already taught me how to 'look at myself and my shadow'. The course was led by David Bick, an Anglican priest, and his perceptive wife Gill. They came over to Cardiff every fortnight, and after input from David we were subdivided into two groups to deal with our inner selves!

Halfway through this course there was an opportunity to have extra input at David and Gill's home. I wanted to go but I needed a lift. Dorothy, who was taking her friend Meg, offered to take me too.

There wasn't enough room at David and Gill's home for us to stay overnight, so we were accommodated in the old Prinknash Abbey – about a hundred yards away and in the same grounds. Everyone else seemed to have a comfortable room, but I found myself in a dark room that was quite separate from the others. When I got up in the night to go to the toilet, I found myself trying to get into a broom cupboard! Added to that, I thought I saw a ghost walking past. I scarcely slept. Even though I was used to that, the ghost and the unfamiliar surroundings disturbed me. When I cautiously mentioned my experience the following day, I was assured. A nun – an icon painter – lived above my room. It must have been her. In spite of my room it was a productive couple of days and we discussed it on our journey home.

I told Dorothy and Meg about the healing ministry and what had happened to me. The following week, Dorothy rang me and said that Meg was having a difficult time. Could she come over to see me? Yes, of course. The two of them arrived and settled in our middle room downstairs. Dorothy was in the room all the time as Meg told me her story. When she had told me everything that was troubling her, I began to pray with her, putting my hand gently on Meg's head. Occasionally I am given words from a passage in the Bible at times like this. I might well have used one of these then – but I honestly can't remember. What I did remember was the fact that Meg was 'drifting off' as if she were losing consciousness. I seemed to know that it was not a medical problem. After a while, Meg revived. I asked her if she was alright and went out to make a cup of tea. As we drank, Meg told me that she had never had an experience like that before. She didn't know what had happened but she felt safe. She knew that, because of what had happened, God was with her in her ordeal. When Dorothy and Meg left, I realised that had Meg been standing she would have fallen to the ground. No one was more surprised than me.

There was still little information around but I had managed to get hold of a leaflet that described a phenomenon known as 'resting in the Spirit' or more dramatically 'being slain by the Spirit'. When this happens the person affected falls in a totally relaxed way and enters a different level of consciousness. The Holy Spirit overcomes the person. I'd have been dismissive of anything like this a year or two earlier, but with Meg I had seen it for myself.

One of the dangers in the healing ministry is that of getting psyched up in a way that can affect the outcome, usually adversely. It's too delicate and sensitive a ministry to be at the mercy of ego trips. So how did I know that this response from Meg was genuine? It's essential to 'test the spirits'. There has to be discernment and it's essential to know oneself. I hadn't expected Meg to respond like that at all. I was taken by complete surprise. I hadn't sought it out. And the fruit was that Meg had felt the presence of God close to her.

After Meg, other people got to know about my 'ministry'. Peter continued to surprise me. When, one day, I questioned my ability to be a channel when I was so flawed myself, he replied, 'If you're only a channel, it doesn't matter if the vessel is cracked.' Dorothy spoke to other people and a steady stream of new people came to see me. Dorothy was then a member of Tabernacle Baptist church in Penarth, and some of the people who came to see me were from Tabernacle. I was taken aback when Dorothy told me that her pastor wanted to see me. There is something intrinsic in me, as a depressive, which immediately assumes that I have done something wrong. So when I went to Penarth to see him I was anxious. The pastor was just intrigued. He told me that I had an innate gift. And he suggested that I should get in touch with a person who was editing a magazine on healing and wholeness in Cardiff. Her name was Elinor Kapp.

I rang Elinor and discovered that she lived quite close to me. She wanted to come and see me. The pastor from Tabernacle had told me that she was a consultant psychiatrist – something that, with my medical history, was a challenge anyway. But, as I gave her directions on how to get to our house, a few familiar bells rang. I realised that Elinor was the wife of Professor Ken Rawnsley. He was the most senior psychiatrist in the area and he had treated me briefly when I first came to Cardiff. I knew that I'd have to tell Elinor the truth – I was prepared for the worst. Before we even began to talk about the healing ministry, I told Elinor all about my background. She seemed to accept it all and merely said,

'People often come to healing from a point of vulnerability. It was sensitive of you to have told me.'

Elinor and I became friends. We had a lot in common and I have had the privilege of listening to Elinor's problems and praying with her over the years. These prayers were needed as Ken's prostate cancer spread – they were certainly needed when Ken was dying. I was walking along a local street called Severn Road one day when I had a 'picture in my head'. It was of Ken being received into heaven. Dr McGill was reaching down to greet him. The words of a hymn came to me at the same time. They were 'Just as I am, without one plea, but that Thy blood was shed for me...' When I got home I rang Elinor. Ken had just become weaker and she was comforted by my 'vision'. 'Just as I am' was one of the hymns chosen for the funeral. Elinor and I are still friends and, apart from all these spiritual matters, we share a liking for zany clothes and eccentric accessories.

31

St Ignatius of Loyola

ONCE THE BASIC counselling and pastoral care course had finished, I decided to take the opportunity of extending it further. David and Gill were looking for a Cardiff venue to facilitate it and Ann, who was also doing the ongoing training, worked at a centre for people with addiction problems, which was our initial base. We met there for challenging and often daunting sessions once a month on Saturdays. They worked something like this. If I (or any of the others) were concerned about a pastoral situation, we had to present that situation, then act out the way we had handled it with one of the others playing the part of the 'client'. Everybody else observed closely. Afterwards, the person acting as the client described any times when he or she had felt uncomfortable. Everybody else challenged and analysed the handling of it. It was a very professional and thorough approach in a safe and confidential setting. Several years later the sessions took place in our home.

I have always needed silence – time to be alone with my thoughts or meditations. This is not an option but a necessity. It had been very difficult to accommodate this when Meleri was little, when I was in hospital or going through a crisis. In the early 1980s I went on a day of meditation in Roath. I met a few people there who used the spiritual exercises of St Ignatius. They were new to me but I joined their group that meets once a month. The format is deceptively simple. We have a silent meditation, then an opportunity to 'share' before enjoying a simple meal. Members of the group have become friends, as prayer binds people together. At the beginning there were Saunders and Cynthia, John and Mary, Ruth, Margaret, and now there are others.

Ignatian spirituality has become central to my way of life. I find it deeply attractive. I went through the exercises, with John Morris as my spiritual director. Then I went a stage further and stayed on a fifteen-day residential course on spiritual direction in Llysfasi, north Wales – an agricultural college opened up for us in the summer holidays. I had saved up £200 to pay for the course – a lot of money for me. The leaders of the course were Graham Chadwick, Gerard Hughes, Lister Tonge, Isobel Gregory and Sisters Mary Rose and Madeleine.

The course was dynamic and interesting. I remember the excitement when Graham (an Anglican bishop) and Gerry (author of God of Surprises and a Jesuit priest) took it in turns to celebrate Communion and invited us all to receive it. This was way ahead of its time and is still not widely accepted. We met in small groups to talk about what was happening (the meditations brought out deep feelings) and were told just to listen to each other. This is quite difficult – no interrupting with counsel, judging, comparing. It was an incredibly powerful approach – and one that I still try to use.

I didn't feel that I'd done well in the course. My three-day silent retreatant didn't want to be led by me – she wanted to go it alone. Fundamentally, I was ditched. This dragged me back to old experiences of rejection – memories of the past came flooding back. Three days was a long time to nurse and search for the healing of negative feelings in silence.

So, on the final day, when we had an assessment from our supervisor (mine was Lister), my heart was pounding. To my total surprise, he said, 'This [spiritual direction] is something you have a natural flair for. Just keep on doing it.'

Back home in Cardiff, Saunders, Cynthia, John, Mary, Margaret, Ruth and I had a wonderful few years working as a team, leading weeks or days of guided prayer, taking our Ignatian spirituality out into the community It was an exhilarating time. I felt that I was doing what I had been led to do.

32

Laying on of Hands

I continued to be very involved in the healing ministry, and Ignatian spirituality was becoming central to my life. Peter was working hard at the university and Meleri was studying for her A levels. Her subjects were mathematics, biology and chemistry as well as AS level music. From the age of eight she had always said that she wanted to be a doctor. It was even more specific than that – she wanted to be a pathologist. She had loved reading Agatha Christie novels as a young child!

She started applying to medical schools. She was given several offers of a place but, a year or so previously, there had been a *Horizon* series called *Doctors to Be* on the TV. It featured students from St Mary's Hospital in Paddington and followed them on their journey from interview to final exams. Lew had recorded each programme on video tape.

Meleri was defensive after her interview at St Mary's. She rang us up from Paddington just before getting on the train back to Cardiff. She didn't want to talk about the interview. I assumed that it had gone badly. I kept my silence. A short while afterwards an envelope arrived for her. I could tell from the details on the front where it had come from. I took it upstairs to her. I said nothing. I went downstairs. Then I heard her shouting,

'I've got into St Mary's!'

She got the A levels she needed and, when the time came for her to start at St Mary's, Peter and I went with her to the station. She left for London a few days before most of the other freshers as she wanted to take part in a music course. Peter and

I waited on the platform and the train pulled out. We walked back along the platform and down the stairs to the exit and our car. Neither of us said much. I guess we were just lost in our private worlds. I had prepared myself for the 'empty nest syndrome' but it was hard to go past her bedroom and know that she had moved on.

We were reminded of how much she had moved on within the week. An elegant invitation had been sent to us from London, inviting us, as parents, to the dean's tea party. Peter and I wanted to look appropriately smart and turned up in a hall where we found Meleri and her new friends. The dean arrived and we discovered that this was the first of the medical jokes that are rife. The 'dean's tea party' was not a delicate affair with cucumber sandwiches. We just had a cup of tea from an urn in a plastic cup. He told us that we were very welcome but any further invitations to visit would have to come from our student offspring. It was not a day for overprotective parents!

Meleri even joined a mountaineering club at first but, outside her medical studies, music remained her primary interest. We had the pleasure and privilege of going up to London for the concerts. She sang with the sopranos in the choir, then, when the St Mary's orchestra was established, she played the flute. Lew and Nancy were always willing and ready to come up with us. Perhaps her major performance was playing the flute as the 'Bird' in Prokofiev's *Peter and the Wolf*. In her final year she told us that there would be a surprise for us in the concert. When the musicians came on stage, she wasn't in her usual position with the flutes – she was leading the timpani. It brought tears to Lew's eyes. As well as performing, she worked as one of the stage managers.

After Meleri left Cardiff, the irony was that I had the time to cook more home-made food. And I took an interest in gardening. There was still the healing ministry of course, and in the next few years I was invited to speak and minister at various churches and chapels. The ministry was still new and people were beginning to get thirsty for what it had to offer. I had been on a weekend course on 'Gifts of the Spirit' where I met and spoke to the leader, Keith Denerley, an Anglican priest. Keith was very experienced – a former chaplain at Burrswood (a healing centre in Kent where the medical profession works in conjunction with the Christian healing ministry), the chaplain at Tymawr Convent and vicar of Penallt with Trelech. Keith invited me to keep in touch. I did and we remain friends. It was Keith who often invited me to minister with him on our visits to various churches.

Steve Glascoe (the GP who had told me that I was a 'healer') kept in touch with me. I was his patient, of course, but I felt that there was a deeper bond which could exist without damaging the professional relationship. One day, I went to see him as a patient. I had heard that his wife, Sue, had breast cancer and told him how sorry I was. He looked down at his desk, then, when he looked up he said,

'I've told Sue about you. She might give you a ring.'

When Sue came over to our house, I had to let go of any apprehensions. I had to let the Spirit flow through me as it is blocked by negative emotions hovering around. Sue was lovely and we had a natural rapport. She told me how she felt and, when she finished talking, I asked her if I could pray with her. She didn't have an active faith but was very open. Something very beautiful happens when there is such trust and we kissed each other goodbye afterwards. Sue came a few times and said how much the sessions were helping her.

When the acute need was over, I just became Steve's patient again. He had given me his phone number at home but I had never used it. Then, sometime later, I felt that I should ring him. As it happened, when I rang, Sue was in America visiting a friend, so Steve was on his own with his young son. He had just heard that there had been a rift at his practice. He needed a friend. He and his little boy came over to our house quite often for a while. When the problem resolved itself, I became Dr Glascoe's patient again. That remained the case until the next time I felt that I should ring. This time Sue had just been told that she was terminally ill. The cancer had returned. I went over to see her at home. The way Sue dealt with her situation was so courageous that it inspired me and many others. Bereaved, Steve needed friends. I spent a lot of time with him – he just called over at our house. He has faced more trials since then but, thankfully, he now has a new wife, Liz.

It was Steve who began referring patients to me. It's hard to believe how much things have changed in the past twenty-five years or so. Then, if a patient had metastases from a primary cancer, they were told little more than 'go home and sort out your affairs'. There was hardly any palliative care or hospice treatment. As a result, several people came to see me who had been diagnosed with liver cancer. I was their last resort. It was a great privilege to have had them with me – usually with a caring relative waiting outside.

I used a particular form of meditation with them, trying to adjust it to the individual personality – so I listened first. Then I did some relaxation and breathing exercises before moving on to the meditation itself. There are some very beautiful passages that can be visualised. Who can't benefit from imagining themselves beside 'quiet waters' or savouring the atmosphere whilst walking along the Sea of Galilee? Each person valued these sessions – and all of them eventually died. They expressed their gratitude and I had letters of appreciation from their families afterwards.

One person (not referred by Steve) who came to see me did have an amazing physical healing but, as so often happens, his condition had been mainly caused by negative emotions lurking in his psyche. On the whole though, I seemed to have the dying, the emotionally wounded and the bereaved coming my way. Dying itself can be healing. Peacefully passing from one world to the next makes such a difference – to the person involved and to the relatives and friends left behind.

There are other aspects of Christian healing described as 'inner healing' and 'healing of the memories'. Graham Horwood was familiar with these and they are ones for which I have been used too. It can be very beautiful and moving. Inner healing comes, for example, when a person who is facing a tough time is given an enhanced sense of peace that enables him or her to manage a situation that has been too difficult to bear. This is what happened to Meg. 'Healing of the memories' is a very sensitive aspect of 'inner healing' – to receive or to offer. It involves listening to another person until a painful memory surfaces. Then, very gently, that person is invited to 'go back to the memory' and imagine that Jesus is there with them. The healing that this can bring is wonderful. Nothing can be forced, so it's important not to let the ego spoil its gentleness.

33

A Glimpse of Heaven

I STARTED WRITING a short autobiography when I was recovering from an unpleasant virus. I finished it in three days. I believe that it was written for me. There were no laptops around, so I typed it out with a few spare carbon copies. I sent one to Keith Denerley. A few days later, he rang me and asked if he and his wife could come round for tea. He wanted to call on their way to see the ballet in Cardiff. He told me that he had read my story and was struck by the light that shone through, but he discerned a few episodes in my life that he thought might still be unhealed. Keith's wife Jane was suffering from ME at the time and her diet was very limited. Not being a natural hostess (especially when I am alone and have to entertain as well as cook), I began to prepare. They arrived and probably had a cup of tea or coffee – I can't remember. We chatted for a short while, then Keith asked if he could pray with me.

He laid his hands on me and before long I was taken somewhere else. I was aware of a brilliant light – silver, white, but more than that. Perhaps the closest way of describing it would be that it was as if I were in the line of a highly-powered torch. The light was pure and it didn't hurt, even though it was dazzling. In that space of light, I saw three faces. They were all smiling at me. The first was that of a young child – a boy. I have no evidence that the baby I lost was a boy, but it was a boy who came to me on this occasion with Keith. And he was smiling at me. The other two faces were those of Daddy Bom and Data – the two grandfathers whom I had loved so much. They were smiling at me too. I have no idea how long I stayed in that place of ecstasy. But eventually I heard a voice inside my head – it was Nana's and she said, 'Don't forget you've got people round for tea.' Ever practical, Nana's voice reminded me of where I was physically. The contrast between what had happened and what I had to do (put food on the table) was so extreme that I said nothing about my experience at all to Keith and Jane. We had our meal and they thanked me before going off to the ballet. A day or so later I wrote to Keith and told him what had happened. He was not surprised.

A few months later I organised a 'quiet day' at Tymawr Convent. I had asked Keith to lead it. During the course of the day he mentioned that he had recently had the privilege of being present when two people (I was one of them) had been lifted up to Heaven. 'It's only for a moment,' he said, 'and, quite often, it's followed by a familiar, practical voice that brings the person back down to earth. It's as if the Lord is saying "Yes – but not yet".'

Lots of people won't talk about experiences such as this for fear of being ridiculed. Had I really had such a powerful spiritual experience? Yes, I had.

I was still going to the extra sessions following the counselling course. Before one of these, I found a friend, Ann, busy copying out extracts from contemporary prophets. She gave me some of them. If the gifts of healing are misunderstood, what about that other very controversial gift – prophecy? In the Old Testament people were given words from God, people such as Ezekiel, Micah, Joel, Nehemiah and Daniel. Very often, their given words were unpopular because they disturbed the comfort of the people to whom they were addressed. They didn't just warn of hard times, they also spoke of God's forgiveness and the restoration that comes with repentance. Repentance is an unfashionable word today – it just means being sorry about wrongdoing and being genuinely prepared to try to put it right. If the prophets of old had had a difficult life, things are just as hard for prophets today.

Are there really prophets in our times? If so, how do we know if someone has really received words from God? Sometimes people think that they have this gift but, for one reason or another, they're deceiving themselves. Like any other spiritual gift, prophecy demands to be tested. Discernment is a key factor. Prophecy never contradicts the Scriptures – it echoes it. Prophecy is needed today because humanity has stepped so far away from the path of peace that the world needs a reminder. I took Ann's copies to my little prayer group to see how we responded to them.

I had been holding a weekly prayer group with Brenda and Eileen for several years. They were my two closest friends from church and we met once a week. We had been trying to solve a problem in our own strength, and the only way forward (we were going round in circles) was to pray it through. It was obvious, but it's surprisingly difficult to do the simple things. The three of us looked forward to these prayer times so much – they were the highlights of our week. Their structure was simple. The three of us listened to each other without interrupting, then we prayed in silence for about twenty minutes. After that, we shared anything that had come directly from the meditation. The way this small group flourished was mind-blowing. Eileen and Brenda both had gifts of prophecy. By this I mean that they were given 'words' or 'pictures' that can't be explained logically. We tested them. At a time when the church was fairly stable, Eileen had a picture in her head of a church falling and crumbling.

When we listened to some of the words from today's prophets, we were overwhelmed. We discerned that some were false and we were unsure about others. Our little group joined up with another at times – we prayed with Judy, Dorothy and Frances. Frances had a gift of prophecy. She was a simple and humble person but, when God spoke through her, she used words that were beyond her normal range of expression and vocabulary. They were always filled with an authority that was both loving and firm. I'd never have believed that I could say something like this earlier in my life but, when Frances spoke through her charisma, I knew that it was divinely inspired.

These personal experiences of prophecy had prepared us for something bigger – something global that is meant for the whole world.

34

Abercynon, the Old Man's Funeral

ABOUT THE SAME time as all this was happening, a friend told me that he was thinking of moving to Abercynon. I asked him why (this was the little town where Nancy had been brought up)? He said that it was a holy place. Again I asked him why, and he told me about an apparition in the 1920s and the subsequent healings. I found it hard to believe, but then I remembered Nancy telling me of how Data had taken her down to the river several times as he thought it had 'healing properties'. I hadn't thought any more about it but, on hearing what Robert said, I realised that there was a connection. I had been unaware of the history of the shrine and its waters until then. I decided to go to visit the place myself. I stepped off the train and made my way over to the shrine. I was disappointed by what I saw.

The gate leading down to the river was locked; the shrine was dilapidated and Japanese knotweed had taken root in the banks. Yet there was something powerful about the place in spite of it all. Below the shrine there is a confluence of two rivers – the Cynon and the Taff. They rush together as if they're pleased to find each other and join forces; the sound of the rushing water is powerful and strong. Someone had left flowers in a jam jar. Someone else had lit a candle. I walked around the town itself and found the house where Nancy and her siblings had been born. Data and Jane's old house was as dismal as the shrine – it was boarded up.

In spite of everything, I felt attracted to the place and, as

I was seeing a lot of troubled people in Cardiff, I wondered if there was somewhere where I could go to be still and pray. At the top of the village was the tiny church of St Gwynno's. After I'd been 'checked out' by the vicar, I was given a key. I wanted some quiet privacy but my plans are not necessarily God's plans. Within the space of a month, I was asked to start a prayer group in the tiny church. I took the train to Abercynon and was sad but very privileged to be there at a very difficult time for the parish. The prayer group continued for a few years; I still have friends there and visit from time to time.

I wondered if anything could be done to improve the state of the shrine and I wrote to the director of the Sacred Lands Project. He and a colleague came down to take a look. The local parishioners of St Thomas' gave us a warm welcome and a pile of food, including the ever-popular Welsh cakes. I hoped that the project would get some financial backing but that didn't happen. What *did* happen was that the local people put the work into action themselves. It happened gradually but, by 2011, it has been wonderfully transformed. The statues have been painted, cleaned and the area around the shrine has been tidied. The bank has been freed from the strangling Japanese knotweed, the paths have been power-cleaned so that they are no longer slippery; the gate down to the river has been reopened and the old stone steps are passable once more. The crumbling Stations of the Cross have been removed and new ones have been installed. There are even a couple of new benches so that pilgrims can soak up the atmosphere, rest and pray. And a stream that had disappeared has surfaced again.

By 1993, Meleri was well into her medical school training, Peter was still busy in his university job – but still on a temporary contract! My life had taken me in unexpected directions but how was my own health? My asthma was well controlled and I had stopped taking Aminophylline. I still have mood swings but they haven't been so severe. As if to fill the gaps left by the improvements in the two health problems that had blighted my life, I developed other conditions.

I had to take medication for high blood pressure. I have an underactive thyroid which is easily managed and treated. Out of the blue, I had two or three episodes of 'cluster headache'. It's a rare condition in which intolerable headaches totally cripple any normal activity. The pain was terrible. When the second episode started I went up to see a neurologist. He agreed with my 'self-diagnosis' and, just to be sure that nothing else was amiss, arranged for me to have an MRI scan. A short while afterwards I received a letter from the neurologist – a copy of the one he had sent to the GP.

The MRI scan showed that I had a hernia in the cerebellum (part of the brain). It was very marked but did not reach the spinal cord. The finding explained the nystagmus which had puzzled doctors since my time in Carmarthen. It also explained my problems with balance, my very lively reflex responses and slightly clumsy coordination. But it didn't explain the headaches!

I have had several episodes of iritis – an eye condition which, if not treated quickly, can lead to blindness. I am grateful to the GP, Alan Stone, for detecting that so promptly. Trying to identify the cause of lower back pain, I was given a bone density scan. I had a degree of osteoporosis and the scan also showed that one of my lumbar vertebrae has partially collapsed, probably as the result of earlier trauma.

I had remained in touch with Dr McGill ever since I left college. But the last time I spoke to him he sounded flat and deflated. He said that he was going to retire to spend more time with his wife and family. He bemoaned the fact that psychiatry had changed so much during his working life that he wondered if he had done anything worthwhile. He was despondent. It was a sad note on which to end a devoted career. I had wonderful memories of him. Apart from his first-class treatment of me professionally, I had stayed with him and his wife – they had both befriended me. They took me over with them to Tenby to one of their favourite pubs. I had babysat for the children. But because of his low mood that day, I was concerned that it

might be intrusive to ring him at home any more. My motive
was sound, although I was probably wrong about this. We lost
touch.

Peter was still doing the graduate enterprise projects, and
when one of them was based in Carmarthen he suggested that
I might like to go with him. He thought that I would enjoy
spending the day in the town. I walked around old haunts,
found some of them – others had inevitably disappeared.
After lunch I was running out of physical stamina, and there
was still some time before Peter's working day was over. I
decided to go along to the Catholic church where Dr McGill
worshipped. I could sit there and be quiet. Some years earlier,
one of the McGill children had been killed and I made a small
contribution towards a stained window in the church in his
memory. Maybe I could see that? But the church was locked. I
walked over to the presbytery to ask if I could sit quietly in the
church. A priest came to the door, took me over to the church
door and opened it for me. I told him of my connection with
the family and he said that he had taken the funeral of the old
man. The old man? Who did he mean?

'The old man,' he repeated. 'He had a bad chest.'

Suddenly, I realised that he was talking about Dr McGill.
Dear, lovely Noel McGill. He only had one lung after
contracting TB when he was younger. As an adult he'd never
been physically robust. The priest, seeing how upset I was, left
me to do my own mourning. If I hadn't found out about his
death directly from the family, I had been dealt with kindly.
I had been told personally, intimately, in private, in the place
where his body had been brought. In spite of the shock, it felt
like a gift. Later that day, when we arrived back home, I wrote
to Margaret, his widow. She replied – my letter had arrived
on the first anniversary of his death. We remained in touch
and I've met up with one of their daughters, Jo, who lives in
Cardiff.

The only other psychiatrist who had really helped me over
the years was David Shaw. He was the person to whom I was

referred after the termination. He came along at exactly the right time for me, even though it took a few years to find the right balance of medication. I took lithium for a while, but it was impossible to get it stabilised. It made me very, very thirsty, and at one time I drank a lot of fluid – pints – to satisfy it.

Whilst the drug regime was still being settled, David Shaw told me that his MRC (Medical Research Council) grant had not been renewed. Of course my own needs were close to my heart, but I thought how short-sighted it was to stop funding him. He was an expert in the field of depressive illnesses – particularly those that had not responded well to the usual treatments. I went into a 'high' determined mood and wrote a letter to inform the authorities that they had to change their minds. I think it was addressed to the Welsh Office; I took it by hand to the building itself and managed to get access to the right person. I was a woman on a mission! Within days, I had a letter from David saying how grateful he was. They had changed their mind.

When he retired from the NHS, David took on private patients for counselling / psychotherapy sessions based at his home. I had no idea how much it would cost but I made an appointment. At the end of the first session I asked him how much I owed him and he said, 'It was a privilege.' The times I spent with him were invaluable. Nothing goes on forever and, several years later, David told me that he and his wife were returning to her native Isle of Man. I stammered out my thanks and wondered how I would manage.

'You've learnt enough to be your own guru,' he said with a smile.

35

A Wedding, Cyprus

IN 1992 LEW and Nancy celebrated their fiftieth wedding anniversary in Llandrindod Wells. It was a happy occasion. Nancy's younger sister, Nesta, came with her husband Bill. Nesta and Nancy were close and Bill and Lew always got on well chatting away with the aid of their cigarettes and pipe. Nancy's brother, Owen, came too with some of his family. I gave a speech and wanted it to be positive. I mentioned how Nancy had posted me parcels of fruit when I first went to college in Carmarthen. The postage probably cost more than the fruit itself, but it was a loving and much appreciated gesture. I told everyone about the time when Lew spent hours making and painting the little farmyard animals for me.

Meleri had come up for the event from London – something that thrilled Lew and Nancy as she had been working the night before on the wards. Even though it was just a day visit, Meleri slipped out to send two postcards. One was for her old friend Rachel who was studying art in Loughborough, and the other was for her boyfriend Huw. That simple act made me realise the seriousness of the relationship. Huw is from Tredegar and was a fellow student at St Mary's. She had gone to London to find a rugby-loving Welshman!

The medical course was long, hard and unremitting in intensity and responsibility. Halfway through her studies, Meleri sandwiched in an extra year doing a BSc degree. Working on the wards was harder than it is today – Meleri was sometimes on call for over a hundred hours a week. Eventually her reward came and she qualified as a doctor.

When she came home shortly afterwards she and I went to Swansea (halfway between Cardiff and Llandrindod) to meet Lew and Nancy. I'm so glad that they both had the opportunity to do this as Lew suffered a stroke shortly afterwards. He was a proud and gifted man and the limitations that the aftermath imposed on him made him deeply unhappy.

Huw qualified and the couple announced their engagement. House jobs began for them both. Meleri worked at St Mary's itself and she had stints at the Central Middlesex and Northwick Park hospitals amongst others. After that, she worked with an eminent team of heart surgeons in Harefield Hospital. She didn't finish this placement because she was offered a new job – as a pathologist with a lectureship at the Royal Free Hospital in Hampstead.

By this time Huw and Meleri had moved into a flat together in London, so we were still going up to visit them as they had so little free time. Sometimes we took Huw's mam, Jean, up with us. Huw and Meleri wanted to marry in Cardiff but, as they were still working in London, most of the arrangements fell to me. The date was set for 25 April 1998.

It was a wonderful day, not without its comic elements. A nervous Huw must have rung up about five times as Meleri and her bridesmaids were getting ready – he was checking that she still wanted to go through with it! Peter said that he had a migraine coming on. Huw told me that he hadn't prepared a speech – he would speak 'off the top of my head'.

Nesta, Bill and their family were sitting in the Roman Catholic church for a while before they realised that they were in the wrong place! They hurried to St John's Church just in time. Huw was very worried about his relatives from Tredegar and Dowlais. They'd booked a minibus to bring them down and they'd started out in good time. He wasn't to know that the bus driver had lost his way in the city! The guests knew that the church was near Canton Police Station and, when one of Huw's cousins saw it, she shouted out 'We're here!' As they had about five minutes to beat the clock, they got off the bus immediately so that they could walk the remaining fifty yards or so. All they had to do was cross the busy Cowbridge Road. Huw's Auntie Kay took direct action. In police mode, she stopped the busy traffic and the little assembly crossed, unperturbed by the rules of the road.

The service was taken by Michael Sserenkuma. Peter's father and stepmother were there and it was good to see them – but I was particularly glad that Lew and Nancy were able to make it. They had invested so much time and love in their granddaughter. After the stroke, Lew was largely immobile and often confused. He was a heavy man and had other associated problems. If he hadn't been able to come, Nancy would have stayed with him back in Llandrindod. It would have broken her heart. In the end, I arranged for them both to stay at a residential home in Cardiff for a couple of nights. They arrived at the church with difficulty – Lew in a wheelchair. After a stroke, emotions can be very pronounced and he cried all the way through the ceremony. Things must have registered to some extent because, as Meleri left the church leaning on Huw's arm, she smiled across at them – and he remembered that moment afterwards. So did Nancy who was glowing.

They both came to the reception but, afterwards, Lew was tired. When he had settled down for the night, Nancy came back for a while to enjoy part of the evening's festivities. Peter and I had booked a room at the Cardiff Bay Hotel simply so that we could change and have a rest if needed during the day. By ten o'clock I was physically and emotionally exhausted. Peter persuaded me to stay overnight – he went back to attend to our cat, Dilys. Once I lay down on the bed, I cried and cried. They were tears of happiness and gratitude.

In Llandrindod life had become increasingly hard for Lew but equally, if not more so, for Nancy. She tried so hard to look after him at home but his illness had made him difficult and sometimes aggressive – he was so frustrated. Lew was largely immobile and sturdy. Nancy looked frail and gaunt. She rang me most days in tears (sometimes it was several times in a day).

Things had to change for them. Loyal to the end, Nancy went to several places until she found a home where Lew might be happy. Nothing could be too good for her Lew! She decided on Bryngwy in Rhayader and it was an excellent choice – the best residential home that I've ever known. It was based in a lovely house with spacious grounds on the banks of the river Wye and was run by a lovely, efficient couple – David and Pam Hunter. It's a pity that Lew was never able to fully appreciate it, but I don't think that anyone could have done more for him.

Nancy stayed in the bungalow and was taken to visit Lew by some of her many friends – Richard, Sylvia, Beryl... She had people such as Kay to help her out at home. Nancy began to put on weight again and seemed much happier. But she had suffered from congestive heart failure for several years and the toll was telling. She often rang me up, breathless and afraid. If I needed to get up there quickly, Peter had to take me up in the car before work and leave me there. If it wasn't so urgent, there was the beautiful but painfully long train journey.

This situation lasted for years and my own health began to suffer. On one occasion Nancy was en route to Hereford Hospital when Lew was acutely ill in Bryngwy. I went with Nancy – she had suffered a small stroke. Another time, when Nancy rang up, she sounded terrible. Peter drove me up but we went in such a hurry that I forgot to take my reading glasses. I stayed overnight and thought that Nancy was safely in bed. I went to bed myself. Then I heard a cry. She had fallen out of bed and I couldn't lift her. She needed her nebuliser, but without my glasses I couldn't read the instructions. I rang the ambulance service. I didn't know what else to do. When they came to put her back into bed, they suggested that I should make other arrangements. Neighbours had been 'links' for the alarm service for some time – but they'd been called out so many times that I felt that their goodwill couldn't be relied upon any more.

Nancy agreed to go into Bryngwy for a 'trial' fortnight. It was the best thing that could have happened to her. She didn't share a room with Lew because of his serious problems. She had a lovely room of her own with plenty of photographs on the wall and favourite items of furniture and mementoes all around her. When I visited, it was almost like going to the bungalow. She even had the sheepskin rugs on the floor! She ate well, enjoyed all that Bryngwy offered – strawberries and cream during Wimbledon week, visits from the vicar for Communion, carol singers, countless visits *from* the community and *to* it. The bungalow had to be sold but not before Nancy took several trips back in a taxi to pick up even more things that she wanted to keep. Huw and Meleri went up to see granny and granddad when they were down in Wales. We all did what we could.

Peter and I were surprised when Huw and Meleri said that they wanted to move back to Wales. Meleri had been away in London for ten years. She came for an interview as a specialist registrar in the pathology department of Llandough Hospital (a few miles out of Cardiff). She stayed with us overnight and didn't think that she'd got the job. But she had.

So she came back to live with us for a short while. Meleri had left just after her A levels and returned as a married, professional woman. I had to adapt to a different relationship. Huw had worked in several London hospitals but had moved on to Wexham Park Hospital in Slough. He came down to Cardiff whenever he was free. It wasn't an easy situation for them and they soon decided to rent a flat in the next street to ours. Huw began to apply for jobs in south Wales. He worked at various hospitals here before deciding to become a GP. There were more exams ahead for both of them.

It took a long time before Meleri sat and passed her professional exams in pathology. Huw had to do the same with his general practice exams. They made new friends in Cardiff but strong bonds had been forged at medical school; they kept in touch with many of their fellow students who remain good friends to this day. Student loans took a long time to pay off but when they were able to consider buying a house, Huw and

Meleri found a small one in Pontcanna – less than ten minutes' walk away from us! Nancy was still well enough to come to Cardiff on the bus sometimes, but I realised how frail she had become when we stood at the end of the road where Huw and Meleri's new house was. It was just a few yards away, she was very curious – but she couldn't make it. They settled in and the first addition to the family was a cat – the lovely, good-natured Sidie.

At about this time there was a big change for me too. I didn't realise until it happened how devastating it would be. Brenda, Eileen and I had kept up our prayer group for years and it was still a source of great encouragement and blessing. It was a key feature in my life. The grief I felt when it had to stop was overwhelming. Eileen, a widow, liked going on exotic holidays, and on one of them she met a man and fell in love. The couple were going to live in Cyprus. Eileen was moving away! I was pleased that she'd found happiness but, personally, I was devastated. Eileen had been giving me a lift home from church every Sunday for years and we stayed in her car for ages talking about everything – life, faith, gifts of the Spirit. I've never had a sister but Eileen and I couldn't have been closer if we had been. We had similar thoughts, the same insights and the same intuition. We both promised to keep in touch regularly and meet whenever she came back to Cardiff to visit her family. We also agreed that we would learn Greek! We kept to the bargain, although neither of us made much progress. Nothing gave me greater pleasure than seeing one of Eileen's letters arrive in the post. Full of love and news, these letters made my day. And we always finished our letters with a little bit of that classical language that is so hard to master.

In church, Graham Horwood retired and we had a new priest at St Luke's. Graham had offered me – and many others – a wonderful depth of spirituality but he retired at the right time. The new priest, Mark Preece, is very different. Decades younger, he is friendly and has great social and managerial skills. He is better equipped to deal with an institution that has had to change with the times. There is more and more administration – yes, unfortunately even in the Church. Before long he was asked to take responsibility for the three Anglican churches in Canton. Although he has the support of a second priest, it's not an easy task.

36

Farewells, Welcome

I'VE NEVER BEEN excited about seeing the New Year in. However, as 1999 came to an end, I was curious about the coming of a new millennium. I certainly had no idea of what its first years would hold for me. My emotions were thrown into complete disarray.

Nancy was very close to her two sisters and brother and they had been very much part of my life too. All four of them were powerful, strong characters and it felt as if they were indestructible. Peggy, the older sister, had been very beautiful and elegant. She had survived a major stroke but died in December 2000.

Just two months later, in February 2001, Nancy's brother Owen died. Nancy was too frail to go to the funeral.

Just two months after Owen's death, Lew's health deteriorated and he was admitted to hospital in Llandrindod. I wanted to do what I could but the stress on me then was so bad that an old enemy returned. I was covered with severe urticaria, my lips and eyes swelled up with angioedema. I needed emergency treatment at A&E twice.

Then I had a call asking me to go up to the hospital in Llandrindod urgently. When we arrived I told the staff nurse that I wasn't well, as if to apologise for not having come up earlier. I was strangely reassured when she said, 'You don't look well!'

We went down to the room where Lew lay, barely conscious. He half-opened his eyes and I said, 'Have a good night's sleep'. I kissed him on the forehead. The following morning I received a phone call to say that he had slipped away quietly. Nancy surprised me – and everybody – by her strength.

My mind was racing from the steroids I was taking but I had to organise the funeral – Nancy wasn't up to it. My father Lew was a proud, passionate, determined and highly intelligent man. He had worked hard all his life in a conscientious and cautious way. Our relationship had often been strained, so I needed the chance to fully honour the man who had given so much to so many. I wrote a poem for the funeral. It wasn't a great poem, it wasn't even a good poem, but it expressed what I wanted to say.

On the day of the funeral Peter and I travelled with Nancy from Bryngwy. I thought that I'd better go to the loo before the service and burial. Nancy decided that she wanted to go too. Pam and David from Bryngwy had her wheelchair in the second funeral car, so this had to be taken out and assembled. The whole affair took some time and, as we helped Nancy back into the car, she replied with typical Valleys humour,

'Oh Lew, this is the *second* time I've kept you waiting!'

My father, my much-loved aunt and my uncle died within the space of four months. I tried to take it all in. Fortunately, there was a very special surprise awaiting me – a *positive* one. I was going to be a grandmother! In January 2002 Meleri gave birth to a little girl – Bethan Nia. She was perfect and, like her mother, she was born with a mop of black hair. I was overawed by her tininess and realised why I had been such a nervous mother at first. Meleri and Huw were far more relaxed than we had been – but times had changed too. Meleri was out of hospital with her baby just hours after the birth. I helped out and so did Peter and Jean (Huw's mam). It was the first good news of the new millennium. I needed it.

I thought that Nancy's health would plummet after losing Lew but she actually thrived as everyone took such good care of her. Of course she was frail and dependent, but far stronger emotionally than I would ever have believed possible. And she had a great-granddaughter to look forward to! We went up to see Nancy when Bethan was six weeks old and, through her tears, there was a huge smile.

'Isn't God *good*!' she beamed. 'A new little human being!'

Peter and I went up to see Nancy as often as we could. In the summer of 2002 I was reluctant to go on holiday abroad in the circumstances but in the end Peter and I decided to go on another short break to Brittany. We enjoyed it and, on the last night, Peter parked the car as usual in the hotel's car park. In the early hours of the morning I heard what I thought was thunder. I woke and went to the window. The noise stopped and we went back to sleep. In the morning Peter took our cases down and returned muttering 'Disaster!'

The sound I had heard during the night was not thunder. It was a motorcyclist crashing into our car. It was a write-off. I had to go to the police station, give a statement, fill in forms. The insurance firm gave us a replacement car to get us home. A taxi took us to the local airport to pick up the car – a left-hand drive. Poor Peter had to test it out around the lanes before braving it on the road. He drove a left-hand drive in France, then, once we were in Plymouth, he had to drive that same car on British roads!

I wouldn't have told Nancy about the accident but, without a car of our own, I had to explain why we couldn't visit her. She promptly decided to buy us a car. When Peter drove it up to Bryngwy for the first time, she wanted to look at it through the window of her room but she was too frail to turn her head that far.

In September 2002 Nancy's younger sister Nesta died. Nancy had been very close to her but there had been such a litany of deaths that I don't think she really took it in. It was another funeral that she had to miss – but the rest of us went. Meleri and I were very fond of our Auntie Nesta and, if circumstances had been different, Meleri would have taken Bethan up to see her. Nesta had prayed for '*yr un fach*' (the little one) every night. In a way, they did meet up. Bethan was held in Meleri's arms for the funeral.

227

Two months' later Nancy's health took a turn for the worse. We'd had so many calls to go up and it was impossible to discern that this would be the final one. Peter drove us up and we spent hours with Nancy. She still had her bright, brown eyes and was delighted to see us. She wanted to hold my hand and I wanted to hold hers. Her breathing was laboured and I watched each rise and fall of her chest, fearing that every breath would be her last. I looked at the familiar features of her face and hands; I talked to her and gave her family news. I said how much we all loved her. Later that evening we stayed overnight in a nearby hotel. Before breakfast the following morning, I rang up to ask how she was. She was much the same. I wondered if this was another 'false alarm'. We went back up to her bedside and stayed for a few more hours. I felt very close to her then. I held her hand again, reassured her that we loved her. I said a prayer. The doctor arrived and looked at her briefly before he spoke to me privately.

'I *liked* her!' he said.

He was using the past tense.

We had spent a long time with Nancy and no one can predict the exact timing of a death. We made our way back to Cardiff for a rest. As soon as we arrived home I rang Bryngwy. Nancy had died shortly after we left. It was as if she had waited until we had gone to save us the distress.

There was another funeral to arrange. When Lew died I needed to be positive for Nancy's sake. But, when Nancy died, there was a very different feel about it. I put my heart and soul into the arrangements. I wrote out a basic history for the vicar but, in addition, I wrote an 'end-of-life report'. Nancy had written so many school reports for her infants; it was time for her to have one herself. The funeral was almost at an end and I was disappointed that they hadn't used the 'report'. Then, to my surprise, I heard it read by the archdeacon, word for word, at the commendation – the moment when the body is blessed and offered to God. It was such a special moment. I felt that

I had done her justice. At the age of ten months, Bethan had been to her second funeral.

Nancy had been a soft and tender girl and woman. She laughed a lot and made other people laugh. She was feisty but vulnerable. Her teaching career had been very successful. She was popular in Essex and, in her retirement, she had made many more friends. People warmed to her. I arranged for a bench to be made in memory of both of my parents and it is in the grounds of the cemetery where they lie. Nancy had been a regular churchgoer in Llandrindod and worked keenly for their leprosy mission. There is a chair in the church in Nancy's memory. She had also worked as a volunteer for the hospital's League of Friends and they had a water feature fitted in its grounds in Nancy's memory.

Lew was an only child but he had plenty of cousins. I had known most of them all my life, was fond of them and, in those same tough couple of years at the beginning of the twenty-first century, they died too. Ray, Jenny, Doris, Margery and Gwendo all passed on as did his lifelong friend, Iris. I was asked to lead the prayers at Iris' funeral and had difficulty in containing my feelings. I asked that Iris might be received in the same way that she had always given out during her life. There was always a warm welcome for me – a 'Hullo, Di' that came from the heart.

I am not an extravert but there had been so much grief that I decided to hold a party to celebrate my sixtieth birthday in 2004. It was a lovely occasion with friends and, at last, as an extended family, we were able to meet on a happy occasion. Meleri and Huw were there with two-year-old Bethan who helped me blow out the candles. I soon discovered that there was going to be another celebration. Another baby was on the way. I was overwhelmed.

37

Losses, a Gain

IT TOOK TIME to recover from all the family losses and deal with the ongoing ones. Before Nancy died, my mother-in-law had treatment for cancer. Peter and I spent a total of fourteen years attending to the needs of our parents. I hadn't expected more blows to strike so soon. Some of Peter's best friends died and so did three of my closest friends.

Rachel and Meleri have always been good friends and we got to know the whole family well – Margaret, Rachel's mother, Roger her father and Eleanor her younger sister. All the family was there for Meleri and Huw's wedding – Rachel was a bridesmaid. Margaret was a very cheerful and thoughtful person. She had come to Nancy's funeral because my mother never forgot her girls' birthdays. It was a typical 'Margaret' gesture. She didn't tell me beforehand that she was coming to the funeral; she sat at the back of the church and she wouldn't stay on afterwards. She just gave me her lovely warm smile.

Peter and I went over to have a meal with Roger and Margaret one evening in April 2005. Within days, Margaret had been admitted to hospital after some kind of 'attack' – it took a while before a diagnosis was made. I spent a lot of time with Margaret in the next few months before she died in the August. If Bethan had been to two funerals in her first year, there was a new baby to attend Margaret's funeral. Catrin Elinor (Cati) – our second granddaughter – was born in May 2005. She snuggled cosily in Huw's arms throughout the service.

Margaret and I had had a lot of fun together. Many years earlier, on a cold, windy day, we went on a Sunday school trip to Weston-super-Mare. The children were fine in the heated swimming pool but, as we watched, Margaret and I were freezing. She produced a thermos flask which didn't contain tea or coffee. The cold didn't bother us after that!

The year after Margaret's death, my mother-in law Pat died in 2006. She had had some kind of a seizure a couple of years earlier. Whatever the diagnosis was, it affected her cognitive faculties and she remained very difficult after that. It was a very gruelling time, especially for Peter.

There was another death in 2006. Eileen – my soul mate – died. Whenever she came back to Cardiff from Cyprus, we always met up. We made up for lost time in our spectacularly long get-togethers. In our favourite café – the food was just a pleasant diversion – we talked about everything under the sun and above it for hours. Whichever way the conversation went, there was always a spiritual dimension. We sometimes knew intuitively what the other was thinking or feeling before anything had been said.

Eileen had always been very slim but she lost a lot of weight after she was diagnosed with coeliac disease. Then she developed chest problems and was eventually diagnosed with bronchiectasis – a miserable combination. The last time I saw her, she had to put a cardigan underneath her to serve as a cushion. As usual, we talked about everything – life, death, children, grandchildren, faith, the beauty of flowers and nature. And we laughed a lot. When we said goodbye I sensed that we might never meet again. I think she did too.

Six weeks later her family phoned me. I couldn't believe it. Eileen – my lovely, bubbly, spiritual friend had gone. The funeral was held in Cyprus. I sent a sympathy card to her husband John, and told him that 'O, Love that wilt not let me go' was one of Eileen's favourite hymns. He could hardly believe it because, not knowing this, he had just chosen it as one of the hymns for the funeral. We held a Requiem Mass for Eileen the following week in St Luke's Church. I felt that we were bringing her home.

The following Sunday I listened to the choir singing after Communion. They sang 'Abba, Father, let me be yours and yours alone...' It really touched me as Eileen had loved this simple song. When I mentioned it afterwards to my friend Brenda, she said that they hadn't sung it. I hadn't imagined it, so I just have to accept that it was a gift – a mysterious gift to me, a compensation for my loss, a reassurance that all was well with Eileen. I often feel her presence close to me. It is light, fragrant and joyful. I think that she might be one of my guardian angels.

The third of my close friends to die in this short space of time was Penny. Penny had originally been Peter's colleague. He introduced us when she began to suffer from asthma – he thought that we could compare notes. Penny and I became good friends and the more we met, the closer we got. Her asthma deteriorated; she retired and was given a car. The two of us became unashamedly 'ladies who lunched'. But we didn't just chat. We discussed everything at length and there was that joy that comes from the knowledge that we could confide in one another safely. Penny was soon diagnosed with COPD (chronic obstructive pulmonary disease). She was unable to walk any distance, so the lunches became very important to her – and to me. Usually, all we had was a bowl of soup but it was a good bowl of soup!

I grieved terribly over Eileen and, to some extent, Penny compensated. But before long, Penny asked me questions about Eileen's disease. She was given the same diagnosis – bronchiectasis. I couldn't believe it! Shortly before she died, when she was dependent on oxygen, Penny was determined to come to see a film with me at a local cinema. She was frighteningly pale and her face had changed shape with the weight loss and the progression of the disease. I rang her afterwards to check that she was alright. She told me that she had had terrible chest pain when the film was showing. It had featured ordinary life in a small Cardiganshire village and a woman was shown making a Victoria sponge for the local fête.

Penny got her breath back at the other end of the line and said, 'But didn't that Victoria sponge look wonderful!'

We met once more – for lunch! I knew that Penny was very ill but I had an intuition the following Sunday that I should call her. It felt urgent – I told Brenda about it and rang Penny's number as soon as I got in the house. There was no answer. The following morning I discovered the reason why. She had been admitted to hospital and died hours later.

As if to balance things after so much loss, I got to know my two little granddaughters. Bethan was already bilingual and articulate – fond of drama and singing. She has a strong personality and I was concerned that her little sister would be overwhelmed. But I hadn't reckoned on Cati! Strong, funny, stubborn, competitive and extraverted, Cati was accomplished at sport and dance even as a toddler. This intrigued me as I had always disliked gym. I was learning about the unique mystery of genetics.

38

My People's Pilgrimage

WHEN LEW AND Nancy died I inherited all their old photos and documents. I had already been interested in family history but now I had so much more information. I discovered envelopes stuffed with medical notes on Daddy Bom's final disease. I had just two photos of Nancy's mother, Jane, so I sent away for some extra certificates and researched the census returns. I visited local museums and did a lot of background reading.

In doing so, I noticed that something significant was happening. I wasn't just recording my own personal family history – I was documenting the plight of a large part of the population of Wales. They were people who had worked on the land in rural areas until the late nineteenth century. Then, farmers used new tools and equipment and didn't need to employ so many labourers. After countless generations of a tough but stable life, they were forced to look elsewhere for work. Some emigrated but many more went to the south Wales Valleys to work in the heavy industries of iron and coal – just like my ancestors.

The research was fascinating and I delved into social history as well. I found myself writing some Celtic poems. I made a note of all my childhood memories of the family. I had had three wonderful storytellers as grandparents so their tales had given me that little bit extra. When I looked at everything in a huge file, I realised that I had the beginnings of a book. It took me a long time to piece it together but it gave me so much satisfaction.

For my grandchildren, the material is *history* – I vividly

remember Data's sister, Sarah, who was born in 1877. I decided to call the book *My People's Pilgrimage* and began to send it away to publishers. One day Lefi Gruffudd from Y Lolfa rang me to say that they would publish it. I couldn't stop thanking him – in Welsh! The book looked good when I saw the first copy in 2008. The weather on the night of the launch was terrible – windy and wet. So I was really touched by the number of people who came out to support me. Instead of reading sections from the book, I told the stories. I had been going to a storytelling circle for a couple of years and had gained enough confidence to do this. The evening went really well, even though Cati couldn't stop helping herself to the Welsh cakes!

One of the unexpected pleasures of preparing this book has been the need to get in touch again with relatives whom I'd known in childhood. We'd lost touch – there had been the geographical distance, dealing with personal life, the lack of transport and money. There was Nancy's family in Pembrokeshire. Janice, Colin, Laurence and Sandra, Maggie, Elmor, Phoebe Ann... I even discovered a distant cousin: Richard is a local historian and he was a mine of information. I am still in touch with them all. On Lew's side of the family I reconnected with Tim and Anne, Margaret, Wally, David, Anne, Janet, Lyn, Ivy, Donna and her family. And it was a delightful privilege to have got to know Betsi and Ted again.

So, although I had lost so many members of the family, there was a real sense that, through the book, I was gaining some too. There are inevitably rifts and misunderstandings in families over the generations and I felt that I had inherited them. I didn't need to be bound by them any longer. It was a healing process and gave me a great sense of freedom.

My own health problems continued. I had a scan to see if my high blood pressure was secondary to another condition. My kidneys were in fact clear but the X-ray showed a fluid-filled sac in one of my ovaries. It was small but the gynaecologist wanted to remove it. He explained that it was going to be keyhole surgery with a convalescence period of about ten days. I was taken down to the theatre. When I woke up I was attached to a drip and had an oxygen mask on my face. The surgeon had made the keyhole incisions but then was unable to remove the cyst so they'd had to open the old hysterotomy / hysterectomy incisions – the tramline right down the centre of my abdomen. I'd had major surgery yet again. It was painful and my convalescence period was extended to three months. I was very weak when I got home but Bethan and Cati came up to see me in bed. Cati was just beginning to talk and, as she looked at me, she said 'cup of tea'. The answer to everything!

Peter was finally made a permanent member of staff at the university in 2005 when he was sixty! He was appointed as senior lecturer in mathematics and statistics. A couple of years later he was promoted again and made a reader in quantitative analysis. I was very pleased for him – he has always worked so hard, even though this came at a time when many people are thinking of retirement.

I recovered from my surgery and we went to the Loire Valley for a holiday. We were able to go on a few Eurostar short city breaks. I loved Paris. Rushing to catch the Metro, I felt good. There was so much to see! We went to Bruges and Lille. Meleri and Huw and their girls had moved into a lovely house nearby. Bethan and Cati were settled in their Welsh-medium primary school. Meleri and Huw's careers were flourishing. Did I dare hope for easier times?

39

Bitter Winds and a Gift

ONE FEBRUARY EVENING in 2010 we were babysitting. Meleri and Huw had gone to a friend's funeral in London – one of their contemporaries at medical school. When they arrived home I asked if it had been a difficult day – it had. Then Meleri and Huw sat down facing us directly. Meleri told us simply and plainly that she was ill herself. She would need surgery. My mind raced at times in the following months. I often felt numb or on overdrive. That episode in my life was surreal.

That winter (2010–11) was bitterly cold with heavy snowfalls as early as November. Schools were closed, cars were stranded, roads and streets were thick with ice. Meleri came over to our house to see us. It was unusual for her to be on her own without the children in tow. I guessed that she had something special to say and my heart skipped a beat. She came into the lounge and sat down. Peter was working late so I was on my own with her. She said, 'I've got some news for you.' I waited for her to tell me what the news was but, in that second before she told me, my mind went on a whirlwind journey. Then I saw that she was smiling at me.

'I'm pregnant!'

Again, my mind went into a state of confusion. She showed me the picture of the first scan. I stared at it and didn't know how to respond. Gradually, I began to get a clearer picture. She and Huw had obviously known for some weeks but they had needed time to deal with the situation themselves. Although she was at high risk of losing the baby after her treatment, they wanted to go ahead with the pregnancy. Meleri had to go for a scan or check-up every other week.

Peter and I continued helping out with Bethan and Cati and life carried on in the grim weather. I was very pleased with myself for managing to get out and about in the snow and ice. On 18 January 2011 the bitter chill was still raw. I got up fairly late (I have always had problems with mornings!) and prepared to go to my Welsh group. I was confident that I would manage the mile-long walk there but, when I stood up from a sitting position on the bed, I seemed to have turned my ankle. I heard a cricking noise and instinctively turned my foot the other way to correct it. I tried to stand, but as soon as I put weight on my right leg I fell to the ground. Even though the pain was excruciating, I assumed that I had a very bad sprain. It had happened so suddenly and simply. I dragged myself over to the other side of the room to get to the phone. I spoke to Peter and said that I didn't think I could get to the GP's surgery. When I described the pain and the fact that I couldn't stand, he said that I needed to go to A&E. He'd come home as soon as he could.

I knew that I'd have to get downstairs somehow so, using the banister as a support, I hobbled along to the top of the stairs. It was undoubtedly shock that made me stop by the bathroom to clean my teeth more thoroughly. I sat on the edge of the bath, then I sat down on the bathroom floor and dragged myself to the top step of the stairs. I felt just as a small child must feel – it seemed such a long way down. I shuffled down one stair at a time on my bottom, holding my damaged foot up with my hands. I felt totally helpless and went over the sequence of what had happened in my mind. Ten minutes earlier, I was going to my Welsh group! I settled on the second stair up from the hall and waited for Peter to come. Even with his help, the pain and weakness made it impossible for me to get to the car. A neighbour had to come to help.

As soon as we arrived at A&E, Peter got out of the car and fetched a wheelchair for me. He pushed me towards the waiting room. I was in agony but still thought that it must be a bad sprain because it had happened in such a simple way. I was taken down to have an X-ray, then Peter wheeled me back into a cubicle for the results. He tried to get the wheelchair straight but the nurse told him not to worry.

'You won't be here long,' she said.

There is something intrinsic in me that makes me think that I am doing something wrong. Was I wasting their time? If I was, I didn't think that I could tolerate the pain. Then the nurse gave me the X-ray results. I had a very nasty fracture. It wasn't a single break – it was a double fracture. The nurse offered me strong analgesics immediately. I refused because I wanted to be fully aware of what was happening. Peter took me down to the plaster room. Even with their experience of dealing with fractures every day, the nurses were surprised when they looked at my X-ray.

'Look at this!' they said.

Peter looked. I looked. My ankle had to be set in plaster before I had surgery. Surgery again! The nurse said that she was going to lift my injured foot onto the little block they have.

'It will *hurt!*' she warned me. When I offered to do it myself, she said, 'You're a braver woman than me.'

I was stunned.

'Hmmm,' one of the nurses said. 'You're not really overweight. That will be a great help. And you look fairly healthy and strong.'

Was it *that* bad?

I was wheeled on a trolley to the surgical assessment unit. Peter followed me. A surgeon came out to see me. Young and smiling, he repeated what the nurses had said. I had a particularly bad double fracture – a double malleolus fracture. It wasn't related to my osteoporosis. It's a freak thing that can happen to anyone. He drew me a picture of it and explained what they would have to do. ORIF was the name of the procedure – open reduction internal fixation. I looked at his drawing. It showed a plate inserted into one side of my ankle and screws into the other. I still couldn't believe that it had happened. I needed to have emergency surgery that same day.

Peter had contacted Meleri at work and she arrived straight away. Visibly pregnant by this time, she looked shaken and said, 'This is not good news, Mum.'

I was taken on the trolley up to a ward but, as soon as I arrived there, I was wheeled down to the theatre. After three hours of surgery I was taken back to the ward, wide awake and alert. As I looked around me, I saw that the other patients were all elderly and immobile. I suppose the same could be said for me! I remained in hospital for six days and, after two or three days of complete bed rest, a physiotherapist showed me how to hop on my good leg whilst balancing the injured one off the ground. An impossible task without support, of course, and to my horror I realised that I would have to use a Zimmer frame to attempt it. I had to keep the weight off my leg in plaster for twelve weeks!

I was desperate to go home, but when I got there I realised how protected I had been in the hospital. The simplest task was very, very hard work. I was extremely nervous of falling. Peter had brought a bed downstairs for me and we had the loan of a commode. Washing, going to the loo, washing my hair – these were all tasks that exhausted me. A district nurse came out every day to give me anticoagulant injections until I was asked and agreed to do it myself. The settee was filled with all my daily needs and, as it was still cold, I covered my legs with a crocheted shawl! Peter tried so hard to look after me. He had to carry on working and, in addition to my needs, he was covering for a sick colleague. He prepared my lunch for me on a tray every day before he set off.

I had to be taken back to the trauma clinic often. The heavy plaster was removed and I had a lighter one. I could choose the colour, so I opted for red – I might as well make a 'statement'! When the red plaster was taken off, I was given a heavy knee-high boot to wear. This was more uncomfortable than the plaster, especially as I had to wear it at night in bed at first. Lying flat on my back, I yearned for the luxury of curling up in bed.

The surgeon told me that I could expect a recovery time of eighteen months. The snow went and the spring flowers began to bloom in the park so tantalisingly close to our house. The only way I could go out to see them in those early months was in a wheelchair. Peter, Meleri and Huw were all working. A friend, Allan, offered to take me out – the pond, the trees, the flowers were so beautiful. Immobile and helpless as I was, I also realised how blessed I was. Streams of visitors came and I think we could have lived off the food that we were given!

When I began physiotherapy in April, I seriously doubted that I would ever walk again unaided. My right leg had already been weakened after my accident in 1979. Now it had an extra challenge. I struggled on two crutches and eventually progressed to one. I remember the day when I first made some steps without any aid at all – just my two legs!

It wasn't just my recovery that I was dealing with. I was also counting the weeks into Meleri's pregnancy. We sometimes met at the hospital briefly. My appointments at the trauma clinic coincided with her scans. Surprisingly, Meleri continued to carry her baby. Bethan, Cati, Meleri and I had all arrived a couple of weeks early, so we all assumed that the pattern would be repeated. This new little baby had other ideas. She was due at the beginning of June. On 31 May 2011, Bethan was performing in a drama presentation at the Urdd Eisteddfod in Swansea, and Meleri had planned on going with a babe in arms. There was no sign of the baby arriving, so she decided to go with the rest of the family, taking her hospital notes with her – just in case. They all had a lovely day at the Eisteddfod and the contractions began on the return journey. Peter and I stayed at their house overnight. We had stayed overnight at their house to look after their cat, Sidie, when Bethan was born. We had stayed in their house overnight to look after Bethan when Cati was born. Now, we were staying overnight to look after Bethan and Cati – and Sidie! Little Gwen Sara was born by normal delivery just after 8am. She seemed a little miracle. From the beginning, Gwen was a loving little child with a sunny disposition.

I continued to have problems with my ankle. Two years after the surgery, the metalwork supporting my ankle was so close to the surface of the skin that it was almost visible externally – and it was still painful. Metalwork is sometimes removed when the bones have healed, so I made an outpatient appointment to see the surgeon. When he saw the state of the repair work, he said, 'No wonder you're in a lot of pain. Can you come in tomorrow?' So, without having the time to worry about it, I was in hospital again for surgery under general anaesthetic. It was just an overnight stay and I returned home with another 'moon-boot' and a couple of months back on crutches!

40

Fit for a Purpose

I HAVE HAD plenty of convalescence time recently in which to contemplate life. And, on the whole, I have contemplated – it hasn't been the empty silence that comes from depression or the inner world of introversion.

In spite of everything, I have survived so far. Peter and I have been together for more than forty-seven years. I won't pretend that it has been easy – for either of us. We are very different people, but we have somehow managed to come through it all together. I never believed that I would have children, yet Peter and I have been blessed with a wonderful daughter. Meleri has been a consultant for twelve years now; she works extremely hard and is a devoted wife to Huw and mum to her three girls. In Huw, we have a kind and loving son-in-law with a great sense of humour. He is a GP in a practice in the Valleys – one of the most deprived areas in Wales. His practice is one of several incorporated into the university medical school, so he teaches medical students as well. It is heart-warming to see the love that exists in their family. I have three grandchildren – all strong characters, extraverts, bright, fascinating, growing fast – each one of them created unique. One day, Bethan, Cati and Gwen will have their own life stories to tell. I cannot write on their behalf.

I still have good friends. Brenda and I have been close for over thirty years. So has Elinor; then there's dear Marion who is as gentle and kind as anyone I know. I have my friends from the Ignatian group. Julie is a soul mate and, even though she has moved away, there is a depth of love, shared spirituality and intimacy when we catch up with each other. I am still in touch with my old school friend, Felicity. We don't speak often but make up for lost time when we do. I meet up with my old college friends – Jean, Lesley and Mary. In 2011, we all went to Carmarthen for a reunion. It was a very special occasion because my other college friends, Kay and Ann, joined us too. From my support group, I have the friendship of Dorothy and Muriel – there is a special bond between people who pray together. Then there is Hywel, Fides, my neighbours, friends from my Welsh group, the storytelling crowd...

These are the facts as they stand now; there is no complacency. There is no room for me or anyone else to be self-congratulatory. We live in challenging times. The generations below me have to deal with the current economic, ethical and ecological crises. My ancestors moved from their homes in search of work. Today, millions of people are wandering all over the world seeking refuge from disasters – and searching for work.

I can hardly grasp the speed of changes that have happened within my lifetime. From rationing, thin cress and salmon paste sandwiches, Heinz Baked Beans, Green Shield Stamps, the search for a bargain turkey on Christmas Eve, to 'eat as much as you can' for £4.99, and then to 'best before' warnings and waste. From coal fires downstairs, freezing bedrooms upstairs, and an outside toilet, to central heating, air conditioning and en suites. From saving small change for bills and Christmas presents to a wallet stuffed with plastic cards. From 'let down hems' and a single winter coat to 'must-have' clothing discarded within a season. The earth cannot sustain this kind of 'progress'. Social structures are collapsing and crumbling under the weight of excessive legislation and bureaucracy. So, no, there is no room for complacency from anyone.

There are seeds of hope – I see them sprouting all the time. I often see them in the eager faces of children. A lot of hard work, common sense and collaboration is needed to nurture these shoots and encourage them to grow. May God help us all on the journey!

41

Listening, Learning, Waiting

DECADES HAVE PASSED since I trained in pastoral care, counselling and spiritual direction. It's a long time since Steve Glascoe surprised me by saying that I was a 'healer'. How has all of this been relevant to my life in the twenty-first century?

Literature and information that was hard to obtain on the healing ministry thirty-five years ago can be Googled now in a couple of seconds. Healing services are in the mainstream worship of lots of churches, chapels and faith communities. On the whole, there is less emphasis on the 'gifts' and more following of prepared data. So things would have changed for me anyway.

My life has had to adapt to changes. There were fourteen years of attending to the increasing needs of my parents and Peter's parents. We seemed to be constantly on the road between Cardiff and Llandrindod Wells or Cardiff and Fishguard. During that exhausting time, there were the other bereavements. I certainly needed time to receive and wait upon healing.

Margaret and Penny were very different people but when they were seriously ill they both found it difficult to be with people outside their immediate family for long. It was a great privilege for me to have been invited to spend so much time with them then. Eileen was always so cheerful with everybody but, when she was so ill, she could let the mask slip with me.

I have been actively involved in many of these twenty-first

century funerals. I led the prayers at Iris' funeral, read a poem at Margaret's funeral, gave a eulogy at Penny's funeral, read at Ivy's funeral, organised the Requiem Mass for Eileen as well as delivering a eulogy. I contributed creatively to Lew and Nancy's funerals. That was all healing. It has been tough but healing often hurts.

I still go to St Luke's Church but I enjoy going to Salem, the local Welsh Presbyterian chapel, too. I like the liturgy, the Eucharistic prayer and the simple chants at St Luke's. It can all transport me to a place beyond myself. I co-lead a silent meditation group with my friend, Andrew. I like the unassuming simplicity in Salem, the depth of the preaching, the prayers and seeing social justice being put into action. I still have the support group at home and I lead a 'quiet day' away once a year. I still take an active part in the Ignatian group and I have become involved in a charity that helps to feed the homeless in Cardiff. I have become more interested in ecumenism between denominations and interfaith issues. God is everywhere and not limited to a building or institution. I have become less attached to a particular place of worship and find that I am becoming more and more contemplative.

I am writing poetry again. When I can, I enjoy doing simple things in a contemplative way. I attend to our small garden, collect its tiny harvests of herbs and dry some of them. I let the bees and butterflies enjoy the lavender before I snip the flowers off with my hands, divide them, sort them with my fingers and either make oil from them or press them into little home-sewn bags. Doing such things, I slow down, meditate and feel in touch with the rhythm of the seasons, the Creator of all that is. It helps me remember how laborious such tasks are without the advantages of our easy commercialism. I feel overwhelmed by our lifestyle and that helps me to focus on the less fortunate. Peter has become a Buddhist and it doesn't worry me at all. He and his group of friends come here for their meditation sessions once a month and I've got to know, like and respect them.

Yes, people do still come to see me, though not as many as before. It is a gentler, more fluid ministry. I feel that I am mainly used these days as a channel for 'listening'. With life moving at such a frenetically fast pace, being available to listen is more important than ever. This ministry often 'spills out' into the streets. I meet people on the road and, if I can, I stay around for the reply when I ask them how they are. It's as simple as that. If anyone wants me to pray with them or for them, I do it. Sometimes, I am 'given' someone for a period of time. When the problem is resolved, they move on and so do I. Occasionally, I am given a 'word' for someone, out of the blue, unsought, unexpected. Regarding this, I recently had a reaction of sheer delight from someone. The words were prophetic in the sense that they came to be. Other gifts with which I am sometimes graced are those of wisdom, discernment, knowledge and prophecy. This is not a boast. They are gifts. I do not possess them. They pass through me.

I am human and I get things wrong. This is where the discernment practices from Ignatius of Loyola help me. I try to examine the motives in my ego. And then I try to let my ego go.

When I talk of being a channel for non-judgemental listening, it needs to be on two levels. I need to listen to what the other person is saying and I need to listen out for the voice of God. Sometimes this comes through a scriptural text or the words of a hymn. Sometimes it comes through silence and sometimes I can't hear it at all.

Life is still teaching me lessons. I realise more than ever that the divisions between success and failure, illness and sickness, life and death can be wafer thin. If I had been well, I would probably have been a high-flyer. I don't regret what has happened to me. I was chosen for a different kind of flight. My feet have stayed on the ground, though I have had the privilege of walking with angels. I hope that my life experiences have taught me empathy – they certainly don't allow any pride to linger.

Every human being has gifts and talents but we all have failings too. It is difficult and embarrassing sometimes to face the dark forces deep inside our psyche. They are usually unattractive, undesirable and primal. But, if we can bear to let them surface, face and acknowledge them, we become more whole as people. We become the person we were designed to be – freed from all that has, for whatever reason, locked us away or trampled us underfoot.

I can't avoid death for ever. Accepting this, I hope that I am liberated into more creative living. We are reminded at most funerals that we bring nothing into this world and we leave with nothing. The inheritance that we endow is what we have been, what we are – not what we have owned. It has nothing to do with status. I hope that I have done the little things here and there. The little things that cause ripples, the effects of which often remain a mystery, reminding us that our life is not focused on us. We are not God.

When I embark on a different kind of journey, I hope that I will still be praying, asking for God's blessing and protection on all those whom I love. Asking Him to help me understand what I have failed to grasp. And I will plead for peace on this troubled earth that has been loaned to us for such a little while.

Acknowledgements

I WOULD LIKE to thank Y Lolfa for publishing this book. In particular, I am indebted to Eirian Jones for her work as my editor. Eirian has been conscientious, exact, helpful and encouraging. I could not have found a better editor and I cannot thank her enough. I am also grateful to Peter Finch for his helpful advice and suggestions over coffee and cake. I am indebted to my husband, Peter, for helping me with the computer tasks that were beyond my grasp. I owe a big thank you to Cati Davies for the cover picture.

Last but not least, I am grateful to my family – Peter, Meleri, Huw, Bethan, Cati and Gwen for being here and to all other relatives or friends (alive or dead) who have shared in my journey.

A family's odyssey from rural to industrial Wales

MY PEOPLE'S PILGRIMAGE

Diana Gruffydd Williams

y Lolfa

£9.95

A Childhood
in a Welsh
Mining Valley

V I V I A N   J O N E S

y Lolfa

£9.99

y Lolfa

Foreword by the Most Reverend
John D E Davies, Archbishop of Wales

A Pilgrimage Around Wales

IN SEARCH OF A SIGNIFICANT CONVERSATION

ANNE HAYWARD

£8.99

JOHN I. MORGANS & PETER C. NOBLE

OUR HOLY GROUND

The Welsh Christian Experience

y Lolfa

£9.99

Fit for a Purpose is just one of a whole range
of publications from Y Lolfa. For a full list of
books currently in print, send now for your
free copy of our new full-colour catalogue.
Or simply surf into our website

www.ylolfa.com

for secure on-line ordering.

TALYBONT CEREDIGION CYMRU SY24 5HE
e-mail ylolfa@ylolfa.com
website www.ylolfa.com
phone (01970) 832 304
fax 832 782

Printed by Y Lolfa
Ask for a quote